World Crisis and the Gandhian Way

About Authors

Anil Dutta Mishra (*b.* 1965) is Deputy Director of National Gandhi Museum, Rajghat, New Delhi. Earlier he was an Assistant Professor in the Department of Non-violence and Peace Studies, Jain Vishva Bharati Institute (Deemed University), Ladnun, Rajasthan. His areas of specialization include Indian Government and Politics, Grassroot Politics, Women's Studies, Ecology and Human Rights.

He is associated with a number of national and international organizations in various capacities including General Secretary of Indian Society of Gandhian Studies, Secretary-*cum*-Treasurer of Alliance for Sarvodaya, Member Board of Studies, Punjab University, Chandigarh and Nagpur University, Nagpur.

He has authored/edited 12 books and published a number of research papers in leading professional journals. His earlier books *Problems and Prospects of Working Women in Urban India* (1994); *Fundamentals of Gandhism* (1995); *Gandhian Approach to Contemporary Problems* (1996); *Decentralized Planning in India: A Study of Objectives and Operational Framework* (1999); *Gender Perspectives: Participation, Empowerment and Development* (1999); *Perspectives on Human Rights* (2002); *Rediscovering Gandhi* (2002); *Patterns of Gender Violence* (2002); *Challenges of Twenty-First Century and Gandhian Alternative* (2003); *India and Canada: Past, Present and Future* (2003); *Public Governance and Decentralization: Essays in Honour of T.N. Chaturvedi* (2003); *Gandhian Alternative to Contemporary Problems* (2004); and *Globalization Myth and Reality* (2004) were well received and widely acclaimed.

S. Narayanasamy (*b.* 1954) is currently Professor in the Department of Gandhian Thought and Peace Science at Gandhigram Rural University. Earlier, he was Director, IDARA—Information Development and Resource Agency for Nehru Yuva Kendras in the Southern Zone. He has authored/edited seven books. Also, he has to his credit 62 articles published in various national and international journals. On academic assignments, he had been to Sri Lanka, Italy and Mauritius. He is both academic and activist who has introduced "Peace Bus Technique" and "Mobile School of Peace" for Communal Harmony.

Gandhian Studies and Peace Research Series-32

WORLD CRISIS AND THE GANDHIAN WAY

Anil Dutta Mishra
S. Narayanasamy

CONCEPT PUBLISHING COMPANY, NEW DELHI-110059

ISBN : 13-978-81-8069-600-8 **ISBN : 10-81-8069-600-6**

First Published 2009

Published and Printed by

Concept
Since 1974

Concept Publishing Company
Regd. Office:
A/15-16, Commercial Block, Mohan Garden
New Delhi-110059 (India)
Phones : 25351460, 25351794, *Fax* : 091-11-25357109
Email : publishing@conceptpub.com,
Website: www.conceptpub.com

Editorial Office:
H-13, Bali Nagar, New Delhi-110 015, India.

Cataloging in Publication Data--*Courtesy:* D.K. Agencies (P) Ltd. <docinfo@dkagencies.com>

Mishra, A. D. (Anil Dutta), 1965-
World crisis and the Gandhian way / Anil Dutta Mishra, S. Narayanasamy. -- 1st ed.
p. cm. -- (Gandhian studies and peace research series ; 32)
Includes bibliographical references (p.).
Includes index.
ISBN 13: 9788180696008 ISBN 10: 8180696006

1. Gandhi, Mahatma, 1869-1948--Philosophy. 2. Sarvodaya movement. 3. India--Politics and government. 4. India--Social conditions. 5. India--Economic conditions. 6. Peace-building. I. Narayanasamy, S. (Sangarappa Naidu), 1954-, joint author. II. Title. III. Series: Gandhian studies and peace research series ; 32.

DDC 954.035 22

Preface

Gandhi was a unique personality in human history. He lived his life with purpose. His all actions were well-defined and followed by masses. He always wrote with a purpose and for common man as well as intelligentsia. He lived simple and dignified life based on truth and non-violence. His life was best example of pristine purity. He rightly said: "My life is my message." In this book an attempt has been made to locate Gandhi in the era of liberalization, privatization and globalization. After 9/11 the world has changed drastically. Everybody is looking forward for peaceful and dignified life, and searching the better alternative and way out. In this crisis, the only hope is to follow the Gandhian path which is based on love, truth, non-violence, *swadeshi* and *swaraj*. The main purpose of this work is to rediscover and reinterpret Gandhi in the context of present crises and provide an alternative.

The great American dreams have shattered. Humanity is undergoing almost a phase of moral collapse and ethical nihilism. Satyam has become asatyam. Service is being given in quest of personal aggrandizement. In the era of the mad rush for power and material gain, the significance of Gandhian principle lies in stressing the permanent value of self-abnegation and to enshrine the primacy of goodness and character in place of the skill of manipulation and self-assertion. Gandhian way is the only hope to solve the problems of unemployment, unequal distribution of wealth, violation of human right, fundamentalism, terrorism and poverty.

The whole world is in search of an alternative. Gandhism provides an answer, an alternative and a way out. Gandhi's relevance is eternal. His political philosophy possesses a variety of meanings ranging from religious purity to political expediency. Politics was, to Gandhi, not a profession but a vocation. He sought to apply moral values to the difficult domain of politics. His moral and political thought is intrinsically linked with his religious and ethical beliefs. Such a thought needs serious study always and more so when the world is so much corrupt and inhuman as the one in which we are living. The ultimate goal, for Gandhi, was the greatest good of all people. Good, to him, means the self-realization and not the material well-being of the individuals or the society. The Gandhian principles are capable of meeting the greatest challenge of the age. The most urgent need of today is the abolition of human suffering as well as of war.

Thus the tragedy of modern India is that the ruling elite could never understand the crux of Gandhian philosophy. Our quest for social justice and sustainability will remain a dream until we realize what Gandhi meant when he said: that economics is untrue which ignores and disregards moral values. He was also convinced that without democratic decentralization and rural development freedom would not mean anything to the masses of India. He continuously emphasized this through his speeches and writings throughout the freedom struggle. He maintained that the country's prosperity and progress depend upon the villages and if the village perishes, India will perish too. The *swaraj* of Gandhi was intrinsically linked with rural development. We would like to remind what Gandhi wrote in the 22nd July 1946 issue of Harijan "Independence must begin at the bottom." Till Indian politics and politicians learn to practice it, the interpretations of Gandhian thought and perspective will need to be reiterated again and again.

This work would not have been possible in the present form without the support and help from friends and well-wishers. There are a number of persons behind the scene whose ideas, comments and suggestions have been included to make the work complete. No words can be adequate in acknowledging their contribution to this work.

The Librarians and staffs of Parliamentary Library, Indian Institute of Public Administration, National Gandhi Museum and Library, Institute of Economic Growth, Planning Commission, Sapru House, British Council, Gandhigram Rural Institute and American Centre have rendered their valuable help and support in the completion of this book. We express our heartfelt thanks to all of them.

Last but not the least, we are grateful to Shri Ashok Kumar Mittal of Concept Publishing Company for bringing out the book in a nice form and that too within record time.

Anil Dutta Mishra
S. Narayanasamy

Contents

Preface *v*

1. Philosophy of Sarvodaya 1

2. Sarvodaya Movement at a Glance 26

3. Role of Youth in Sarvodaya 35

4. Gandhian Vision of Society 48

5. Gandhi and Environmental Crisis 52

6. Gandhi and Crisis in 21st Century 62

7. Political Crisis and Gandhian Solution 70

8. Value Education and Crisis Today 84

9. *Satyagraha* and World Crisis 90

10. Panchayati Raj: A Gandhian Perspective 119

11. Disability Management: A Gandhian Perspective 127

12. Ecology: A Gandhian Perspective 133

13. Rural Development: The Gandhi Way 141

14. People's Participation and Sustainable Development 154

15. Voluntary Organizations and Reconstruction of India 176

16. Gandhian Concepts of Social Work and its Application 185

17. Mosaics on Constructive Work 202

18. Constructive Work: Futuristic Trends 267

19. Creative Programmes for Peace 272

20. Gandhi's Thought for Ending world Crisis 281

Bibliography 296

Index 305

1

Philosophy of Sarvodaya

Introduction

Sarvodaya, today, does not represent a mere vision or utopian notion but makes an attempt of reorienting the human mind to reconstruct human society. It has assumed the dimensions of a movement and a socio-economic force of great potentialities. It is a dynamic philosophy, which can make possible the advent of a radically transformed humanity. Sarvodaya seeks to build a new society on the foundations of old spiritual and moral values of India and attempts to meet the challenge of contemporary problems[1]. The world has witnessed the propagation, experimentation and implementation of various socio-economic ideologies—capitalist, socialist and communist, from time-to-time. But, in overall consideration, sarvodaya is undoubtedly far more superior to other attributive models. It envisages a well-balanced and integrated development of the nation with no distinction among have and have-nots, privileged and under-privileged, ruler and ruled. The issuance of sarvodaya thought lies in socializing matter through the strength of the spirit. Dogmas have no place in sarvodaya. "The philosophy of sarvodaya is not a set of dogmas, in its issuance, it is compatible with an attempt of the spirit to prevail over matter and to socialize itself"[2]. Sarvodaya is a redeemer's philosophy of social and political orientation, where suffering is, sarvodaya goes to mitigate it. It is the culmination of human emotional integration and the highest intellectual aspiration. It is a symbol of platonic detachment and Gita's Anasakti[3]. It is the highest manifestation of love and attempts at a mental transformation of the people.

Gandhi denounced the utilitarian principle of the greatest good of the greatest number, and advocated the sarvodaya philosophy.

Gandhi did not originally coin sarvodaya. Even before him, the idea of sarvodaya was found in religious books *Vedas, Upanishads, The Ramayan, The Gita, Quran* and many others. It was also preached by Indian and Western saints as well as philosophers. But Gandhi gave to these age-old principles and ideals an extended meaning and application. In fact, after the death of Gandhi, the word sarvodaya came into greater prominence, when his fellow-workers assembled at Sevagram (Wardha), in March 1948, and decided to form an organization named 'Sarvodaya Samaj'. This name was chosen in preference to that of 'Sarvodaya Mandal' (*Satyagraha* Circle) because the word 'Satyagraha' had come to acquire a restricted meaning which did not include constructive work. Since then the school of thought which accepts Gandhi's philosophy in all its aspects and of which the central figure is Vinoba Bhave, has come to be known as the 'Sarvodaya School' and its philosophy as the 'Sarvodaya Philosophy'[4]. The prominent thinkers of this school were Acharya Vinoba Bhave, Kishorlal Ghanshyam Mashruwala, J.C. Kumarappa, Kaka Kalekar, Shankerrao Deo, Dhirendra Mazumdar, Loknayak Jayaprakash Narayan and Acharya J.B. Kripalani. Except Jayaprakash Narayan, all of them had been associated with Gandhi in his constructive work.

Sarvodaya: Meaning and Genesis

'Sarvodaya' is Sanskrit in origin which is comprised of 'Sarva' meaning all and 'Udaya' meaning rising. The etymological meaning of Sarvodaya is the rising of all. This all includes all living beings[5]. In other words, sarvodaya as the word means welfare of all. The word first appeared in the form of the title for the Gujarati translation of John Ruskin's book entitled *'Unto This Last'*[6]. *Sarvodaya* was the title of series of nine articles, which Gandhi wrote and got published in Gujarati in the *Indian Opinion* weekly in South Africa in 1908.

Sarvodaya is essentially a spiritual activity which has two meaning, viz., negative and positive. As a negative concept, sarvodaya is not limited to one person or to one group of persons.[7] Nobody is excluded from enjoying anything from other[8]. It is not something which one man or set of men can gain or enjoy to the exclusion of others[9]. As a positive concept sarvodaya implies the participation of all kinds of people irrespective of class, caste, creed and religion. It also stands for the total blossoming of all the facilities—physical, mental and spiritual of the human being. It is an activity in which all may partake and it is tantamount to a full realization of the human faculties of the human soul[10].

According to Acharya Vinoba Bhave, the term sarvodaya commands a two-fold meaning. *Firstly,* sarvodaya means making all happy by removing suffering and poverty with the help of scientific knowledge. *Secondly,* establishing a world state full with divinity, kindness and equality is called sarvodaya[11]. Sarvodaya aims not at the rise of the few or the many, or for that matter the rise of the greater number. It is not utilitarianism, which stands for the greatest good of the greatest number. It contains the germ of minority and majority. Contrary to utilitarianism it stands for the good of one and all, of the high and the low, of the strong and the weak, the intelligent as well as the dull. As against the *Laissez-faire* theory, that is the survival of the fittest, sarvodaya believes in the survival and development of all. To Vinoba, "The idea of sarvodaya, as preached by the *Gita* is to merge oneself in the good of all"[12].

Apart from connoting the welfare of all, sarvodaya commands two more meanings, *firstly,* the universal welfare and *secondly,* the integrated development of all. The *laissez-faire* philosophy stands for the exploitation of many by a few. The utilitarian school supports the majority, totally neglecting the minority. Sarvodaya rejects these theories, which stand for the joy of few, advocates the welfare of all, irrespective of class, costs, creed, colour, race, region or religion. The philosophy of sarvodaya makes the attempt at reorienting human mind of reconstructing human society. It means welfare and prosperity of all. All must progress together without collision of interest[13]. Interpreting the purport of sarvodaya Dada Dharmadhikari said: "Sarvodaya is a term with a wider connotation since it conceives of assimilation of all and not only of many or most[14]. Sarvodaya is a philosophy, which provides checks against the imperfections of human mind and soul.

As regards the meaning of the word sarvodaya is concerned, there are broadly two views: the first, in its micro-form, means simply the rise of one. Secondly, the macro-form connotes the rise of all, the universal welfare and the all round development of all[15]. But it connotes several other meanings. In its negative sense, it never omits even a single person from enjoying anything from the rest of the mankind. As a positive concept, it promotes the development of all the faculties of man. According to Vinoba Bhave, it stands for not only making all happy by eliminating suffering from all but also for bringing a world state based on equality. For Gandhi, Sarvodaya as a broader concept stands for the merger of one in all with self-sacrifice and a selfless service. It aims at not only fulfilling the minimum material needs but also developing the ethico-spiritual aspects of all people.

Sources of Sarvodaya

The following sources helped Gandhi to develop his concept of Sarvodaya. These were—Ruskin's book *'Unto This Last'*, Tolstoy's *'The Kingdom of God is Within You'*, Thoreau's *'Civil Disobedience'*, *The Bhagvad Gita*, *Isavasyupnisad*, Buddhism, Jainism and Islam.

Ruskin's 'Unto This Last'

The Gandhian philosophy of Sarvodaya can be traced to the central teachings of India's spiritual and religious heritage although Gandhi admits the fact that he had immediate inspiration from Ruskin's *'Unto This Last'* of which the term sarvodaya is his rendering[16]. The welfare of all became the basic idea of Gandhi's philosophy right from the days when he wrote in Gujarati his most world famous thirty thousand word book *'Hind Swaraj* or Indian Home Rule' in 1909.

Gandhi called one of the chapters of his Autobiography

'The Magic Spell of Book' wherein he describes the effects of Ruskin's *'Unto This Last'* (meaning uplift of the last). He translated it later into Gujarati claiming it sarvodaya. It is a book from which Gandhi drew great inspiration and he at once determined to change his view of life in line with the ideals embodied in Ruskin's book *'Unto This Last'*.[17]

The central teaching of *'Unto This Last'*, according to Gandhi are:

(i) That the good of the individual is contained in the good of all.
(ii) That a lawyer's work has the same values as the Barber's in as much as all have the same right of earning their livelihood from their work.
(iii) That a life of labour, i.e., the life of the tiller of the soil and the handicraftsman is the life worth living.

There is a controversy with regard to the meanings of the term Unto This Last and Sarvodaya. Though Gandhi himself acknowledged that he translated it later into Gujarati, entitling it Sarvodaya. On the one hand, Benudhar Pradhan opines that the idea of welfare of all formed a part of his mental make-up even before he read this book[18]. This view is further strengthened from what Gandhi has expressed in his own words—"*the first of these I knew*" [19]. On the other hand, Geoffery Ashe doubted whether the idea of sarvodaya is contained at all in Ruskin's *Unto This Last*. Persons like Benudhar affirms that "it will be a travesty of truth to say that the objective of 'welfare of all' does not remain couched in the pages of *Unto This Last* of Ruskin"[20].

Ruskin and Gandhi both, were earnestly concerned with social welfare. While Ruskin aimed at the social welfare of 'the greatest number', Gandhi aimed at the welfare of all. Therefore, Vinoba Bhave feels that Gandhi is the real author of the term sarvodaya, since the term, 'Unto This Last' would mean only the uplife of the last (*Antyodaya*). In fact, one has to accept that Ruskin's *Unto This Last* has directly or indirectly profound influence on Gandhi in fulfilling the ideal of sarvodaya, which he had already cherished as his life's mission.

Leo Tolstoy's 'The Kingdom of God is Within You'

Gandhi was greatly influenced by Leo Tolstoy, through his book, '*The Kingdom of God is Within You*' and his essay on 'Christianity and Patriotism'. Tolstoy's simplicity of life and purity of purpose influenced Gandhi deeply. His views on Christianity, its church, its teachings roused Gandhi's feelings. Tolstoy accepted love to be the law of life. The principles of non-violence, is based on love for the entire mankind. Tolstoy and Gandhi, both adopted the instrument of love to solve all problems in their lives. In his celebrated book '*The Kingdom of God is Within You*', we find a political force creating an indelible mark on Gandhi. Gandhi confessed that its reading cured him of the scepticism and made him a firm believer of *Ahimsa*. Both Tolstoy and Gandhi firmly believed that non-violence could cure all social maladies, remove political ills, and establish peace on the earth and goodwill among mankind. In fact both Tolstoy and Gandhi believed in the efficacy of love for the cure of evil and suffering in this world. Tolstoy perceived the truth, love and non-violence and Gandhi grasped the essence of these virtues and led his life directed towards these paths[21].

Tolstoy also impressed upon Gandhi's mind the importance of bread labour. For Tolstoy, the man who abstains from manual labour is a thief of the society. Gandhi acknowledged his debt to Tolstoy. He says, 'the laws that to live man must work, first come home to me upon reading Tolstoy's writing, 'On Bread Labour'—only those man deserve to eat bread who actually till the ground, spin cloth and produce things'. Tolstoy says, 'let us get off the shoulder of our neighbours' and Gandhi adds that if everyone performed that simple operation, he would have rendered all service God requires of him. Since every man has an obligation to himself as well as to the society, bread labour becomes an imperative duty which must be performed by each and every man[22].

Gandhian philosophy of Sarvodaya comes very close to Tolstoyan philosophy of anarchism. The pure ideal of Gandhi's conception of sarvodaya is an ideal of philosophical anarchism, a stateless society marked by voluntary co-operation. Profound faith in God, commiseration from the exploited, inherent aversion to violence, deep-rooted belief in the dignity of man led the two philosophers to the same goal and objective. But Gandhi is not a through-going Tolstoy. The difference between the two philosophers arises out of the fact that Gandhi is far more practical than Tolstoy. Tolstoy recoils from all expressions of violence. Gandhi permits violence, provided of course, that motive for violence is not anger but true love. Thus the moral content of Gandhi's doctrine of *Ahimsa*, which forms the fulcrum around which the entire doctrine of Sarvodaya ideology is based, has a higher significance than that of Tolstoy's. This is due to the fact that Gandhi was greatly influenced by the *Gita* ideal of *nishamakarma*, i.e., action in without attachment[23].

Thoreau's Civil Disobedience

The American pacifist Thoreau was the champion of the free spirit and was repelied by the established political and economic routine of time. In his we discover an element of moral individualism culminating in his concept of 'Civil Disobedience'. Thoreau used the term in his speeches in 1849. It is obvious that Gandhi did not derive his idea of 'Civil Disobedience' from the writings of Thoreau. In fact, the resistance to authority in South Africa preceded before Gandhi got the essay of Thoreau on 'Civil Disobedience'. This movement was then known as 'Passive Resistance'. Gandhi was not satisfied with the term 'Civil Disobedience' because it failed to convey the full meaning of the struggle. Hence, he adopted the phrase 'Civil Resistance'[24].

Thoreau did not believe in narrow sectarianism and felt that man is meant to experience God, not to theologies about him. Man according to Thoreau is a social being who is generally disposed to co-operation with fellow beings for social good. He felt that the moral institutions of the state supported by coercive authority hamper the individual's moral and spiritual freedom. He, therefore, visualized a society in which government will disappear. 'That Government is best which governs not at all', or, 'which governs least'. Like Thoreau,

Gandhi also held that the democracy could be realized only in a stable society based on Truth and Non-violence. And Gandhi described it as sarvodaya, which promotes not only social welfare but spiritual upliftment. Thus Gandhi heard an echo of his own thought in Thoreau[25].

The *Bhagvad Gita*

Gandhi drew his primary strength and inspiration from the *Bhagvad Gita*. To Gandhi, the *Gita* is the 'Eternal Mother'. According to him, the theme of *Gita* is self-realization. He says: "self-realization and its means is the theme of the *Gita*"[26]. Again he affirms, "To one who reads the spirit of the *Gita*, it teaches the secret of non-violence the secret of realizing the self through the physical body"[27].

The sole aim of the *Gita* is to suppress unrighteousness and to establish *Dharma*. It wants to bring prosperity and peace to all. It presents in concise from the Hindu view of life, which in turn stands for the universal brotherhood of all beings. It also highlights the importance of all selfless service for the promotion of the welfare of the whole creation since God and the creation is one. Through *Svadharma*, the *Gita* aims at *Sarvabhutahita* or the good of all beings[28]. In this way, *Gita* preaches the message of the welfare of all or sarvodaya, which influenced Gandhi's thought, and action.

Isavayopanisad

The first verse of *Isavayopanisad* deals with the ideology of sarvodaya. The first part of the verse contains the principles of equality and fraternity. And second part reveals the ideas of renunciation, non-acquisitiveness, non-exploitation and service to the society. According to Gandhi, since the entire universe is pervaded by God, the verse preaches the philosophy of equality and fraternity, which are the fundamental principles of the welfare of all. He confirms, "Universal brotherhood not only brotherhood of all human beings but of all living beings, I find in this mantra..."[29].

Buddhism

According to Lord Buddha, all life is suffering. Suffering has to be extirpated in order to enjoy the bliss of nirvana, which is the highest goal in Buddhism. Nirvana is both individualistic and universal or cosmic. It may be realized in his life, here and there. It may also be known as full and perfect enlightenment for the sake of all beings. All can obtain nirvana if they meticulously follow the Noble Eight-Fold Path of Buddha. Gandhi was highly influenced and deeply impressed by the Buddhist philosophy, which preached universal love, non-injury to living beings, sacrifice and renunciation for the sake of promoting the welfare of all. The Buddha stressed on purity of means which in turn influenced Gandhi who constantly maintained that there is indissoluble relationship between pure means and noble end[30]. Buddha preached about the middle path. Similarly in sarvodaya it is understood that no one should take an extreme step.

Jainism

The ideal of the welfare of all forms is the corner stone of the Jainism. *Ahimsa* forms one of the five vows. The positive aspect of non-violence is the love for fellow brings, not only human but also all creatures. A Jain Tiruthankara's duty is to devote his whole life for showering happiness on all the beings of the whole universe. About the place of sarvodaya in Jainism, Benudhar Pradhan states: "The concept of welfare of all was so much an integral part of Jaina Philosophy that the term 'Sarvodaya' was used by one Jaina teacher Samantabhadra even before the Christian era"[31]. Further, Benudhar Pradhan argues that though the word sarvodaya is used by the Jaina Saint Samantabhadra for the first time, yet Gandhi's use of the word is completely his own. According to him, the term sarvodaya came to Gandhi "as if in a flash"[32]. Therefore he maintains that "the word Sarvodaya...was purely his own coinage"[33].

Islam

Gandhi had a great respect for Islam. He learnt the message of universal brotherhood from it. As for Islam, Gandhi declares that in his view, 'the point of brotherhood is manifested in no other religion as clearly as in Islam'. The reading of the holy Quran convinced Gandhi that the basis of Islam is not violence[34]. In fact, Gandhi shows remarkable catholicity and sympathetic and reverential attitude towards all religions of the world.

Apart from *Unto This Last, The Kingdom of God is Within You*, the *Upanishads*, the *Gita*, Buddhism and Jainism, Gandhian Sarvodaya concept was also influenced by Vaishnavism, Zoroastrianism and Christianity. The revival of the ancient teachings by Gandhi and incorporating them in his philosophy of sarvodaya is perhaps his greatest contribution to the world of thought. Gandhi attempted the synthesis of the ideas of Vedanta, Buddhism, Jainism, Christianity and the teaching of prophets life Tulsidas, Tolstoy, Thoreau, Ruskin and national leaders of the Indian Renaissance movement. The philosophy of sarvodaya takes up the Gandhian synthesis and tries to work out the implication of their ideas at more critical and analytical levels[35].

Ends and Means in Sarvodaya

Morality is the essential means to achieve spirituality and good society or good ends. But communists like Machiavelli maintain that end justifies the means. This reveals that through any impure means like cunnings, hypocrisy, hatred or violence one can get one's own desired end. To them, ends and means are watertight compartment. End is everything, no matter what or how the means are. Means become good if they serve the end. J.P. Narayan observed impartially: "In Marxism any means are good means provided they serve the ends of the social revolution"[36].

For Gandhi means determine the end. He says, "As the means so the end"[37]. Means are as important as the ends. In a way, his unique contribution to the world lies in his maintaining "that the means are more important than the ends"[38]. His emphasis on means rather than on the end is based on the doctrine of *niskamakarma* which holds that a person can have control over actions and not on their fruit. Gandhi is fully convinced that man can only strive but cannot command results. He maintains that "means are after all every thing. There is no wall of separation between means and ends. Indeed the creator gives us control over means, none over the end. Realization of the goal is in exact proportion to that of the means. This is a proportion that admits of no exception"[39]. Gandhi's stress on the strength of the means is based on the following reasons:

1. He believes in the progressive evolution of man;
2. He fixes the end of man as self-perfection;
3. He feels that the end is always out of man's grip till it is attained; and
4. He is convinced that if means are subordinated to ends, the ends to which means are subordinated are likely to be less effective. All the above conviction made Gandhi to held the view that man must have complete control over means, despite both means and ends are various and contradictory[40].

According to Gandhi, the end justifying the means is dangerous in practice and unsound ethically. If it is accepted, it permits resource to violence, fraud, untruth, opportunism, etc. Gandhi viewed human beings as supreme. They are ends in themselves. If the means are pure, the end also becomes pure. When we take care of the means, the end will take care of itself. By emphasizing only the means, Gandhi does not intend to give a secondary place to the ends. To him, means and ends are inseparably connected just like seed and trees are connected.

By considering means and ends as a continuous process, Gandhi dissolved the age-old opinion of viewing both as water-tight compartments. The difference between them is imaginary[41]. Therefore, he takes them as an organic whole. In a way, he proposes that both means and end must be homogeneous. He also holds that the extreme of means is itself the end. That is, the end progressively realizes itself through the means. The end can never result all of a sudden out of the means. In fact, when means slowly progresses, it turns itself into the end. The means apart from leading to an end shapes the end. In Gandhian philosophy, self-realization or spiritual freedom is the end of all human actions. Gandhi throughout his life tirelessly tried to use sarvodaya social order as the means to achieve spiritual freedom. Sarvodaya society guarantees moral freedom to every individual. This moral freedom, in turn, progresses itself into spiritual freedom, when it is followed meticulously placing faith in the supremacy of God. Moral freedom as means and spiritual freedom as end forms a continuous process or organic wholes. They cannot be divided into water-tight compartments. Their difference is only imaginary. Both are convertible terms. That is what Gandhi too reveals. What is needed is understanding and practicing ethics as God has given. Sarvodaya, as it enjoys ethico-spiritual basis, it can also be equitable both moral freedom and spiritual freedom. Thus, the problem of ends and means, as an organic whole, occupies a unique place in Gandhian thought, contributing to sarvodaya, moral freedom, spiritual freedom, political freedom, and spiritual economic freedom.

Sarvodaya Social Order

Gandhi with his many-sided personality had a clear vision and definite approach to the problems, which faced India of his time. Indian society was full with deep-rooted evils. It had totally degenerated socially, politically, economically and educationally. Penury had further ruined India social conditions which were already corroded with caste-conflicts, child-marriages, untouchability, *sati*, *pardha*, negation of education to women, dowry, polygamy, corruption, exploitation, etc. Gandhi tried to find immediate solutions to all these problems[42].

In Sarvodaya society, there is no scope for exploitation, discrimination, inequality, and violence, Gandhi envisaged that Sarvodaya society should also be free from evils like 'politics without principle', 'wealth without work', 'knowledge without character', 'commerce without morals', 'science without mankind' and 'service without sacrifice'. It should not be divided into watertight compartments called social, political and religious where all these act and react upon one another. His aim of Sarvodaya made him to establish a close correlation among these problems. The Sarvodaya society is an indivisible whole. In order to establish a democratic and free society Gandhi suggested every individual to imbibe the spirit of love, tolerance, kindness, fearlessness, non-violence, etc. A non-violent society, however small it is, is the strongest one. Non-violence as the law of life includes individuals, societies and nations. To him, non-violence as the law of life includes individuals, societies and nations. To him, non-violence is both a personal and social virtue. A society built on the basis of complete *Ahimsa* is the purest anarchy[43].

For Sarvodaya mentality, certain attributes are essential. Gandhi has offered the 'eleven vows' to discipline oneself so that a disciplined society could emerge. Self-sacrifice is the essence of sarvodaya social order. Every individual is to be ready and willing to sacrifice his happiness for the sake of others. Every one is to follow the policy of giving and not taking. He is to work for others and not expect anything in return for the same. Through sarvodaya he wanted to rebuild the nation "free the bottom upwards" and establish a new social order based on freedom, justice, equality and fraternity. Gandhi's ideal (Sarvodaya) society will be marked by following characteristics:[44]

- There should be no coercive state power in it and social cohesion should be maintained through the citizens' sense of social obligation like the obligations of *Varnashram dharma* in ancient India.
- It should consist of villages or rural agricultural settlements in which wants are few and co-operation, conservation and decentralization are the governing norms of social, civil and economic activity.
- Besides agriculture, other production should be based

on cottage industries and handicraft. Even education should be handicraft-centered.

- The ruling principles of decentralized and handicraft-centered production, three other economic norms should be maintained or practiced, namely, village self-sufficiency, bread-labour (i.e., winning one's bread through work done by one's own body labour), and non-possession (acquiring or using the minimum possible articles of consumption). Heavy machines and heavy transport will have no place in this society.
- In such a society, disputes or conflict (generally arising out of the craze for power, property or possession) will be few and far between. But in order to deal with such disputes, as may possibly or occasionally arise, village Panchayats should be organized. In the unlikely event of the failure of Panchayats, recourse may be had to Sarvodaya.

Gandhi had set up his first sarvodaya community on a farm near Durban and called it Phoenix (c. 1904), followed by another one (c. 1910), near Johannesburg named after Leo Tolstoy. The idea behind these two settlements was that the inmates had to perform all chores of running the farms, whatever is their avocation, on living wages, so that they become self-reliant and self-sufficient. In fact, through the pursuit of sarvodaya ideals, Gandhi wanted to chart out an alternative course. The ideas on Sarvodaya social order find their fullest expression in his constructive work programme that began to unfold itself on his arrival in India from South Africa. Khadi, communal amity, removal of untouchability, promotion of village industries, village sanitation, basic education, etc. came one after another and so did the supporting organization. Some of these organization were: All India Spinners Association, All India Harijan Sewak Sangh, Hindustani Prachar Sabha, Hindustan Talimi Sangh and Akhil Bharat Sewa Sangh. The Sarvodaya society is an ideal society and an ideal can not be fully realized. Gandhi also believed that an ideal is never fully realized in life[45].

Sarvodaya Political Order

Sarvodaya as a political doctrine is mildly anarchist. In fact the political ideal of Sarvodaya is an anarchism of its own variety. It concedes that a fully stateless society is beyond the reach of man, and the goal of human endeavour can only be to reduce the power and sphere of the state to the minimum. The politics of sarvodaya is politics of *Lokniti* instead of *Rajniti*. *Lokniti* is a comprehensive term, which denotes simultaneously a way of life a form of social order and a method. As a way of life, it stands for the self-regulation of individual conduct and for a habit to act on one's own initiatives. As a form of social order, it envisages a society in which police and military will have little to do and the law will interfere least with life. A man will have the utmost freedom of action. As a method, it stands for social change in a manner that would maintain men's freedom of action[46]. The Sarvodaya Political Order is based on certain fundamental political assumptions:

(i) All individuals are equally born.
(ii) People are the custodians of the supreme power in the State.
(iii) Political power should be decentralized both at individual and the village legal.
(iv) All must train themselves for self-rule.
(v) All should believe in the divinity of every individual and strive for the welfare of all people[47].

The ultimate goal for Gandhi is the greatest good of all people. Good, to him, means only the self-realization but not the material well-being of the individuals or the society. A study on the nature of sarvodaya political order demands a brief survey of his view on State, *Swaraj*, *Satyagraha*, Democracy, Nationalism, Internationalism and *Ram Rajya*.[48]

In sarvodaya political order tyranny of majority rule has no place. Vinobaji writes "Political science lays down that everything should be decided by majority. It started counting votes. If there are fifty-one votes in favour and forty-nine votes in opposition, then the former must have an over-riding voice." Similarly, to quote Jayaprakash Narayan, "Because fifty-one people out of hundred decide to do a certain thing in a certain manner, why should the forty-nine people who do not agree with that, be forced to accept that decision? What kind of democracy is this? The laws passed in this way the majority vote are not only oppressive to the minority, but also violate the principle of human unity and dignity as they consider the individual as one of the many rather than as a unique individual possessing a personality. It thus tends to dehumanize humanity". The advocate of sarvodaya also points out that a representative democracy strengthens the bureaucracy in the country and that is not a desirable thing. Therefore, sarvodaya society is to be self-regulated and self-managed in small communities, whether urban or rural. There is to be no political coercion and also no coercion of any kind. People in sarvodaya society are bound together in love and by love. Every individual is to live for others and all others are to live for every individual. The dirty party politics have no place in it. Similarly, there is no place for the philosophy of *laissez-faire*. Sarvodaya stands for national unity and solidarity and there is no place for provincialism and religious fanaticism. Sarvodaya aims to replace thoroughly the manipulative politics of power by the participant politics of co-operation.[49] It emphasizes mutualistic activities spontaneously engaged in by the people. According to Vinoba Bhave,[50] there are ten criteria of an ideal polity:

(i) International fraternity.
(ii) The conscious, spontaneous (as far as possible) and hearty co-operation of all the inhabitants of the country.
(iii) The identity of the good of the capable minority and the general majority.
(iv) The orientation towards the universal and equal development of all.
(v) The widest dispersion of political sovereignty.
(vi) The least amount of government.
(vii) The easiest availability of tantra or justice (?)—(*Sulabhatama tantra*).

(viii) The least possible expenditure.
(ix) The lowest degree of external protection.

Sarvodaya Economic Order

Gandhi had adopted an integral approach to human problems. His basic aim was to reduce economics to terms of religion and spirituality. For him, ethics and economics are not two different entities. Economics that hurt the moral well-being of an individual or a nation are immoral and therefore sinful.[51] True economics, according to Gandhi "stands for social justice, it promotes the good of all equally including the weakest and is indispensable for decent life"[52]. He mainly wants to formulate such an economic constitution to both India and the World that no one suffers from want of food, clothing and shelter. All necessities of life "should be freely available to all as God's air and water are or ought to be"[53]. Such an economic constitution, he aims at building not on material wealth but on spirituality. This is only possible when every one shows more truth than gold, greater fearlessness than pomp of power and wealth, greater charity than love of self.

Gandhian sarvodaya economic order is based on simplicity, decentralization, self-sufficiency, co-operation, equality, non-violence, sanctity of labour, human values, self-sufficient village units, nationalization of basic industries, swadeshi, and the theory of trusteeship. These, in turn, will solve the problems pertaining to labour, capital, production, distribution and profit, etc.

In Gandhian economic order, dependence on others is slavery and self-sufficiency is freedom. Regional self-sufficiency is must in sarvodaya economic order. People should produce their own needs of life. Production must be in accordance with the need.

In Sarvodaya economic order, man is totally free from material bondage. He never becomes a slave to material wants. He lives above his greed and amassing of riches. He views work as service. It is divine for him. He cherishes the principles of self-suffering, sacrifice, dedication and renunciation. His eating, clothing or dwelling shows no superiority or inferiority. He finds no difference between the rich and the poor. Really sarvodaya economic system is practical, realistic and humane.

Socialism, Communism and Sarvodaya

Gandhi called himself a socialist and even a communist but for him socialism and communism were transcendental forms of egalitarian social philosophy that find their fulfilment and culmination in Sarvodaya[54]. Although the situational background from which socialism and sarvodaya have emerged is different, still their humanist idealism is almost similar[55]. According to Jayaprakash Narayan, sarvodaya represents the highest socialist values. Socialism arose in the west as a philosophy of the industrial proletariat and challenged the pretensions of the contemporary state, which bolstered the interests of the capitalists.

Socialism and communism are basically idealistic, ethical and humanitarian in nature. They are concerned with the illumination of the misery of the millions, elevation of the status of poor, unfortunate and downtrodden and founding a society based on the principle of economic equality and social justice. Sarvodaya stands for the just society free from all types of exploitation and human miseries. According to Rajendra Prasad, sarvodaya represents an aspiration "towards a society based on truth and non-violence in which there will be no distinction of caste or creed, no opportunity for exploitation and full scope for development both for individuals as well as groups". Jayaprakash Narayan writes about Sarvodaya, "What we desire is the establishment of a society in which there will be no exploitation, there will be perfect equality and each individual will have equal opportunities for development". Sarvodaya aims at a "classless, casteless and non-exploitative society"[57]. Vinoba said "There is no permanent conflict between the two ideologies-Marxism and Sarvodaya. Whatever differences there might be between Gandhism and communism, there are also points of similarity between these and these too are important. The cause of the have-nots is the basic sentiment running through both. Both Gandhism and communism regard the well-being of the poor and the oppressed with the intensely loving regard of the Mother". K.G. Mashruwala, prominent Gandhian observes, "the common point between Gandhi and Marx is the extreme concern of both for the suppressed and the oppressed, the resourceless and the ignorant, the dumb and starving section of humanity". Similarly, Jayaprakash Narayan said "If we are true socialists, we would be true follower of sarvodaya as well".[58]

In spite of some fundamental similarities between socialism and sarvodaya, there are great differences between them on the question of means and methods. From the sarvodaya stand point there are two shortcomings in the socialist philosophy. First the basic technique for effectuating socialism is supposed to be nationalization. But nationalization may entrench the control of the bureaucrats and may be another name for state capitalism. According to Sarvodaya, the socialist belief in positive state action as the sovereign remedy for human ills is unfounded. Sarvodaya pleads for villagization while socialism believes in nationalization, sarvodaya accepts village ownership. Secondly, socialism adheres, at least in some cases, to the concept of violent revolution. But sarvodaya has no place for violence in its philosophy and technique.[59]

The difference between sarvodaya and communism are far more basic and fundamental. Communism advocates a violent technique for a change over in favour of egalitarian society, a society free form exploitation and privilege. Sarvodaya, to the contrary believes in persuasion and change of heart. Both Marx and Engels expressed their conviction that "violent overthrow of the bourgeoisie lays the foundation for the sway of the proletariat". Lenin and Mao used the technique of violence to bring about a change in the Soviet Union and China respectively. While Gandhi has taught the ethics of self-suffering to convert the opponent because violence can never be the foundation of a just and equal society[60]. Violence breeds counter-violence. And on the basis of violence it is not possible to establish the just social order. In fact a new form of exploitation of man has come into existence and that is exploitation by the party bosses, bureaucrats and the state machine.

The Sarvodaya avoids the evils of legislative or legal coercion in democratic socialism and violence and physical coercion involved in communism. It relies on the technique of conversion for bringing about social transformation in the direction of a non-exploitative and egalitarian society. Gandhi was concerned with the welfare of all and hence rejected the view that the welfare of all can ever be attained by physical, intellectual and moral coercion perpetrated by a section of the people against the rest of the community. Gandhiji believed that sarvodaya could be realized only by the application of a moral and ethical method. Gandhi believed that through the application of the technique of persuasion and appeal to the innate good sense of the rich and the privileged, they might be made to renounce their privileges and apply their superfluous wealth for the welfare of the community. Such renunciation of wealth and privilege was to be for the good of the poor and the rich. "The essence of the revolution contemplated by sarvodaya is that it plans its faith on human approach, at the root of which stands the concept of revolution by human beings for the proliferation of human values and human virtues, and through a method that is strictly humane"[61].

The advocates of sarvodaya also differ from the communists and socialists in respect of the role of the state. Both the communists and the socialists have their faith in the potency of the state of bring about equality in society. In the economic sphere, the communists and socialists advocate centralization and concentration of economic powers in the hands of the state and the proliferation of the economic activities of the state. To quote Jayaprakash Narayan, "Democratic socialists, communists as well as welfarists are all statists". The concentration of both political and economic power in the hands of the state leads to too much of bureaucratization, dehumanization and loss of individual freedom. To quote Jayaprakash Narayan, "The democratic state remains a Leviathan that will sit heavily on the freedom of the people".

The state is still worse under communism. It is true that the communists talk abut the withering away of the state in the long run, but during the transitional period, the state is not only tolerated but also becomes more and more powerful. It devours the lofty ideals of classless society-liberty, equality, fraternity and fellowship. Jayaprakash Narayan writes, "The remedy is to create and develop forms of socialist living through the voluntary endeavour of the people rather than seek to establish by the use of the power of the state. In other words, the remedy is to establish people's socialism, rather than state socialism".

Considering from all angles, sarvodaya is a far nobler, subtler, loftier, broader, deeper and transcendental concept than socialism or communism. According to Vinobaji, "Sarvodaya is a better word that 'socialist', it is also our own native word, born from our own soil and carrying a noble meaning. We don't use the word because we are a little doubtful if we can live up to it. So we prefer the word 'socialist'. But our goal is in fact sarvodaya and our people are being prepared for absorption into the sea of sarvodaya". It is true that socialism and communism can realize their true meaning and fulfil their objective by merging their identity with sarvodaya. Jayaprakash Narayan writes, "Socialism as we understand it today, cannot take mankind to the sublime goals of freedom, equality, brotherhood and peace. Socialism no doubt gives promise to bring mankind closer to those goals than any other competing social philosophy. But I am persuaded that unless socialism is transformed into sarvodaya, those goals would remain beyond its reach." Vinoba writes, "There is no permanent conflict between the two ideologies—Marxism and Sarvodaya. As the Ganges becomes wider and wider and moves on and finally merges in the ocean, I hope Marxism will merge in sarvodaya one day".

Sarvodaya and Contemporary Crisis

The Sarvodaya principle is capable of meeting the greatest challenge of the age. The most urgent need of today is the abolition of human suffering as well as of war. Even Sarvodaya will be very important in the 21st century due to complexity of human behaviour. Sarvodaya by laying stress on the goodness of human nature, unity of mankind, service of man, application of moral principles considered valid for individuals to group life and inter-state relations, the non-violent process of change, social and economic equality, economic and political decentralization, tries to resolve the various kinds of tensions that disturb domestic and international harmony. Sarvodaya is capable of strengthening the forces of love, creativeness and joy of life. Sarvodaya takes a whole view of man and emphasizes his spiritual nature. In modern context the concept of sarvodaya can be interpreted as the "awakening of one and all". Thus, in addition to the awakening of everyone, it refers to the awakening of the total human spirit and personality. Sarvodaya is also related to achieving the highest level of self-realization in which one sees one's manifestation in all others.

Our political, social and economic life has been siezed with a malady. The malady of our times perhaps of all times, is mad quest for power, whether it is political, social or economic. Service is being given up in quest of personal aggrandisement. Humanity is undergoing almost a phase of moral collapse and ethical nihilism. In the era of the mad rush for power, the significance of sarvodaya lies in stressing the permanent value of self-abnegation. Sarvodaya is giving expression to a moral principle of cardinal importance because it wants to enshrine the primacy of goodness and character in place of the skill of manipulation and self-assertion. Sarvodaya appeals to the mind and heart in terms of values and goals. The decadence and corruption, which in fact organized institutional mechanism, can be removed only by the reassertion of moral and spiritual values and their ever-growing incorporation in social, political and economic life. Sarvodaya is the only way to solve the problems of unemployment, unequal distribution of wealth, growing corruption in public life etc. The moral collapse and prostration of our world needs the revitalizing notion of ethical idealism and stress on the moral approach to social and economic problems, which sarvodaya envisages.

Summing Up

The philosophy and sociology of sarvodaya, based on the insights and experiences of Gandhi, is a reassertion of the valuation and moral approach to the problems of mankind, which has been a part of ancient Indian culture for ages. Vinoba Bhave rightly said "Sarvodaya stands for not only making all happy by illuminating suffering from all but also for bringing a world state based on equality"[63]. For Gandhi, sarvodaya stands for the merger of one in all with self-sacrifice and a selfless service. His sarvodaya ideal, apart from standing for the meaning of the welfare of all, implies the meaning of the universal welfare and integrated development of all. As a universal ideal, it aims at not only fulfilling the minimum material needs but also developing the ethico-spiritual aspects of all people. The great contribution of sarvodaya in the present century lies in the reassertion of the Gandhian moral approach to the problems of mankind.

NOTES

1. V.P. Varma, *The Political Philosophy of Mahatma Gandhi and Sarvodaya*, Lakshmi Naryan Agarwal, Agra, 1980, 4th Edition, p. 279.
2. J.N. Mohanty, "Sarvodaya and Aurobindo—A Rapprochement", *Gandhi Marg*, Vol. 4, No. 30, July 1960, p. 211.
3. B.P. Pandey, *Gandhi, Sarvodaya and Organizations*, Chugh Publications, Allahabad, 1988, pp. 20-21.
4. Vishwanath Tandon, *The Social and Political Philosophy of Sarvodaya After Gandhi*, Sarva Seva Sangh Prakashan, Varanasi, 1965, p. 2.
5. Anil Dutta Mishra, *Fundamentals of Gandhism*, Mittal Publications, New Delhi, 1995, p. 5.
6. Mahajan, P. Mani and K.S. Bharathi, *Foundations of Gandhian Thought*, Dattsons, Nagpur, 1987, p. 68.
7. *The Collected Works of Mahatma Gandhi*, Vol. 8, pp. 239-41.
8. K.M. Rathnam Chetty, *Sarvodaya and Freedom: A Gandhian Appraisal*, Discovery Publishing House, New Delhi, 1991, p. 46.
9. B.S. Sharma, "The Philosophical Basis of Sarvodaya", *Gandhi Marg*, Vol. 4, No. 3, July 1960, p. 259.
10. *Ibid.*

11. K.M. Rathnam Chetty, *op. cit.*, p. 47.
12. *Harijan*, 13.2.1949.
13. B.P. Panday, *op. cit.*, p. 14.
14. Dada Dharmadhikari, *Sarvodaya Darshan*, Sarva Seva Sangh Prakashan, Varanasi, p. 18.
15. K.M. Rathnam Chettu, *op. cit.*, p. 48.
16. *Ibid.*, p. 38.
17. *Ibid.*
18. Benudhar Pradhan, *The Socialist Thought of Mahatma Gandhi*, G.D.K. Publications, Delhi, 1980, Vol. I., p. 284.
19. M.K. Gandhi, *An Autobiography: The Story of My Experiments with Truth*, Navajivan Publishing House, Ahmedabad, p. 224.
20. Benudhar Pradhan, *op. cit.*, p. 285.
21. K.M. Rathnam Chetty, *op. cit.*, pp. 39-40.
22. *Ibid.*, p. 40.
23. *Ibid.*, pp. 40-41.
24. *Ibid.*, p. 41.
25. *Ibid.*
26. M.K. Gandhi, *Young India*, 12-11-1925.
27. *Ibid.*
28. K.M. Rathnam Chetty, *op. cit.*, pp. 42-43.
29. Anil Dutta Mishra, *op. cit.*, p. 11.
30. *Ibid.*, p. 11.
31. Benudhar Pradhan, *op. cit.*, p. 294.
32. *Ibid.*, p. 301.
33. *Ibid.*, p. 302.
34. K.M. Rathnam Chetty, *op. cit.*, p. 45.
35. *Ibid.*
36. J.P. Narayan, *Socialism, Sarvodaya and Communism*, A.P.H. Bombay, 1964, p. 149.
37. M.K. Gandhi, *Young India*, p. 364.
38. S. Gopalan, Means and ends: The Gandhian View, *Gandhi Centenary Volume*, 1969, p. 70.
39. M.K. Gandhi, *Young India*, 17.6.1924.
40. B.G. Tendulkar, *Mahatma*, Vol. II, Government of India, New Delhi, p. 299.
41. M.K. Gandhi, *Harijan*, 27.2.1949.
42. A.D. Mishra, *op. cit.*, p. 14.
43. *Ibid.*, p. 15.
44. S.C. Gangal, *Gandhian Thought and Techniques in the Modern World*, Criterion Publications, New Delhi, 1988, pp. 158-59.
45. *Ibid.*, p. 159.

46. Vishwanath Tandon, *op. cit.*, pp. 124-25.
47. K.M. Rathnam Chetty, *op. cit.*, p. 66.
48. Anil Dutta Mishra, *op. cit.*, pp. 16-17.
49. Jayaprakash Narayan, *From Socialism to Sarvodaya*, Akhil Bharat Sarva Seva Sangh, Kashi, 1958, p. 48.
50. V.P. Varma, *op. cit.*, p. 295.
51. N.K. Bose, *Selection from Gandhi*, NPH, Ahmedabad, 1994, p. 40.
52. *Harijan*, 9.10.1937.
53. M.K. Gandhi, *Young India*, 15.17.1928.
54. V.D. Mahajan, *Modern Indian Political Thought*, S. Chand and Company, New Delhi, 1986, p. 569.
55. Jayaprakash Narayan, *Socialism to Sarvodaya*, Socialist Book Centre, Madras, 1956, p. 96.
56. V.P. Varma, *op. cit.*, p. 283.
57. V.D. Mahajan, *op. cit.*, pp. 569-70.
58. *Ibid.*, p. 570.
59. V.P. Varma, *op. cit.*, p. 285.
60. Vinoba Bhave, *Swarajya-Shastra*, Sasta Sahitya Mandal, New Delhi, 1953, pp. 58-68.
61. V.D. Mahajan, *op. cit.*, pp. 573-4.
62. *Ibid.*
63. Anil Dutta Mishra, *op. cit.*, p. 17.

2

Sarvodaya Movement at a Glance

Introduction

Nelson Mandela's prophetic words that the twenty-first century belongs to Gandhi appear to be more than a mere ripple among today's intelligentsia. Gandhi gave to the world new and revolutionary concepts such as *Satyagraha,* i.e., truth force Sarvodaya, i.e., welfare of all and *Shanti Sena,* i.e. peace brigade. These concepts are bound to gain greater relevance and currency as years roll by. Gandhi borrowed the word "Sarvodaya" from a Jain text by Acharya Samantabadra, who lived about two thousand years ago. Sarvodaya represents a higher moral idealism, a more dynamic political ideology and a more radical culture. Sarvodaya movement is a people's movement to carry forward the ideas and programmes sponsored by Gandhi for the welfare of all and the awakening of all. Sarvodayites, as the term used by both Kapoor (1974) and Hans Wismeijer (1981) are the leaders, constructive workers and Gandhiites engaged in the Sarvodaya movement. Sarvodayites are also known as *Sarvodayavadis*.

The foundations of the Sarvodaya movement have been firmly laid by Gandhi based on the principles of truth, non-violence and love all of which have eternal value. Success of any movement depends on its leadership. Vinoba's charismatic leadership constituted a potential strength for the movement. Jayaprakash Narayan undoubtedly had his own personal charisma and it has been shown on many occasions, particularly on the occasion of his grand declaration of *Jeevadan,* i.e., life gift, meant the dedication of one's whole life and energy to the cause of the movement.

The basis of sarvodaya according to Vinoba, rests on the three-fold programmes— *Gramdan, Khadi* and *Shanti Sena*. They are indivisible and the three would revolutionise the life of man and build a new world, believed Vinoba. According to Ostergaard, the sarvodaya movement in India represents an attempt to apply to the task of social reconstruction, the ideas originally developed by Gandhi.

Based on the two basic principles of truth and non-violence, Gandhi developed the concept of constructive programme in early 1930s. The constructive programme resulted in the eighteen-fold activities and reforms. After the assassination of Gandhi in 1948, Vinoba took the mantle of the movement. In 1951, Vinoba started his famous *Bhoodan*-Campaign and later it grew as a popular movement.

Sarvodaya in Tamil Nadu

Sarvodaya movement in Tamil Nadu is as old as it originated in India in the early 1920s and spread to Sri Lanka in 1958. Sarvodayites of Tamil Nadu have their links with their counterparts in Sri Lanka and the rest of India. Sarvodaya Mandal established in Tamil Nadu at the fag end of 1956, continues to play the lead role in the movement as such and it is said to be the nerve centre of its activities. As per the Directory (1986) of Gandhi Smarak Nidhi, New Delhi, there are 146 Gandhian constructive institutions including Sarvodaya Mandal in Tamil Nadu.

Sarvodayites and their Movement

Sarvodayites, who include both leaders and constructive workers, play a vital role in a significant social movement, which is in the making and in the process of social reconstruction. Sarvodayite is otherwise known as Anna—"Brother" and Akka—"Sister" a common form of address among sarvodaya workers in Tamil Nadu. Since a study on sarvodayites and their movement would facilitate a deeper understanding of their lives and trend of the movement as such and pave way for solutions, the present attempt has been made with the following objectives:

(i) To explore the growth of Sarvodaya movement in Tamil Nadu as evinced by the sarvodayites.
(ii) To study the impact, if any, of sarvodaya leadership on the political scenario.
(iii) To understand the nature of involvement with people among those in the Sarvodaya movement in Tamil Nadu.
(iv) To analyse the process of perpetuation of leadership in the Sarvodaya movement.
(v) To visualize the global perspectives vis-à-vis the trends of Sarvodaya movement.

Methodology

There were 503 constructive workers in Tamil Nadu as per the Directory (1973) of the Gandhi Smarak Nidhi, New Delhi. In addition, 126 workers were listed out in Vol. 2 of the constructive workers who's who (1978) in Tamil Nadu. Based on the above Directories, participation in the various meetings including seminars and conferences and personal correspondence with different sarvodayites, the researcher prepared the final list of sarvodaya workers for the study purpose. As a result, 252 members were identified and finalized as the total number of constructive sarvodaya workers in Tamil Nadu. A total of 252 sarvodayites in the entire state of Tamil Nadu constituted the universe, from which 97 responses were recorded through mailed questionnaire method. Four respondents were marked as dead and eleven of them were untraceable at the said address. Thus the remaining eighty-two (82) respondents provided data for the major analysis in the study.

Tools of Data Collection

Questionnaire method was used as the main tool in conducting the study. Personal case study method and non-participant observation methods were also adopted in collecting data. Besides this, the researcher attended several meetings and also visited sarvodaya centres and Gandhian constructive institutions; publications, reports and documents of various institutions were used for secondary data. Twenty-one individual interviews were completed from among those who had responded to the mailed questionnaire. Seventeen prominent sarvodayites were also interviewed outside the questionnaire; both primary and secondary data were thus gathered in this shape.

The Trend of Sarvodaya Movement

The youth group 15-35 years in the Sarvodaya movement constituted six per cent and the rest ninety four per cent were between 36 and 85 years. Thirty-five per cent among the respondents were degree holders. Thirty four per cent high school passed, fifteen per cent primary school passed, twelve per cent middle school educated and four per cent of them have completed the intermediate under the old pattern. Of all the respondents, eighty one per cent were sarvodaya workers, seventeen per cent constituted supervisory and managerial staff working in the Gandhian constructive institutions and the rest two per cent were founders of the Gandhian Institutions in Tamil Nadu. As regards the duration of working of the respondents in the Sarvodaya movement, eighty three per cent of sarvodayites had gained rich experience over a period ranging from 21 to 40 years and the rest seventeen per cent had below 20 years of experience. In the case of an annual income, fifty two per cent of the respondents fell under the income group of Rs. 11,000 to 20,000, thirty one per cent of them had Rs. 21,000 to 30,000 and the rest sixteen per cent had an income ranging from Rs. 31,000 to 70,000 except the only one per cent who hailed from the category of below Rs. 10,000.

While analysing the respondents' living conditions, it was observed that forty five per cent of sarvodayites lived in the urban environment and the rest thirty three had chosen to live in rural areas, and the 'urban' (semi-urban) constituted twenty two per cent of the respondents. Sixty-one per cent lived in their own houses, twenty-one per cent used housing quarters provided by the management and the rest eighteen per cent of them lived in rented ones. Eighty-one per cent of the sarvodaya workers opined that there is nothing wrong in having an individual savings/bank account and the rest objected this rather strongly.

Sarvodaya Work vis-à-vis Family Life

Nuclear families comprised fifty-one per cent while the remaining were joint families, except the one per cent of Ashram type. Twenty-four per cent had one to three members, fifty-one per cent had four to six members, twelve per cent had seven to nine members and five per cent had more than ten members and the rest eight per cent belonged to the category of children's home-*cum*-ashram type for the benefit of orphan boys and girls run by the committed sarvodayites. Sixty-five per cent of the families stated that none of their family members are involved in the activities of the Sarvodaya movement, twenty eight per cent indicated that at least one member had been associated with the movement and the rest seven per cent pointed out that 2-3 members were fully involved in the on-going activities of the movement. Fifty-one per cent of the sarvodayites were influenced by the elders and leaders of the movement, thirty four per cent by their self-interest and the rest fifteen per cent by their parents.

Sarvodayites had evolved their own personal code of conduct within sarvodaya movement. The respondents in general were in favour of the daily use of *khadi*, strict vegetarianism, and the use of public transport to their place of daily work. Majority of the respondents remained as spiritualist.

Current Status of Performance

Of all the respondents, forty three per cent of them had a darshan and meeting with Gandhiji whereas the rest fifty-seven per cent had no such opportunity. In order to strengthen the sarvodaya movement, forty-seven per cent of sarvodayites had inducted 100 to 500 male and female members separately. Twenty-eight per cent enrolled male members and the rest (18.28%) inducted neither male nor female members, seven per cent do not remember the number of men and women members enrolled.

As for the encouragement of their involvement in the Sarvodaya movement, sixty-three per cent of the sarvodayites stated that both rich and the poor encourage and provide necessary assistance for carrying out sarvodaya work, seventeen per cent felt that only the rich supported them whereas twenty per cent were appreciated by the poorer sections of the society. As regards the coverage of villages by the individual sarvodayites, fifty-seven per cent of them reported that they covered below 100 villages, seven per cent 701-800 villages, four per cent 301-400 villages, one per cent 201-300 villages and five per cent 101-200 villages and the remaining twenty-six per cent had not specified the number of villages covered by them. In the case of beneficiaries of sarvodaya twenty-three per cent of the respondents revealed that people ranging from 501-2500 in number were benefited and from 2501 to 5000 persons received benefits from twenty per cent of respondents. Thirty per cent of them opined that the people who benefited were only below 500 persons and the rest twenty-seven per cent were not maintaining any register showing the details of beneficiaries.

Methods of training people committed to sarvodaya include campaigns, *padayatra-vahana yatra*, conference, exhibitions, public meetings, *Shanti Sena* camps, wearing *khadi* and using village products, formation of Gandhi Mandram in villages, nurturing Gandhian values, arranging wall newspapers, screening videos and documentaries and organising cultural programmes.

Factors Influencing Sarvodaya Movement

The following are the positive and negative factors influencing the Sarvodaya movement as spelt out by the respondents in the study. The positive factors which influence sarvodaya movement are working for the casteless and classless society, experiments with non-violence, pledging to work for the last man, adoption of simple life and use of *khadi*, encouraging inter-caste marriage, empowering women, faith in partyless democracy, commitment for *Gram Swaraj*, freedom from bossism, working for national unity and purity, organising *shramdan*, encouraging youths in the movement and organising periodical conferences and special events.

The factors that affect the image of the sarvodaya movement are groupism and casteism, lack of tolerance, hunger, for power, thirst for publicity, lack of devotion and commitment, gap between leaders and workers, practice of hidden dowry system, misusing foreign aid and hidden corruption, frustration among workers, lack of unity and taking shelter under political parties.

There are three popular magazines of Sarvodaya movement i.e., *Sarvodayam* (Tamil monthly 500 copies), *Sarvodaya* (English monthly 500 copies), and *Grama Rajya* (Tamil weekly 3000 copies). These magazines are the mouth pieces of the movement.

A Comparative Profile of Elder and Younger Sarvodayites

The following are the details of the age group of the respondents:

Mean age — 58.8 years (N=82)
Standard deviation of men — 12.9 years

Aspects	*Elder*	*Younger*
Education	Discernibly low percentage of graduates	Significantly high percentage of graduates
Marital Status	A little over a third unmarried	No single unmarried person
Occupation	Sarvodaya work as full time occupation	Sarvoraya involvement as part time interest
Economic level	Economic standing long and firm enough to bring regular income	Irregular income
Family size	Large family background	Small family

As per the above definition, there were fifteen who belonged to the elderly age group and fourteen to the younger. A comparative profile of elder and younger sarvodayites, identified in the study is given below:

- The elder and younger Sarvodayites were identified respectively as those above the level of mean plus standard deviation on the one hand and below the level of mean minus standard deviation on the other hand.

However, the place of current residence did not throw up any notable difference between the two in terms of rural, semi-urban and or urban.

The blue-print for expanding the sarvodaya movement will include the following:

- Like UNO, there should be a world body for sarvodaya movement.
- There could be sarvodaya charter like Earth charter to be followed by all the nationals.
- Sarvodaya ideology to be taught in the schools and colleges, *Shanti Sena* to be formed as part of UNO.
- A strong network among the centres working on the lines of sarvodaya.
- Sarvodayites to be honoured properly by recognising their works.
- Representation of sarvodayites in the State Assembly and Parliament.
- Sarvodaya Kala Kendras to be created as part of cultural dimensions of Sarvodaya movement.

Conclusion

While concluding the present study, it may be stated that the choice before us now is between sarvodaya and 'sarvanasa' extinction of mankind. There are tremendous opportunities to promote a sarvodaya society in which sarvodayites can continue to play a paramount role. Problems confronting the sarvodayites emerge from their community, work place and their non-sarvodaya neighbourhood. To reduce their burdens, problems and to better the movement, the present study highlights the current trend as a movement of the aged and offers a blue-print for expanding and strengthening the sarvodaya movement in Tamil Nadu. It is suggested that a sarvodaya society will be achieved not by making Gandhi a myth of the bygone days but only when we practice sarvodaya ideology and Gandhian way as a living philosophy of life.

REFERENCES

Aram, M., *Future of Mankind,* Shanti Ashram, Coimbatore, 1989.

Augustine, Thottakara, *Gandhian Spirituality,* Centre for Indian and Inter-religions Studies, Italy, 1992.

Balasubramaniam, K., *Directory of Gandhian Constructive Workers,* Gandhi Peace Foundation, New Delhi, 1996.

Copley, Antony and George Paxton, *Gandhi and the Contemporary World,* The Gandhi Foundation, London, 1996.

Detlef, Kantawsky, *Sarvodaya—The Other Development,* Vikas Publishing House Pvt. Ltd., New Delhi, 1980.

Devadoss, T.S., *Sarvodaya and the Problem of Political Sovereignty,* University of Madras, Madras, 1974.

Dinakaran, T.R., *Tamil Nadu Sarvodaya Conference,* Special Number, SOUVENIR, Sarvodaya Publication, Aruppukottai, 1984.

Gupta, Devendra Kumar, *Constructive Workers' Who's Who,* Part One, Gandhi Samarak Nidhi, New Delhi, 1973.

Jain, Pratibha, *Gandhian Ideas, Social Movement and Creativity,* Rawat Publications, Jaipur, 1985.

Kanagasabapathy, A., *12th State Level Sarvodaya Conference,* SOUVENIR, Special Issue, Tamil Nadu Sarvodaya Mandal, Trichy, 1995.

Kapoor, A.C., *Principles of Political Science,* S. Chand and Co., New Delhi, 1974.

Sinha, Archana, *The Social and Political Philosophy of Sarvodaya,* Janaki Prakashan, Patna, 1955.

Tandon, Vishwanath, *Sarvodaya after Gandhi,* Sarva Seva Sangh, Varanasi, 1965.

Wismeijer, Hans, *Diversity in Harmony: A Study of the Leaders of the Sarvodaya Shramadana Movement in Sri Lanka,* Department of Cultural Anthropology, Netherlands, 1981.

3

Role of Youth in Sarvodaya

The purpose of this paper is to specify and analyse some of the issues relating to youth of today and their possible role in Sarvodaya movement towards 21st century. The coming century needs to be a century of Gandhi and Sarvodaya in which youth groups must be given paramount importance. The modern youth are expected to play a vital role in establishing Sarvodaya social, political and economic order in the society in which they live and anyone would agree that every movement has been spearheaded by the young generation. A global socio-economic order is inconceivable and impossible without adoption of Gandhian concept of Sarvodaya. Because—

Mahatma Gandhi	Minus	Sarvodaya is Zero
Development	Minus	Peace is Zero
Development	Minus	Youth is Zero

Hence, the realization is that the youth force has to be effectively nurtured and utilised in the social, economic, political, moral, spiritual development of a country. Specially in developing countries like India, the role of youth has become very important at this crucial juncture of human history. The declaration by the United Nations of 1985 as the "International Year of the Youth" assumes great significance in this regard, thereby providing an opportunity to analyse and reassess the role and involvement of youth in the Sarvodaya Social order, Sarvodaya Political order and Sarvodaya Economic order.

Nationally the age group between 13 and 35, falling between adolescence and middle age, can be treated as youth. Youth are energetic, enthusiastic, creative, dynamic and virile. Capable of achieving good results provided their energies are properly channelised. No development can be sustained for long, without developing youth to be physically fit, mentally alert and socially responsible and responsive citizens, capable of maintaining social equilibrium.

Broadly, the youth can be divided into two categories viz., student and non-student youth. The former are well organised and youth services are made available to them in university and college campuses; whereas the latter who are in no way organized, have remained neglected for long. Little attempt was made so far to involve them in creative and constructive activities even though the non-student youth comprise 33.5 per cent of the entire population and the non-student youth component is seven out of eight. It is well known that the non-student youth living in villages and slum areas are either unemployed or under-employed and they have got to be organized in their own habitat and social conditions so that they could reconstruct their own villages and better their living conditions.

Need for Change

Besides organising the youth for constructive activities, our education system has also to undergo an inherent change to meet the needs of our non-student youth community. Practical knowledge in keeping with the realities of life in rural areas may be imparted. What is taught to them in university campus is of little relevance. Academic achievements continue to be the main criterion in obtaining arm chair assignments, while socio-economic factors, contribute to early "drop outs" from schools, creating a helpless situation for the poor youth.

There is ample scope for their development through self-employment in villages; but owing to the failure to exploit the village resources to the optimum, there has been a large-scale exodus of the youth from villages to the urban areas. This has not only hampered proper development, but has created problems of over-population in the urban areas. There is an urgent need to overcome this difficult situation, by creating suitable self-employment opportunities for rural youth, and by bringing about the needed reconciliation between theory and practice. It would be appropriate to quote Pandit Jawaharlal Nehru, in his address at the Inter-University Youth Festival, New Delhi on October 23, 1955. He said, "The more the action and the thought are allied and integrated, the more effective they become and the happier you grow... The happiest man is he, whose thinking and actions are coordinated."

In a way, the Government is well set to meet the co-curricular and extra-curricular needs of the student youth, in the form of NCC, NSS, Guides, Sports and other service and personality building activities. The non-student youth community in the far flung areas of our country demands a more concerted attention.

The Ministry of Youth Affairs and Sports has sponsored a number of schemes and programme for both the student and non-student youth. They have the National Service Scheme for the college youth and Nehru Yuva Kendras for non-student youth. These two are very important and prestigious schemes of the Ministry.

The quality of gold is known only when it is put to fiery test, so is the valour and dignity of youth of a nation is revealed while facing the challenges of the nation.

It is said that a youth is he/she who is adventurous in spirit, resistant against vested interests, and who lives by fair means, and above all youth is he who thinks dispassionately and acts in a detached manner for the nation's good and is imbued with dynamism.

Despite the problems India has been facing, it should be remembered that we have inherited a great cultural heritage, and have a glorious vision for our country. Nothing worthwhile is achieved without strenuous effort and hard work. It is up to us to build a society free from wants; a society which can bring about a change through law and consent; a society which finds fulfillment in the happiness and equality of its citizens; a society which ensures a life of enlightenment and fulfillment in consonance with national values.

Gandhi's Vision of Sarvodaya

To understand the Gandhian conception of Integrated Rural Development, we may have to go back to the year 1908 when Gandhi wrote his little book *Hind Swaraj* (Indian Home Rule) in South Africa. In his unusual work, Gandhi characterized modern civilization as a 'disease'. It made "bodily welfare the object of life". It had no place, for 'morality or religion'. Gandhi also condemned modern machinery, which helped exploitation of the poor and caused the ruination of Indian handicrafts. He advocated non-violence as a superior ideology.

Gandhi described the cities as "a snare" where various social evils flourished. On the contrary, the village was a wholesome place where "simple living and high thinking" was possible. He praised the virtues of rural life, which was the cradle of Indian civilization.

In South Africa, Gandhi was introduced to the British writer John Ruskin and his book *"Unto This Last"*. This book cast a magic spell on Gandhi who decided immediately to transform his life and conduct in accordance with its three principles: (1) The individual good is contained in the social good. (2) All occupations have equal value. (3) The life of labour is really worth living.

Gandhi translated Ruskin's book into Gujarati, his mother tongue. The English title, *"Unto This Last"* (Welfare for all) was translated into an Indian word Sarvodaya which in course of time, came to be the ideal of Gandhi's conception of non-violent, decentralised, equalitarian social order. He describes it in the following memorable passage:

> "In this structure composed of innumerable villages, there will be ever-widening, never-ascending circles. Life will not be a pyramid with the apex sustained by the bottom but it will be an oceanic circle whose centre will be the individual, always ready to perish for the circle of villages, till at last the whole become one life composed of individuals never aggressive in their arrogance but ever humble sharing the majesty of the oceanic circle of which they are integral units".

A Revolutionary Mass Leader

Mahatma Gandhi was one of the giants of the twentieth century and all his ideas, philosophy and techniques will inspire generation after generation. Also he was a champion and saviour of human kind who applied his mind to socio-economic, political and other problems affecting every facet of human endeavour. His public life was spread over fifty eventful years and from that vantage position he developed a deep insight into contemporary socio-economic problems. As a revolutionary mass leader he commands the loyalty of vast millions of his country and even many more in different parts of the world.

He gave to the world new and revolutionary concepts such as *Satyagraha* (truth force), *Sarvodaya* (Welfare of all) and *Shanti Sena* (Peace brigade). In the years to come, particularly in the coming 21st century, these concepts are bound to gain greater relevance and currency. After Gandhi passed away it was given to Acharya Vinoba Bhave to pick up the thread and give a creative impetus to the Gandhian Movement. He discovered *Bhoodan* (land gift), developed it into *Gramdan* (village gift) and the movement began to manifest new dimensions. All these ideas and concepts are appreciated and also borrowed by other countries and particularly Sarvodaya Movement in Sri Lanka has developed the concept of *Shramadan* under the dynamic leadership of Dr. A.T. Ariaratne who started this movement. *Shramadan* is the instrument through which the movement satisfies the basic needs of the poor, weaker sections and rural community.

Sarvodaya, today does not represent an utopian vision, but has assumed the dimension of a global movement and a socio-economic phenomenon. Sarvodaya represents a higher moral idealism, a more dynamic political ideology and more radical culture. Thus it is to denigrate both Gandhi and his Sarvodaya to say: "All his ideas are right, but he is two hundred years ahead of his time."

In fact, Gandhi is more relevant today than before. We have to choose between Atom and *Ahimsa*. Sarvodaya and *Sarvanasa* (total annihilation). The creation of a social system, free from social ills was Gandhiji's ultimate aim. His quest for such a social system brought him to his conception of Sarvodaya society, identifying it with the perfectly non-violent, stateless, classless and casteless society. Gandhiji says that "...a society organized and run on the basis of complete non-violence would be the purest anarchy" (*Harijan*, 21.07.40).

Youth Development

Youth development is a vast and complex subject. The approaches made by governmental or non-governmental organisations to develop youth are conditioned by the different conceptual or ideological positions that each of these organisations take when defining what is meant by Development of Youth. The youth programmes they develop are also varied, for example, from a "Beach Dance" organised by a sophisticated youth group in the city at one extreme to a purely traditional spiritual development programme organised by a saintly monk on the other extreme. This subject is made more complex by the fact that the social milieu, in which this whole youth development exercise takes place is also constantly undergoing rapid changes.

A Four-fold Approach

The Sarvodaya *Shramadan* Movement considers development of youth as an integral part of a total plan for the development of men and society. This necessarily has to have four components. They are:

(i) The youth as a person and helping him or her to nurture himself or herself into consciously treading a path of building up an awakening personality within the cultural setting in which he or she lives.
(ii) The role of youth as a member of a family or village or (urban) group in awakening the latter into a total development process according to the needs of its specific situation.

(iii) The active participation of youth as the biggest segment of the national population in identifying the problems of the nation, designing solutions, learning the required techniques and skills for nation building and finally playing the most dynamic role in national development, and

(iv) Youth as builders of a new world order where economic justice, mutual cultural respect, international brotherhood and peace prevail.

The Sarvodaya Youth programmes always lay emphasis on social and physical environment within which the youth grows, learns, works to interact with others and develops. And this environment is strongly influenced by the traditional cultural factors of group conduct, namely, sharing Pleasant Speech.

Mass participation in well-organized manual work programmes helps the individual youth to develop the qualities of Constructive Activity and Equality in Conduct in a group setting. *Shramadan*—voluntary sharing of labour—is primarily a psychological technique for personality awakening and secondarily it is an essential process in building up an economic infrastructure in the community where there is less capital and plenty of ideal labour.

Sarvodaya for example, has seven major development education institutes and nearly fifty development education centres to train youth for community leadership and vocational skills that are required for its village development programmes. The age group of youth who are trained is between 18 and 26 years. Already several thousands of youths have gone back to their villages after training.

What strikes me most (after a visit to Sri Lanka) is that Sarvodaya does not regard unemployed youth as a liability as most societies do, where they are a drain on the economy and can be volatile and destructive. Some how Sarvodaya has been able to turn them into an asset (World Bank).

Youth and Gandhian Values

Gandhi looked at life as a whole and as a unity and on

education as the only revolutionary instrument of lifting life continually to something better, richer and fuller materially, culturally, morally and spiritually. Nearly thirty years ago, he deliberately gave his educational programmes the name '*Nai Talim*', meaning New Education. Under *Nai Talim*, education became life-centred, instead of textbook-centered and *Nai Talim* was defined as education for life, through life and through out life. *Nai Talim* became divided into Pre-basic, Basic, Post-basic, University and Social Education. Pre-basic was the nursery school part, Basic was elementary education for a period of eight years, between 7 and 15 years of age, Post-basic was high school education and social education became adult education in the widest and most relevant sense.

Sarvodaya seeks to achieve justice for everyone through peaceful methods. It stands for revolution by consent and not by coercion of any kind. Among all the peaceful methods of revolution, education is the most potent. It is the number one weapon in the entire arsenal of non-violent revolution. And justice once achieved should be maintained and nourished only through democratic processes.

Youth and National Development

In a country like Russia, all the youth are given an opportunity to learn more about Marx. In the same way, the youth in our country must be encouraged to understand Gandhi and Sarvodaya. For the benefit of non-student youth, Gandhian ideology and Sarvodaya may be propagated through Social/Adult/Non-formal Education Centres. In order to take Gandhi to schools, colleges, Universities, a suitable syllabus as core subject must be introduced. A system must be devised to enable youth to imbibe Gandhian values and qualities.

Participation of youth in national development is a much theorized subject. For macro-planners, this is a pet phrase in most developing countries. The elite make the plans and expect the youth to participate in implementing these plans. They mistakenly presume that the youth also do get motivated by the same theoretical considerations. Most of the attempts to get youth willingly involved in development have failed.

The motivation for youth to participate in national development has to be inculcated from their young age and should begin from the grassroots in society. Educational institutions in cooperation with voluntary community service and community development organizations can play a key role in this. It should form an essential element in the educational process.

In our country excellent opportunities exist for youth participation in national development. Under national development we may include every aspect of welfare and development activities, man-power training and educational and mass participation in major constructional efforts.

An effective impact on national development can be brought upon by youth participation only if the Government sets the pace for it. However much a voluntary agency tries to help the nation at this level all such efforts can be killed by an arrogant bureaucracy. The Sarvodaya movement is an excellent example for this. The movement has always kept itself out of power politics but was always deeply involved with youth and development.

For over twenty years the movement has tried to offer respective governments its services in this field but to this day it has failed to get genuine co-operation from the bureaucracy inspite of pious utterances.

The entire world order is changing. In rich countries there is a strong segment of youth who are struggling against the old order in their countries. They want to get away from materialist affluence and revert back to pre-industrial human values. They want to enlighten their own communities about the injustices the old colonial system and the present trade system had imposed on poorer countries and correct the imbalances with their participation. Our youth should be ready to work with them with the same concern and enlightment. Their task is to destroy all vestiges of imperialism and building a new world economic order. Sarvodaya movement has established a variety of schemes such as village link-up programmes and people to people direct trade links as practical programmes in this field.

Problems of Youth

"Youth problem, youth unemployment, youth unrest, youth revolt" are some of the expressions we hear from all parts of the world. There is no uniform agreement with these categorization of youth out of context of the broad social situation in which they live. If they are a problem, then the family, the society and even the nation becomes a problem.

There is need to look at youth in relation to the whole social context. The integration between youth and their family and their village community has to result in a forward looking progressive attitude in both and not in confrontation and conflict.

We have a close look at the situation regarding the pernicious evils of drinks, alcohol and drugs which deprive human beings, especially youth. The National Congress organization in its earliest days declared with a fanfare its policy for complete prohibition to ensure the health of body and mind of all Indians. But a few years after *Swaraj* the Congress governments installed by the votes of the people completely forgot all about it, perhaps on account of the pernicious lust for power and the lure of the excise revenue. Now there is a free flow of intoxicating drinks into the throats of the people and a free flow of money from the pockets, especially of the poor and the hungry, into the exchequer of governments. The ostensible policy of the Government should be the welfare of the poor of the land.

Towards 21st Century—Some Issues

Necessary steps may be taken by Sarvodaya leaders mainly to activise the Sarvodaya movement and gear it up towards 21st century and every one's wish is for a century of Sarvodaya in the coming future.

Youth of today may be encouraged to play a desirable role in the Sarvodaya movement of proper and effective training.

So as to take the second line leadership in the Sarvodaya movement in India effective steps must be taken to provide an opportunity for youth with a view to imbibe Gandhian values.

Films on Sarvodaya and Gandhi may be made available more in number so as to attract and educate the children and youth for their future participation in Sarvodaya movement.

Sarvodaya leaders may enlist the cooperation of the media men to produce films based on the principle of Sarvodaya and non-violence. It is because of the films of the day more number of murders are taking place in our society. This may be prevented and may be given a new and good direction.

The motto of the 28th Sarvodaya Conference is Science + Spirituality = Sarvodaya. Youth of today ought to be given spiritual training. Spirituality cannot be a casualty. Youth Development should not be divorced from Spiritual Development.

Our Sarvodaya leaders in India may take necessary steps to organize National *Shramadan* camps. State level *Shramadan* camps, District level *Shramadan* camps, Village level *Shramadan* camps and International *Shramadan* camps in which youth can share their energy and thoughts.

Sarvodaya leaders may initiate to organize World Sarvodaya Conference (WSC) for every three years or five years so as to assess and review the various types of work in progress.

Sarvodaya leaders may particularly appeal to the United nations to declare one of the coming years or decades as the International Year of Sarvodaya (IYS) or Sarvodaya decades like Disarmament Decade so as to popularize it and also deliver more benefits to the youth of today.

The governments both at the state level and national level must be made to understand the paramount importance of Sarvodaya ideology and programmes in today's situation.

Gandhi wanted to establish a society based on Love, Truth, Non-violence and *Dharma* and a society free from corruption and free from laziness. Also he wanted a society to be free from seven deadly sins. If you go to the Gandhi Sȧmadhi at Rajghat, you will find the seven deadly sins enumerated. They were written by some American writer whom Gandhi came across early in his life.

The seven deadly sins are:

Commerce	Without	Ethics
Pleasure	Without	Conscience
Politics	Without	Principles
Knowledge	Without	Character
Science	Without	Humanity
Wealth	Without	Work
Worship	Without	Sacrifice

In conclusion, I wish to emphasis that youth should try to keep aloof from all the above sins and also they should try acquire the knack of maintaining a society based on love, truth and non-violence and a society free from evils, which will lead to "Zero Conflict" and peace in the nation and world at large. However the author emphasizes that youth is the backbone of any movement in particular Sarvodaya Movement in India for which the youth of the country need to be oriented periodically under the umbrella of the Gandhian movement.

REFERENCES

Aram, M. 1989, *The Future of Mankind*, Shanthi Ashram, Coimbatore.

Ariaratne, A.T., 1980, *Sarvodaya Concept of Youth Development*, Sarvodaya Movement Leaflets-3, Moratuwa, Sri Lanka.

Arunachalam, K. and Jayapragasam, S., 1987, *Gandhian Techniques for the Liberation of Weaker Sections*, Sarvodaya Ilakkiya Pannai, Madurai.

Discussions with Sarvodaya leaders and workers on different occasions both at Gandhigram and during visits to various Gandhian Institutions in Tamil Nadu and beyond.

Diwakar, R.R., 1985, A Journey to Sarvodaya, *Gandhi Marg*, July, Vol. No. 7, No. 4, pp. 197-208, Gandhi Peace Foundation, New Delhi.

Government of India, 1982, *Youth Bulletin*, Ministry of Education and Culture, New Delhi.

Macy, Joanna, 1984, *Dharma and Development—Religion as Resources in the Sarvodaya Self-Help Movement*, Kumarian Press, 29, Bishop Road, West Hartford, Connecticut D6 119.

Mukherjee, Dhurjati, 1985, Role of Youth in Social Change, *Gandhi Marg*, March, Vol. No. 6, No. 12, pp. 837-44, Gandhi Peace Foundation, New Delhi.

Palkhiwala, N.A., 1984, *Relevance of Gandhi Today*, Gandhi Peace Foundation, New Delhi.

Raja, K.C.R., 1964, *Thoughts and Talks of G. Ramachandran*, Gandhigram on the 60th Birthday of Dr. G. Ramachandran, Madurai, Tamil Nadu.

4

Gandhian Vision of Society

On the occasion of the bursting of nuclear bombs on Hiroshima and Nagasaki, Gandhi exclaimed that non-violence alone could save humanity. The apostle of non-violence martyred himself for the cause he preached and practiced through out his life time. But his very martyrdom is the seed of a faith which is bound to grow for the survival of humanity.

Gandhiji's greatest contribution to human thought and practice is his concept of non-violence. He taught his countrymen a new way of revolt. He would meet violence with non-violence, untruth with truth, hatred with love. On the basis of this tool Indian people would overthrow the almighty British power.

Historically or chronologically speaking Gandhi's active non-violence emerged as a result of his experiences in South Africa, especially his painful experience at Maritzburg.

Non-violence literally means non-killing or non-injury to anybody. It signifies non-injury in thought, word and deed. Violence is committed if one thinks ill of or utters a harsh word to anybody, though one might not have caused any physical injury. The votary of non-violence may bear self-suffering or may even be ready for self-sacrifice but he could never cause hurt to any living being on earth. "I cultivate in my soldiers" he said, "the courage of dying without killing". Non-violence in its dynamic condition means conscious suffering. It does not mean submission to the evildoer, but it means putting of one's soul against the will of the tyrant.

Though the term non-violence is negative in form, it is not merely a negative virtue. It involves the positive doing of good as much as the negative refusal to cause harm. It is a positive force—the universal law of love. In its active form it stands for goodwill towards all that lives. It is supreme love, supreme kindness, and supreme self-sacrifice.

Non-violence is an active force of the highest order. Final victory of the practitioner of non-violence is perfectly certain. "Working under this law of our being, it is possible for a single individual to defy the whole might of an unjust empire to save his honour, his religion, his soul and lay the foundation of that empire's fall or its regeneration—non-violence is soul-force or the power of the Godhead within us".

Gandhi lays down certain conditions for the practice of non-violence. An imperfect man cannot grasp the whole of that essence, he would not be able to bear its full blaze, but even an infinitesimal fraction of it, when it becomes active within us, can work wonders.

These conditions are:

1. Consciousness of the living presence of God within one is undoubtedly the first requisite.
2. Non-violence demands on the part of the practitioner perfect humanity. If one has pride, egoism, there is no non-violence. "It was only when I had learnt to reduce myself to zero that I was able to evolve the power of *Satyagraha* in South Africa" says Gandhi.
3. Purity of heart
4. Courage
5. Forbearance
6. Fearlessness
7. Complete abstention from exploitation
8. Non-possession.

Gandhi had immense historical sense to prove that non-violence is the law of our species as violence is the law of the brute. The history of mankind is witness to the fact that man has been steadily progressing towards *Ahimsa*. Development of mankind shows signs of progressive *Ahimsa* and diminishing *himsa*. "Had it been otherwise the human species should have been extinct by now ever as many of the lower species have disappeared".

Gandhiji's non-violence is not for the weak. He believes in the non-violence of the brave. "Non-violence is the summit of bravery". There is no room for cowardice in Gandhiji's scheme of non-violence. Where there is a choice between cowardice and violence, Gandhiji would prefer violence. "I would risk violence a thousand times than the emasculation of a whole race. Violence offered in self-defence, or the defence of the defenceless, even if not lawful, is an act of bravery far better than cowardly submission". Gandhiji's non-violence was thus the non-violence of the brave. "Non-violence", says Gandhiji "is infinitely superior to violence, forgiveness is more mainly than punishment. But abstinence is forgiveness only when there is the power to punish; it is meaningless when it pretends to proceed from a helpless creature". Physical capacity is not essential for the non-violence of the brave. What is essential is an indomitable will where strength proceeds from.

The religion of non-violence is not merely for the *rishis* or *saints*. It is meant for the common people as well. According to Gandhiji, the salvation of mankind lies only through non-violence. There is no alternative to it. In the violent war, if it starts at all, if there is a victor left, the victory will be a living death for the nation that emerges victorious. Thus Gandhiji taught the message of non-violence not only for individuals but also for groups and nations.

We can't sustain a victory obtained through terrorism, violence, bloodshed and secrecy without further violence and terrorism. Witness the Russian Revolution, for instance. The Bolsheviks came to power through a violent, bloody revolution and, in turn, they themselves imposed a "*dictatorship*" of the proletariat. The long reign of terror unleashed by Stalin was exposed by his own successors, like Khrushchev and others.

Thus non-violence on logical, historical and psychological grounds is the law of human life and as such identical with truth or *Satya* is now recognized by both the superpowers (U.S. and U.S.S.R.). Recently the I.N.F. treat, Delhi Declaration, reduction of nuclear weapons and Indo-Srilanka peace agreement is a positive sign in this direction. A new world order of peace and prosperity can only be ushered in through non-violent means. The attitude that leads one to violence when channelised into other means can lead to peace and happiness. When we talk about non-violence, we do not only mean absence of physical violence. Non-violence can be seen as lack of love. In other words peace and happiness. However, non-violence has to be willed and not obtained by default. As Leonard Sidney Woolf put it "Anyone can be a barbarian; it requires a terrible effort to be or remain a civilized man". An effort in this direction for the people of South Asia is the SAARC. Giving up mutual suspicion, hostilities and jealousy can lead to a real awakening of this region. This will also provide a model for other regions to follow.

Now, I conclude my discussion by saying that if mankind is to be saved from cataclysmic catastrophe and further extinction, path shown by Gandhi along non-violent lines is the only way out for the survival of humanity.

5

Gandhi and Environmental Crisis

Introduction

As the 20th century is slowly receding to the past and 21st is only 9 years old, human beings under severe strain, are compelled to sit up and reassess their own environments, nature, culture and future[1]. Today humanity faces a crisis of global dimensions. It is a crisis that threatens the survival of all alike, the poor as well as rich. Environmental degradation throughout the world is proceeding at an alarming rate—all in the name of more and more development. Development as a process of modernization has proved inimical or antithetical to our environment. The more development means the more environmental deteriorations. In fact we have eaten up the bread of coming generation's of 21st century by way of over utilization of natural resources. Looking to the present way of solution of environmental problems faced by the world, one can hardly have an optimistic view for the better solution of these problems. In such a situation only ray of hope lies in the Gandhian Approach.

Environment is a global concern and its protection is one of the most challenging tasks facing mankind today. "Consumption for today and conservation for tomorrow" has become the slogan of humankind all over the world. The present environmental crises are consequences of past follies (follies of greed, exploitation and domination). Therefore, the present exigency demands that one acquires the basic wisdom of Nature, that is, to follow its laws and learn to manage according to its principles. Gandhian Approach is natural and simple. Therefore, all over the world Gandhism, is being seen as a panacea for the solution of all human problems, be it social, political, economic or ecological. In other words Gandhian way of life is thought to be the only path of salvation for mankind.

The Problem

Mother Earth is the only planet, in our planetary system, which supports life-air, water, land, flora and fauna. All these related elements are interlinked and interdependent and the entire process is self-generating and auto-sustainable. So long as human kind, as a part of this system, worked in harmony with nature and used the resources for its normal sustenance, damage to the system was minimal. With the process of development, human activities assumed such enormous dimensions that the life support system could no longer sustain these[2]. Accordingly, the waste generated through uncontrolled human activities was much more than the system could absorb or assimilate, and resulted in the environmental threat.

Today unscientific and careless urbanization, industrialization and agriculturisation lead to major environmental challenges to our survival than even nuclear holocaust and nuclear stock-piling all over the world. Even two decades back the Stockholm Conference (1972) suggested that "the protection of the environment is a major issue which affects the well-being of people and economic development throughout the world. The relationship between economic growth and environment is a complete phenomenon. Economic growth is dependent on environmental factors. It often feeds on the environment, transforming environmental resources into capital in other forms, at the same time generating "residual wastes" into environment. Thus, economic growth, while increasing the supply of goods and services, brings about changes in the environment and can produce undesirable side effects directly or indirectly."

A crisis of survival has arisen with man's over exploitation of nature. Nature is not only destroyed but Earth is also steadily transformed into a degenerated planet. A society, which eats up all its resources for its development has no future. In fact the growth of population and its growing urban ratio taking away good agricultural land, severe degradation of earth, soil, deforestation, rapid rise in transport, non-availability of well-managed waste disposal system, pressure of human numbers on agricultural land, stock-pile of explosive materials for defence purposes, and testing of nuclear devices etc. have posed the worst threat to the existence of all the living species. If the damage is temporary, there is enough resilience in the life support system which does not return to the original situation and leaves scars behind[3]. It is correct to say that no technological fire, however brilliant, no socio-economic reform however profound will be able to save us from this catastrophe if living natural resources are reduced below the sustainable levels and the environmental elements are degraded to the point of becoming bedysfunctional[4].

In developing countries both poverty and economic growth pose serious environmental challenges. Nothing can possibly be worse for environment than say, hunger, destitution and famine. In their desperate attempt to survive today, people are forced to forsake their tomorrow and overuse their environment. Uncontrolled economic growth, urbanization, and industrialization can rip apart forests, mines and land, overuse groundwater systems, dam rivers, pollute water and air, and stuff the land with unknown poisons[5].

Almost all the consumer items that are being promoted in developing countries by the developed countries to sustain their economic growth have significant environmental impacts. In totality, the encouragement of consumerism, as it is being done in developing as well as undeveloped countries, are antithetical to the concept of sustainable development. With our huge and growing population and rapidly depleting natural resources, we should pioneer innovative, environmentally sustainable models of development. Instead, we are following a path that will be even more disastrous for us, than it was for its original proponents[6].

The major threat to the environment in terms of promoting

agricultural products, has been through the replacement of traditional food crops by high yielding hybrid crops. Degradation of land, pollution through pesticides and fertilizers, and loss of biodiversity have been some of the more disturbing environmental impacts[7].

Of the 1,604,000 species known to inhabit the earth (human are just one of them), an estimated one-fourth to one-third is likely to become extinct within the next few decades. A species a day, perhaps as high as a species an hour, is the current toll—the result of the extensive habitat changes wrought by mankind. Rainforests, home to half of the world's life forms, continue to be destroyed at the rate of our 10,000 sq.km. every year. The majority of the world's population still depends on wild plants and animals for their daily food, medicine, housing and household materials, agriculture, fodder, spiritual sustenance and intellectual stimulation. For these billions, the loss of biodiversity is a direct and irreversible attack on their livelihood and social security. But no one knows how many species we have already lost. There must be hundreds, perhaps, thousands of species, which have gone forever, unsung and unrecorded either because they were not 'glamorous' enough or because we simply did not know them[8].

Nearly 424 nuclear reactors are operating worldwide and more planned for future, which are neither safe nor friendly with the environment. More than 5,000 nuclear warheads are in position and the arms race continues unabated. In fact we are living in a world today, with sixty thousand missiles ready round the clock with a total capacity of destroying our planet thirty times over within minutes. The future of mankind is uncertain and survival is the issue in question. Nuclear waste generated from reactors and dumped into the sea is posing a serious environmental threat not only to coastal people but to entire humankind. The chemical industries alone results in the dumping of about 44,000 chemicals in the USA every year and about 33,000 in the Europe. Over and above this 300 to 3000 new chemicals are introduced in the United States alone every year[9]. Power stations are spewing tonnes of fly ash into the atmosphere. The unwanted smoke from industries pollutes the air resulting in acid rain.

In brief, the principal factors behind environmental degradation have been the need of the poor, greed of the rich and careless application of technology.

There is, therefore, a golden mean, a balance, as in all things ecological between poverty and wealth, between developed economy and developing economy, between need and greed[10].

The Gandhian Approach

Man and nature are interrelated and interdependent. So it is everybody's duty to save nature and protect it at any cost. To me solutions are not likely to be technical, or economic, or social or spiritual alone but a combination of all. In other words the ultimate solution to the threat of ecological disaster in a world of escalating human wants and an increasing population growth is nothing less than Gandhian.

Mahatma's ideas about the danger of western civilization have assumed significance in the context of several issues concerning the survival of the mother earth. The issue of contemporary crisis has been framed in terms of relationship between development and environment, but in fact, it extends to the vision of a human life rooted in cooperation and contentment, peace and non-violence, and in harmony between man and man, and between man and nature[11].

Gandhi saw clearly the moral degradation and cultural decay as well as environmental problems, long back. The *Hind Swaraj* of Mahatma Gandhi published in 1908, long before the negative consequences of industrial civilization were exposed to the common experiences, must have appeared to the generation of his times, a book of reaction and retreat from modernity and civilization. The fact is that long before the industrial west awakened to the perils and limits of unrestrained economic growth and technological innovations, the Mahatma pointed out the pitfalls of industrialisation and the damage to nature and man. His clear, firm and uncompromising stand on the western civilizations as 'Satanic' or as part of a 'dark age' was based not on some obscurantist objection to the use of machine but to enslavement and alienation of man in the industrial civilization[12]. Gandhi emphasized austerity and the moral principle in development. In development his priorities focused on the poor, antoyadha, the poorest of the poor, because poverty is the greatest polluter of the environment. He believed in denying oneself what could not be shared with the least. Gandhiji practiced what he preached. His life is itself a message for people to save our environment.

Our life styles are based on high level of consumption. And high consumption levels ultimately lead to high environmental damage. I like to recall some of the words of Mahatma Gandhi regarding more and more wants. He rightly said "we have to learn to put a curb on our material wants. The mind is a restless bird, the more it gets the more it wants and still remains unsatisfied. Our forefathers knew that if we set our hearts on such things we would became slaves and lose our moral fibre"[13]. We cannot ignore the environmental ethics. We need a new world order based on Gandhian philosophy and techniques to safeguard the environment and Mother Earth. The message is clear and straightforward. Much earlier the *Isa upanishads* had said: "All in this manifested world, consisting of moving and non-moving are covered by the Lord. Use its resources with restraint. Do not grab the property of others, distant and yet to come". I think there could not be a better motto for modern environmentalists and conservationists than this. In modern times Gandhi's approach to nature, man and development was essentially the same emphasizing not only the distant but also the current interdependence of all animate and inanimate objects of nature.

Sarvodaya

Gandhian concept of Sarvodaya will be very useful for solving environmental challenges of today and tomorrow. The concept can be interpreted as the "awakening of one and all". In addition to the awakening of everyone, it refers to the awakening of the total human spirit and personality. Sarvodaya is also related to achieving the highest level of self-realization in which one see one's manifestation in all others[14]. The main theme of the Sarvodaya in context of environmental protection is beautifully analysed in the following Vedic verse:

Sarve bhavantu sukhinah, sarve santu niramaya
Sarve bhadrani pashyantu, ma kaschit dukhbhag bhavet.

From the above verse, we can see that the Sarvodaya concept stresses duty of individuals to themselves and beyond their immediate families to the entire world. "Sarvodaya believes that by tapping their inner most beliefs and values, one can awaken people to their *swa-shakti* (personal awakening or power) and *Janashakti* (collective awakening or people's power)" in order that their *Dharma* can be realized[15]. Sarvodaya movement's vision of development is equally applicable in the case of environmental protection and conservation. It requires that the total well-being (including moral and cultural as well as economic) of the people must be achieved. This development also requires the rejection of capital intensive, machine-oriented, and import-based economy, because these western notions of development foster a style of living and a value system that is intrinsically opposed to the ones which the Sarvodaya movement, and the *concept* of *Dharma*, try to instil within a community[16]. In fact, as a universal ideal it aims at not only fulfilling the material needs but also developing the ethico-spiritual aspects of all people[17].

Swadeshi

Swadeshi is another concept, which will be very useful for the conservation of environment. Gandhi was convinced with not only the merit, both moral and economic of *Swadeshi* principle, but also the feasibility of its practice by the people of poor countries. He also delineated the *modus operandi* of the *Swadeshi* in terms of limited wants and the capacity of the local surroundings and resources to meet the needs of the people[18]. In his famous sentence Gandhi laid down his dicturn: "Nature produces enough to meet the needs of all the people but not enough to satisfy the greed of anyone". Dr. J.C. Kumarappa, one of the disciples and exponents of Gandhian economics wrote nearly sixty years ago"...nature enlists and insures the cooperation of all its units, each working for itself and in the process helping other units to get along their own too—the mobile helping the immobile, the sentient, the insentient. Thus all nature is detailed together in a common cause. Nothing exists for itself. When this works out harmoniously and violence does not break the chain, we have an economics of permanence"[19]. Economics of permanence was the Gandhi term for what we call sustainable development today. But it was a more profound and a more comprehensive concept[20]. In fact solution lies in the application of *swadeshi* in every field and every where. Motto must be "think globally and act locally".

A life of simplicity with self-respect, which will emerge only with the application of *swadeshi* in solving the people's problem, is any time better than a life of luxury for few brought with loss of self-esteem, independence and environment. That is why Gandhi rejected both the liberal individualism and socialist collectivism, both of which were abstractions and artefacts without an anchor in the actual life of people, their needs, and concerns, and their symbiotic relationship with nature.

Satyagraha

Satyagraha will be also an important means by which individuals and groups can have an immediate effect on environmental policy processes. Individuals and groups can organise the people and draw the attention of the government and masses on issue of big dam, power projects, etc. for the conservation of local environment. At a personal level lot of people can work. To operationalize '*Satyagraha* for conservation and better future', it would be desirable to bring like minded people under one umbrella to fight for environmental protection. Environmental groups could gain from non-violent acts designed to disrupt economic activity and environmental degradation.[20]

In a nutshell, the Gandhian approach to environmental problem is based on maximum labour-intensive, employment oriented and minimum capital-intensive industry, thus avoiding the unnecessary and excessive use of machine and the ever-rising spiral of industrial and technological expansion.

Conclusion

If there is anything that can solve our environmental problem, in the Gandhian approach, along with the opportunities which have emerged from modern science and technology. Our whole approach to development and economic growth must be harmonized with human value. Our aim should be to have a worth living place and worth living life which can be achieved through change of our life style and controlling over our unlimited needs and greeds. Hence we need a new living style. We must follow the example of Indian tradition, which believe in the philosophy of *Bahujan Hitaya, Bahujan Sukhaya*. The task is difficult, as the analysis of economic, political and technological sustainability would show, but the Indian culture has a great resilience and Indian mind a great capacity to overcome hurdles. We have to start somewhere to come to right path, the Gandhigram path. Still it is not too late to make a beginning to save our Mother Earth for future generations. The spiritual leader Dalai Lama said, "If we care for Nature, it can be rich, bountiful and inexhaustibly sustainable." Similarly P.N. Haksar said, "There is need to reiterate Gandhian values and instead of merely garlanding the portraits of Gandhiji, Indians must translate his ideals into real life."

NOTES

1. E.P. Menon, "Mahatma Gandhi and Environmental Challenges" in Anil Dutta Mishra (ed.), *Gandhian Approach to Contemporary Problems*, New Delhi, Mittal Publications, 1996, p. 201.
2. T.N. Khoshoo, *Environmental Concerns and Strategies*, Delhi, Indian Environmental Society, 1984, p. 60.
3. *Ibid.*

4. *Gandhi Marg*, September 1981, p. 367.
5. Anil Agarwal, "The best solutions are home-made", *The Hindu Survey of the Environment*, 1993, p. 7.
6. Shekhar Singh, "Budgeting for Environment", *The Hindu Survey of the Environment*, 1993, p. 11.
7. *Ibid.*, p. 14.
8. Ashish Kothari, "For Those Vanishing Species", *The Hindu Survey of the Environment*, 1993, p. 44.
9. T.N. Khoshoo, *op. cit.*, pp. 60-61.
10. Anil Agarwal, *op. cit.*, p. 7.
11. Ali, Ashraf, Gandhian Approach to Sustainable Development in Anil Dutta Mishra (ed.), *Gandhism after Gandhi*, New Delhi, Mittal Publications, 1999, p. 17.
12. *Ibid.*, pp. 18-19.
13. Kamala Choudhary, "Buddhism and Environmental Activism", *IJPA*, Vol. XXXIV, No. 8, July-September 1993, p. 582.
14. O.P. Dwivedi, "Global Dharma to the Environments", *IJPA*, Vol. XXXIX, No. 3, July-September 1993, p. 572.
15. *Ibid.*, pp. 572-73.
16. U.P. Dwivedi, *op. cit.*, p. 572.
17. Anil Dutta Mishra, *Fundamentals of Gandhism*, New Delhi, Mittal Publications, 1995, p. 17.
18. Ali, Ashraf, *op. cit.*, pp. 22-23.
19. J.C. Kumarappa, *Economics of Permanence*, Kashi, Akhil Bharat Sarva Seva Sangh, 1958.
20. K.R. Narayanan, "Greening of Development: Problems and Prospects", in P.R. Trivedi and U.K. Singh (ed.) *Global Environmental Education Visions of 2001*, New Delhi, IIFC, 1993, p. 2.

6

Gandhi and Crisis in 21st Century

Introduction

Few years back the world entered into the 21st century. The world's present status of developmental picture is dark and likely to further deteriorate and put the coming generation in more trouble. The area in which world is going to suffer most can be in the direction of peace, non-violence, socio-economic growth and pollution free atmosphere. In fact we have eaten up the bread of coming generation of 21st century by way of over utilization of forest, water, land and air, etc. Looking to the present way of solution of these problems faced by the world, one can hardly have optimistic view for the better solution of these problems. In such a situation only ray of hope lies in the Gandhian way of solution of the problems.

In this paper an attempt is made in brief to highlight the relevance of the Gandhian way of problem solving likely to appear in the 21st century with special reference to the above mentioned major problem areas.

Gandhism is a living thought for solving the social, economic and political problems of the day. Gandhism is becoming more and more relevant with the passing of time due to the use of moral principles in each and every field. In fact, the future generations will recall Gandhi's idea particularly in two broader specific areas: firstly, the use of non-violent methods and for reflecting violence for the resolution of social and political conflicts; and secondly, for trying to come to grips with the problems of the culture of "consumerism" in the post industrial era[1]. Not only that, his ideas will be relevant in 21st century because the combined theory with practice, individual religious outlook with life-affirmation, morality with public activity, non-cooperation with evil with adherence to non-violence, developing methodology of action with effective force but without malice towards the opponents and rational and experimental attitude together with the fundamental acceptance of an ethical position[2].

The Predicament

Violence became a cult in contemporary world, whether it is east or west. Twenty million people were killed in some 150 wars since 1945, more than the soldiers killed in Second World War[3]. Even domestic violence has increased tremendously. We are living under the shadow of violence and no life is safe on this earth.

The developed countries in the name of national security spent twenty times as much on military expenditure as they provided for economic aid. Seventy per cent of world military spending is by six major military powers, 15 per cent is by other industrialized countries and remaining 15 per cent by developing countries. The world military expenditure doubled between 1960 and 1983 to reach 800 billion dollars per year[4] and by the beginning of the 21st century it will be doubled again. We will be surprised to know that just one-fifth of annual arms expenditure could abolish world hunger by the year 2000 from the entire world.

For over 1 lac people in the world there are 556 soldiers but only 85 doctors. For every soldier the average world military expenditure is $20,000 and for every school age child the average public education expenditure is $380 only[5]. According to the SIPRI report, the nuclear weapons currently in the world's arsenals have a total explosive capacity roughly equivalent to that of about a million Hiroshima-type atomic bombs. Near about 424 nuclear reactors are operating worldwide, and many more are planned for the future, which are neither safe nor friendly to the environment. The nuclear waste generated from these reactors is dumped into the sea and is posing a serious environmental threat not only to coastal people but to entire humankind[6].

Almost all the consumer items that are being promoted to sustain the economic growth have significant impact on society directly or indirectly. Take for example, India. India has 32 million uneducated adults, 36 million unemployed adults and 44 million child labourer[7]. There are 2.4 million women forced into prostitution in 1100 red light areas of major and small cities in India[8]. Child prostitution is on the rise. It is interesting to note that the hub of the child sex industry is in Asia, and that India accounts for 4 lacs children who are sexually abused.[9] Statistics reveal that a women is molested every 26 minutes, one raped in every 47 minutes, one eye-teasing in every 6 minutes, one kidnapped in every 44 minutes, 7 dowry-death in every 24 hours and every 7 minutes one act of criminal offence against women is committed in this country[10]. The statistics show that in 1980, the number of reported rape cases was 0.7 per lac in the country. In comparison, the United States witnessed the highest of such cases (36.1 per lac), followed by Sweden (10.7), Canada (9.6), France (3.5), Italy (3.3), Britain (2.5), Japan (2.2) and Bangladesh (0.3).[11] Today 25 per cent of reported rapes are of girls under 16. In fact, there is a rise of 30 per cent rape in major cities in India. If we look carefully all adolescent girls are visually raped by men[12].

The progress in areas like health, education and housing is slowed by the diversion of previous human resources for national security, military purposes and in combating terrorism, and separatist movements. Most of the major problems facing humanity today like economic disparities, inflation, over population, unemployment, terrorism, pollution, malnutrition, illiteracy, hunger are due to maldevelopment. We should not forget that there are 870 million adults who cannot read and write, 500 million people who have no jobs or are less than fully employed, 130 million children who are unable to attend primary school, 450 million people who suffer from hunger and malnutrition, 12 million babies who die every year before their first birthday, 42 million people who are blind or nearly so, 200 million people who do not have safe water to drink and 250 million people who live in urban slums or shanty towns[13]. By 2,000, about three billion people would be living in urban area. The 21st century will be still more urban. By 2020, about two-third of the human race would be living and working in urban settlement[14]. Not only that the persistence of hunger in a world of plenty, with 750 million men, women and children going hungry everyday in the world's poor countries, is one of the most daunting development challenges facing the global community according to World Bank Report on "Reducing poverty and hunger"[15].

The Gandhian Solution

Mahatma's ideas about the dangers of western civilization have assumed a significance in the context of several issues concerning the survival of the humanity and evolution of a just and viable world order. Gandhi saw clearly the moral degradation and cultural decay long back. The *Hind Swaraj* of Mahatma Gandhi published in 1908, long before the negative consequences of industrial civilization were exposed to the common experiences, must have appeared to the generation of his times, a book of reaction and retreat from modernity and civilization. The fact is that long before the people in 21st century will be awakened to the perils and limits of unrestrained economic growth and technological innovations, Gandhiji pointed out the pitfalls of industrialism, and the damage to nature and man. He strongly criticized the emerging trends of consumer culture in future in all spheres of life and emphasized austerity and the moral principle in development, which is essential for tomorrow's world.

Sarvodaya

Gandhian concept of Sarvodaya will be very useful for solving the social problems of today and of 21st century. The concept can be interpreted as the "awakening of one and all". In addition to the awakening of everyone, it refers to the awakening of the total human spirit and personality. Sarvodaya is also related to achieving the highest level of self-realization in which one sees one's manifestation in all others[16]. The main theme of the Sarvodaya in the 21st century will be same as exemplified in the following vedic verse:

Sarva bhavantu sukhinah, sarve santu niramaya
Sarve bhadrani pashyantu, ma kaschit dukh-bhag bhavet.

From the above verse, we can see that the Sarvodaya concept stresses duty of individuals to themselves and beyond their immediate families to the entire world. "Sarvodaya believes that by tapping their inner most beliefs and values, one can awaken people to their *swa-shakti* (personal awakening or power) and *Janashakti* (collective awakening or people's power)" in order that their *Dharma* can be realized[17]. In fact, Sarvodaya will be very useful for establishing ideal society i.e., free from evils like 'politics without principles', 'wealth without work', 'knowledge without character', 'commerce without morals', 'science without mankind' and 'service without sacrifice'[18]. The Sarvodaya ideal, apart from standing for the meaning of the welfare of all, implies the meaning of the universal welfare and integrated development of all. As a universal ideal it aims at not only fulfilling the material needs but also developing the ethico-spiritual aspects of all people[19].

Swadeshi

At the same time *Swadeshi* will be the greatest tool for solving the economic problems of the 21st century. *Swadeshi* means self-reliance in every field. In other words, *Swadeshi* is service, and if we understand it, we shall simultaneously benefit ourselves, our families, our country and the world. Gandhi delineated the *modus operandi* of *Swadeshi* in terms of limited wants and the capacity of local surroundings and resources to meet the needs of the people. In his famous sentence he laid down his dictum: "Nature produces enough to meet the needs of all the people, but not enough to satisfy the greed of anyone". A life of simplicity with self-respect is anytime better than a life of luxury for the few bought with loss of self-esteem and independence to other nations[20]. Our motto in 21st century should be simple living and high thinking so that we can stop the evils of the society.

In fact, *Swadeshi* movement may become a part of renaissance in 21st century. Because it conveys the idea of returning to one's own country—to its culture and heritage, its own genius and tradition and serve the needs of the next-door neighbour. This is the appropriate time for us to understand the concept of *Swadeshi* and implement it in every possible manner and we will be doing this progress by making ourselves self reliant and self-sufficient in every field and we would be free from moral degradation, economic exploitation and political subjugation[21].

Satyagraha

Satyagraha will be also an important means by which individuals and groups can have an immediate effect on government policy and programmes. Individuals and groups can organize people and draw attention of the Government and masses on issues of terrorism, exploitation, deteriorating law and order, pollution, poverty, malnutrition, etc. to save society. At a personal level also lot of people can work. To operationalize the '*Satyagraha* for better future', it would be desirable to bring like minded people under one umbrella to fight against injustice and wrong governmental policy which is creating social tensions.

In a nutshell, the Gandhian approach to 21st century economic problem will be based on maximum labour-intensive, employment-oriented and minimum capital-intensive industry, thus avoiding the unnecessary and excessive use of machines and the ever-rising spiral of industrial and technological expansion. In social field, it will be based on 'politics with principles', 'wealth with work', 'knowledge with character', 'commerce with morals', 'science with spirituality' and 'service with sacrifice'.

Summing Up

If there is anything that can solve problems in the 21st century, it is the Gandhian path, along with the opportunities which will emerged from modern science and technology. Our approach to development and economic growth must be harmonized with human value. Our aim should be to have worth while of living place and worth while of life which can be achieved through change of our life style and controlling our unlimited needs and greeds. We must follow the Indian tradition of self-sacrifice. We require a proper synthesis of science and spirituality to usher in an era of welfarism in 21st century i.e., *Bahujna, Hitaya, Bahujana Sukhaya*. The task is difficult, as the analysis of economic, political and social situation would show, but the Indian tradition has a great resilience and Indian mind a great capacity to overcome hurdles. We have to start somewhere to come to right path—the Gandhian path. Still it is not too late to make a beginning to save 21st century for future generation.

NOTES

1. K.P. Karunakaran, *Gandhi-Interpretations*, New Delhi: Gitanjali Publishing House, 1985, p. 1.
2. *Ibid.*
3. N. Radhakrishnan (ed.), *Multiple Streams of Peace Movement*, Dr. G.R. Institute of Non-violence, 1986, p. vi.
4. *Ibid.*
5. *Ibid.*
6. Anil Dutta Mishra, *Environmental Challenges and the Gandhian Solution*, paper presented at 16th Annual Conference of ISGS at Kanyakumari, 2-4 Sept. 1994.
7. *The Hindustan Times*, April 5, 1995.
8. *The Hindustan Times*, April 22, 1995.
9. *The Hindustan Times*, April 5, 1995.
10. *The Hindustan Times*, April 27, 1995 and *The Navbharat Times*, January 4, 1995.
11. *The Hindustan Times*, March 29, 1995.

12. Anil Dutta Mishra, "Status of Women and Girl Child in India", *Teaching Politics*, Vol. XX, No. 1-4, 1994, p. 122.
13. N. Radhakrishnan (ed.), *op. cit.*
14. *The Hindustan Times*, April 12, 1995.
15. *The Hindustan Times*, April 27, 1995.
16. O.P. Dwivedi, "Global Dharma to the Environment", *IJPA*, July-Sept. 1993, Vol. XXXIX, No. 3, p. 572.
17. *Ibid.*, pp. 572-73.
18. Anil Dutta Mishra, *Fundamental of Gandhism*, New Delhi, Mittal Publications, 1995, pp. 14-15.
19. *Ibid.*, p. 17.
20. Ali, Ashraf, "Gandhian View of Sustainable Development", *IJPA*, July-Sept. 1993, Vol. XXXIX, No. 3, p. 274.
21. Anil Dutta Mishra, *op. cit.*, pp. 85-86.

7

Political Crisis and Gandhian Solution

Introduction

As the 20th century is slowly receding to the past and the 21st century is at civilization's doorstep, human beings under severe strain are compelled to sit up and have a fresh look at their political system, political culture and the future of their nation. The present world is passing through value crises which have pervaded all spheres of human life, whether it be political, social or economic. There is a crisis in every system, everywhere, and Indian political system is no exception. Decay of moral standards and norms in the democratic system has become a major problem throughout the world. Due to this moral degradation the constitutional system in India is undergoing great stress and strain. It seems that there is a standing threat to Indian democracy both from within and outside.

In this paper an attempt has been made to highlight the problem that face Indian democracy. An attempt has also been made to show how Gandhian method can be a way out to solve those problems.

Corruption

The foremost problem that afflicts our nation is that of corruption. Corruption has seeped into every pore of this country's life. From top to bottom, from Prime Minister in the highest office to a peon in any department, we are told by the press that they are soaked in corruption. It should be a matter of national shame to hear that India is rated as one of the countries in which corruption is all pervasive.[1] Mr. T.N. Seshan rightly said that "there is not even an inch of land in this country that is not wet by corruption," and that the country had lost its character.[2]

People in a democracy should get their legitimate things done in the normal course but instead they have to run from pillar to post to get their work done by greasing the palms of officers and the staff. Those involved in corrupt practices are many. It is very painful to learn that 13 ministers had to be dropped from the cabinet on charges of corruption. Besides this there are allegations against some others. Here is a situation where there are scams galore involving thousands of crores, but the issue of collective responsibility of the cabinet is not raised.[3] There are scandals after scandals and people ask as to how in India only two ministers have gone to jail on charges of corruption since Independence despite a plethora of inquiry commissions, committees, judicial pronouncements, parliamentary probes and public clamour. On the contrary in countries like Korea and Japan, Prime Ministers and Ministers are punished for graft. US President Richard Nixon had to resign after the Watergate scandal. In Italy, many politicians had been in prison for corruption and their links with mafia and two former Prime Ministers are being prosecuted.[4]

If the top is not clean, obviously the bottom is bound to be unclean. Corruption has become an all pervasive phenomenon in India. It is widespread and is found spreading in a frightening manner. There is hardly any area of activity that has remained wholly free from the impact of corruption. In fact, corruption has now been institutionalized and has become a commonly accepted way of life. This is the state of corruption in India today, a bleeding sore in the body politic of our nation.

Decline in Party System

The party system in India is rotten. The growth of intra-party, inter-caste, inter-personal and inter-organisational conflicts has become a common phenomenon in India. It appears that the corrupt-criminal-communal nexus has acquired a solid grip on the system and there is no readiness on the part of any party to cleanse the system.[5] Every party fields candidates of doubtful character and integrity, there being little difference between them in this respect, and yet the voters have to choose between such candidates only.[6] In fact the voters have very little choice. Now the parties are controlled by mafia. There is also decline of party ideology. Elected legislators change parties like clothes in summer to become minister. Party representatives shift their loyalty and no party is an exception. The representatives have now become a saleable commodity. The JMM leaders sold themselves to save the Congress government during the no-confidence motion. The case is still pending in the court. The CBI arrested all the 4 JMM former MPs on 6th September 1996.

The gravity of the situation can be gauged from the fact that intense horse trading before and after the election has become a common phenomenon for almost all parties. That is why persons of dubious character are allowed to get party tickets and made ministers when they win elections.

Irrespective of which party or individual wins or loses at the hosting, or what means are employed and what practices indulged in by those who win or lose, the hard fact is that today every party wants to win elections at any cost. The malady is not confined to the ruling parties at the centre or in the states. Its tentacles have spread far and wide and embrace almost all-political parties.[7]

Rajni Kothari is of the view that "If the party system is allowed to further degenerate, there are going to be many types of disintegrations at work, not all of them of the secessionist variety, but nonetheless tearing the social-political fabric of India in different directions."[8]

Unholy Alliance between Politicians, Bureaucracy and Businessmen

There is an unholy alliance between politicians, bureaucracy and businessmen. Politicians help bureaucrats and *vice-versa*. It appears that the IAS officers who have been given constitutional protection have simply become an extension of political parties, spineless and subservient.[9] The unholy alliance between these three has given way to series of scams, pervasive corruption and break-down of the rule of law and order. The decline in the conduct of bureaucracy is the single most potent cause of decline in Indian polity.[10]

How far the rot has gone and how hopeless the situation has become is best brought out by the confession of Indrajit Gupta, presently the Union Home Minister. He told his party's national council, "there is nothing we can do to end the unholy nexus between criminals, politicians, policemen and bureaucrats. All we can do is pass legislation which cannot be implemented. I see no end to the problem in the country, especially as there are criminals in all sections of society."[11] If the system has driven him to such despair, what hope is the common man left with?

Civil servants who had been the steel-frame of Indian administration, have been reduced to pulp. Attempts to get them committed to the ruling party, their unbridled ambitions and their willingness to stoop to picking up crumbs have broken the back of bureaucracy. Their objectivity is lost because of this unholy alliance and they have become partisan. The fodder and dress scams of Bihar are best examples of this type of nexus. We learn that even our Prime Ministers use the personal planes of businessmen proudly before taking the oath of office. The administrative machinery is often misused to settle political scores. At times public servants doing their duty become the plaything of factional politics. Criminalisation of just administration at a point of time is curable but when it inundates the entire machinery of the state it poses a grave threat to democracy. The feeling is growing that the Rule of Law is only a camouflage for double standards and doublespeak. There is the usual talk of politicization of crime and criminalisation of politics. In fact, it has assumed the form of commercialization of both crime and politics. In the corridors of power, the charlantans and rasputins continue to strut majestically to the utter dismay of the common man.[12]

Decay of Legislatures

The quality, moral and intellectual of our present day legislatures creates misgivings in the public mind. It becomes a matter for self-introspection as to why and how the words *politics* and *politicians* even as popular representatives have acquired pejorative connotations. The elected representatives are the chief instruments of promoting and defending the general public interest. On them squarely rests the responsibility of government, the responsibility to make public policy and serve the general public rather than any special interest or particular group. With the deviations from law and bending of rules to suit their interests, criminality breeds within and outside the system, and then it feeds on it. Accountability of the legislators, the very heart and soul of a democratic polity seems to have became altogether irrelevant for the parliamentary system.

According to press reports and the Election Commission, 180 out of the 425 legislators in U.P. have criminal records. During the Bihar assembly elections in 1995, the local police said that 243 candidates had criminal charges pending against them in law courts. There are reports also of nexus between the under-world dons and goons and legislators of different parties. Even the official report of the Home Ministry's Vohra Committee has confirmed this in no uncertain terms. According to this report, criminal syndicates with political patronage are running parallel governments in some states.[13]

It was not long ago when a well known history sheeter was nominated to the Rajya Sabha against vacancy reserved for eminent persons who distinguished themselves at national level in arts, literature, science or social service. There was also the case of a person being prosecuted for being a paramour and an accomplice in muder, having a seat in Parliament and made a Minister in the Central Cabinet. As per press reports such past records appear to have been surpassed. It is alleged that 84 members in the present Lok Sabha have criminal antecedents.[14]

To add insult to injury, one of them was even appointed a Minister of State in Home Ministry. It was only strong public outrage that forced him to resign. However, the matter does not end here. This Minister recently made a demand for the creation of Purvanchal or Seemanchal State consisting of 15 districts of Bihar and West Bengal. Taslimuddin reportedly met the PM on August 11, 1996 and submitted a memorandum on this subject and the PM is said to have assured him that he would consider the issue seriously.[15] If legislators with a criminal background are allowed to come to the top, India will surely go deep down in all areas of human activities—political, economic, educational and cultural. The disease is still at the nascent stage and hence curable.

The functioning of legislatures has also declined. The quality of debates and discussions in Parliament has gone down. The state assemblies are literally becoming battle grounds of warring politicians. This is reflected in the behaviour of legislators, particularly of state legislators in U.P., Bihar and Gujarat. Now this is becoming a common phenomenon. Late Kulkarni, an honourable MP of Rajya Sabha, himself a man of great integrity, once said during a debate in the Rajya Sabha a few years back that earlier they used to come to Parliament House in auto-rickshaws, later in hired taxis and now many come in air-conditioned cars. Fortunes of some "leaders of the poor" have obviously improved in a free-for-all political environment of "see no evil, hear no evil and speak no evil."[16]

Legislatures which could enforce accountability have themselves become unaccountable. The bills and budgets both at the centre and in the states, are passed without meaningful discussions, generally by near empty houses.

Ethical Decline

History shows that the standards of conduct and behaviour of people in political authority have their malignant influence in other walks of life in society. The ethical dimensions of how influential and powerful people conduct themselves in private life and the public domain set a precedent for the lesser human beings and groups in society follow or to have justification for their own self seeking even scandalous conduct.[17]

There is a widespread feeling that in the present context all over the world, more so in our country, is such that the facets of legislator's behaviour in public life merit scrutiny. The scandals and cases of corruption, kickbacks, bribery, extortions, lying and deception by government all over India are too many and too well-known and are coming to public notice every day. If present ethical standards of behaviour in public life is allowed to degenerate, the gap between the haves and have-nots will widen, social conflicts proliferate, unethical activities become a way of life and India will be on the cross-road of chronic political instability and moral degeneration.

The top functionaries of the government are not working according to prescribed norms. Every day they are violating norms to the benefit of their kith and kin. There is lack of ethical commitment from top to bottom. Public officials have an obligation to serve the public in a manner that strengthens the integrity and processes of a democratic society.

Public life is in a desperate state today, with vice-regal regalia dominating it with its fierce ferocity and crushing criminality, sounding the death-knell of morality and value system. There is dire need to save it. Public men at whatever station of life they function—must be 'men' for the public, leaders must lead; and most importantly, politicians must stop 'politiking'.[18] Action against the unethical behaviour of persons, howsoever high and mighty he may be, must be taken without any delay. Jyoti Basu rightly said that "morality is becoming casualty in politics. Democracy would not survive if this trend continues. It is a matter of great regret that the Supreme Court has to intervene in every matter because morality has taken a back seat. If politicians do not have a sense of morality how could they aspire to rule? Politicians should show the proper path by their conduct and behaviour."[19]

Vote Bank Politics

Today our nation is in great social disarray due to vote bank politics. Vote bank politics has divided the country once again on caste and communal lines. The greatest damage, however, has been done to social harmony by the valueless vote bank politics. The dying institution of caste has not only been revived but also revitalized by accepting and implementing the Mandal Commission Report. It has enabled caste leaders claiming closer affinity to particular castes to lay claim on their votes.[20]

Vote banks are sought to be created through caste alliances, communal appeal and interest articulation of the peasantry, slum dwellers or sub-nationalist groups.[21] People have now been taught to assert for separate caste and communal identities and rights. The caste like the Brahmrishi Sena of Bhumihars, Lorik Sena and Shrikrishva Sena and Mandal Sena of Yadavs, Bhoomi Sena of Kurmis, Sunlight Sena, Ganga Sena, Kuer Sena, Samajwadi Krantikari Sena, of Rajputs, Azad Sena of Brahmins are active in different parts of Bihar under the patronage of well-known politicians. It is not for nothing that well-known novelist Shiva Naipaul called Bihar "the end of earth."[22]

Appeasing different castes and communal groups for their votes by all political parties has greatly undermined social and communal harmony. Encouraged by such special treatments, more social, economic and political demands are being made by different groups at the cost of others. Caste and communal violence has become order of the day and it poses a great threat to national unity.

It is not that all constitutional institutions have gone under cloud. The judiciary is still shining and doing an excellent job for the purity of public life. Institutions of the Comptroller and Auditor Generals are been doing their jobs conscientiously though their strong reports against the governmental lapses always remain a cry in wilderness. The institutions which have failed the country are the political parties, the executive and the legislatures. There is no accountability on the part of the executive, grown callous and indifferent over the years.[23]

The apex court has left no stone unturned to ensure that fairness and the rule of law prevail in administration. But it cannot administer the country which is essentially the function of the executive. Nor can the Election Commission succeed in making the system of elections pure, by being extra-vigilant. The apex court and the Election Commission can only lend to the ailing institutions a helping hand by showing them the right path. The cure of the malady lies in the emergence of "a set of honest men who will have the interest of the country before them."[24] Pandit Hriday Nath Kunzru rightly said in the Constituent Assembly on June 14, 1949: "If we fail to get honesty from persons in high positions, the foundation of the republic will be shaky."[25] And shaky it has become. It is high time to think on these issues.

The Gandhian Solution

In this background Mahatma Gandhi's ideas about the danger of corruption have assumed significance in the context of several issues facing Indian democracy today. Only four days before his assassination Mahatma Gandhi warned the country during his prayer meeting: "The subject of corruption referred to by the correspondent is not new. Only it has become much worse than before. Restraint from without has practically gone. Corruption will go when the large number of persons given to the unworthy practice realize that the nation does not exist for them but they do for the nation. It requires a high code of morals, extreme vigilance on the part of those who are free from the corrupt practice and who have influence over corrupt servants. Indifference in such matter is criminal. If our evening prayers are genuine, they must play no mean part in removing from our midst the demon of corruption."[26]

Unfortunately the warning went unheeded. Gandhi's uninvolved and reverberating voice of truth and compassion can still help to galvanize the country if the common man asserts himself.

Half a century ago on the eve of Independence, Gandhi and Nehru had exchanged views as to the goals and direction independent India should take. Although they agreed on objective like "sufficiency of food, clothing, housing, etc. as minimum requirements for the country," their vision about the future of India was very different. Gandhi was deeply concerned about the 'dumb millions' and wanted to focus on the abolition of poverty, misery and fear. He said that "I shall work for an India in which the poorest shall feel that it is their country, in whose working they have an effective voice, an India in which there is no high class or low class of people, an India in which all communities live in harmony. Woman will enjoy the same rights as men." But what has happened to Gandhi's dream. The differences between the rich and the poor, the rural and the urban have increased; there is violence and terrorism in communities everywhere; and the status of women in spite of much talk seems worse.[27] All these happen because we forget the path shown by Gandhi.

Need for organization, activation, articulation, assertion of public opinion and enlightened citizenship is the life-breath of any vibrant democratic system. Citizen apathy leads to moral decay. Like that Apostle of Truth Mahatma Gandhi, Thomas Jefferson provides a guideline for men concerned with public affairs so that there is no deviation and departure from rectitude in public affairs. This is as follows: "whenever you are to do a thing, though it can never be known but to yourself how you would act were all the world looking at you, and act accordingly."[28]

It is high time for the country to change the chemistry of politics, and work for the promotion of constitutional democracy on Gandhian lines. Otherwise, if the present state of affairs is allowed to continue unabated, then India will soon be entering a Dark Age of her own making.

Gandhi saw clearly the moral degradation and cultural decay long back. His clear, firm and uncompromising stand on various issues should become guiding principles for us to save Indian democracy. Mahatma Gandhi's noble idea of a society, based on the principles of truth and non-violence and which upholds ethical actions and moral conduct, is what one must strive for the betterment of our country. Gandhiji had once said that whenever there was difficulty in solving a problem he had prescribed a talisman, which is at that particular moment think of the poorest person in the country and how his problems can be solved. It means that the administration will be fair and just in its action so that the people can have faith and trust in it.[29]

Sarvodaya

Gandhi's democracy stands for Sarvodaya and it can be interpreted as the "awakening of ours and all." Literally speaking 'Uday' means awakening and 'Sarva' means all, entire or total. Thus in addition to the awakening of everyone, it refers to the awakening of the total human spirit and personality. Sarvodaya is also related to achieving the highest level of self-realization in which one sees one's manifestation in all others. The Sarvodaya movement's vision of democracy is equally applicable in the case of preservation of democratic institutions in India. India of today should seek inspiration from the values enshrined in the ideal of Sarvodaya. India can get rid of the problems of corruption, criminalization of politics and casteism by following the underlying principles of Sarvodaya Society.

Satyagraha

Satyagraha will also be an important means by which individuals and groups can be moulded to the ways of democratic process. By resorting to the techniques of *Satyagraha* as taught by Mahatma Gandhi individuals and groups can organise the people and draw the attention of the government and masses on issues of communalism, terrorism, nexus between politicians and criminals, poverty, population explosion, malpractices in election, misuse of government machinery etc. for the revival of democratic institution. At a personal level also lot of people can work and take up local issues along with national issues. To operationalise the '*Satyagraha* for better polity,' it would be desirable to bring like-minded people and NGOs under one umbrella to fight against the wrong deeds of corrupt legislators and executives who are responsible for creating mess in Indian polity.

Swadeshi

At the same time the spirit of *Swadeshi* should be the surest means for solving the economic problems of India. *Swadeshi* means self-reliance in every field of life. In other words, *Swadeshi* is service and if we understand it, we shall simultaneously benefit ourselves, our families and our country. Our motto should be simple living and serve the country with dedication and thus remove the evils of the polity and society. In fact, *Swadeshi* movement may become a part of a new Indian renaissance to combat the evils of economic corruption. This would bring Indian democracy on the right path. This is the appropriate time for us to understand the concept of *Swadeshi* and implement it in every possible manner. In this manner we will make ourselves reliant and self-sufficient in every field. Only through such a way we would be free from the kind of moral degradation, economic exploitation and political corruption prevalent in the country today.

Revival of the Idea of *Swaraj*

Swaraj at one time meant Independence. But today *Swaraj* means elimination of poverty and hunger, equality between classes and sexes, freedom from fear, and hope for a better future. The *Swaraj* of Gandhi's dream remains a dream unfulfilled. Today we can pledge to return to Gandhi's dream. If we do, we can say with utmost confidence and conviction that we would be on the road to achieving real *Swaraj*.

Summing Up

In spite of the encircling gloom, it is wrong to think that all is lost or that the decay in Indian political system is irreversible. To remove the evils that face our polity today, there is need for moral education, electoral reforms, campaign ethics, transparency in governance, improved parliamentary practices, demystification of governmental processes, greater public awareness of public issues, strict enforcement of rule of law, scientific method of reward and punishment in public services, fairness and firmness in public dealings, better understanding of both rights and duties by citizens, measures for improvement in functioning of political parties, disclosure of assets by people in authority, stress on accountability, greater emphasis on efficiency, responsiveness and sensitivity in administration, expeditious investigation and early disposal of court cases and appointment of Lokpal etc.[30]

True, the task is very difficult. But we have to start from somewhere to overcome the hurdles coming in the way of Indian politics. Still it is not too late to make a humble beginning at an individual as well as society level to save our decaying institutions. This would usher India into 21st century free from all types of social, political and economic maladies. The wise and good men of India should learn to shed their apathy and be ready to participate in the political processes of our democracy.

NOTES

1. Justice R.S. Pathak, "Ethics in Public Life—Some Observations." *IJPA*, July-September 1995, Vol. No. 3, p. 265.
2. Rakshat Puri, "Are Politicians Blameless?" *The Hindustan Times*, July 17, 1996.
3. Lt. Gen. (Retd.) S.K. Sinha, "Electing a Prime Minister." *The Hindustan Times*, April 13, 1996.
4. T.N. Chaturvedi, Editorial, *IJPA*, July-September 1995, Vol. 1. No. 3, p. xv.
5. Rajni Kothari, "Politics: Collapse and Regeneration." *The Hindustan Times*, April 14, 1996.
6. Rajni Kothari, "A Desperate Election", *The Hindustan Times*, May 2, 1996.
7. K. Ganesan, "Crime and Politics." *The Hindustan Times*, August 17, 1996.
8. Rajni Kothari, *op. cit.*, May 2, 1996.
9. Bindheswar Pathak, "Judicial Activism: It's right, My Lord." *The Hindustan Times*, April 28, 1996.
10. *Ibid.*
11. S.S. Gill, "Democracy under Stress." *The Hindustan Times*, August 27, 1996.
12. T.N. Chaturvedi, *op. cit.*, p. xv.
13. U.C. Agarwal, "Politics of Crime, Corruption, and Waste Caste and Creed." *IJPA*, July-September 1995, Vol. No. 3, p. 467.
14. Lt. Gen. (Retd.) S.K. Sinha, "Electoral Reforms Act", *The Hindustan Times*, August 20, 1996.

15. T.V. Rajeswar, "A Flood-gate of Demands Opened." *The Hindustan Times*, September 3, 1996.
16. U.C. Agarwal, *op. cit.*, p. 464.
17. T.N. Chaturvedi, *op. cit.*, p. ix.
18. Bata K. Dey, "Ethics in Public Administration—Maladies and Remedies." *IJPA*, July-September 1995, Vol. 3, p. 461.
19. Hardwari Lal, "Criticism of Judiciary." *The Hindustan Times*, August 21, 1996.
20. U.C. Agarwal, *op. cit.*, p. 468.
21. Ash Narain Roy, "It's time to Tide over the Crises." *The Hindustan Times*, April 29, 1996.
22. Ved Marwah, "Caste Sevas Rule Bihar", *The Hindustan Times*, July 31, 1996.
23. Hardwari Lal, "The System under Strain." *The Hindustan Times*, May 1, 1996.
24. *Ibid.*
25. Bindheswar Pathak, *op. cit.*
26. M.K. Gandhi, *Delhi Diary*, 26.1.1948.
27. Kamla Choudhary, "What are We Celebrating Today?" *The Hindustan Times*, August 15, 1996.
28. T.N. Chaturvedi, *op. cit.*, p. xix.
29. S.K. Pachauri, "Natural Justice and Ethics in Administration." *IJPA*, July-September 1995, Vol. 3, p. 553.
30. T.N. Chaturvedi, *op. cit.*, p. xviii.

8

Value Education and Crisis Today

Swami Vivekananda, the great philosopher of modern India explaining the universal significance of education, once said, "The education which does not help the common mass to equip themselves for the struggle of life, which does not bring out strength of character, spirit of philanthropy, and the courage of a lion—is it worth the name?" No society will attain prosperity unless it is managed by the people of high moral character. This can be done only through providing value-education to the children. There is casual relationship and interdependency between perfect education and character building. In fact both are the two wheels of the same cart.

Education and values are closely related and the prosperity and progress of a mankind rests on these pivots. If these are removed the society will fall flat and people become destructive. Burke rightly remarked, "education is the chief defence of the nation". While Henery Peter remarked: "education makes people easy to lead, but difficult to drive, easy to govern, but impossible to enslave".

The French sociologist, Emile Durkheim[1], saw the major function of education as the transmission of society's norms and values. But so far as Indian education system is concerned it fails to do so. He maintained that, "Society can survive only if there exists among its members a sufficient degree of homogeneity; education perpetuates and reinforces this homogeneity by fixing in the child from the beginning the essential similarities which collective life demands". Without these 'essential similarities', cooperation, and social solidarity, social life itself would be impossible. A vital task for all societies is the welding of a mass individuals into a united whole, in other words, the creation of social solidarity.

Education system in India, some how or other is not egalitarian in character and form, conservative in attitude and a product of Britism cultural imperialism. Unfortunately education has been equated to merely acquiring academic qualifications. Education has been confused with literacy. That is why education has lost its utility and modern youths are getting lost. There is a class dimension to Indian education pattern, which cannot be undermined so easily. According to Prem Kripal, "between the class education and mass education we have neglected the masses, especially the need of rural areas. Between the education of children and the education of the adults we have favoured the children of the well-to-do families. Between those who can afford fulltime education and the working population, India has exercised the choice in favour of the privileged ones". So long as class distinction and elite and sophisticated culture persists the form and context of the present education system is not going to contain the forces of growing resentment. It is generally observed painstakingly that the higher the level of education the lower is the academic acquisition in the real sense of the term. On the basis of many empirical evidences, one is, but, compelled to say that, with the ascendancy of the level of the education, corrupting forces get themselves strengthened and academic excellence virtually gets reduced to unproductive magnificence year after year.

In fact, education today has become something of status symbol—a privilege. It promises job for the few people. What people as a whole fail to realize is that true education is that which produces the perfect human being. Samuel Johnson said, books without the knowledge of life are useless. Academic education is only a means to hasten true education. And true education is one that makes people of character and high caliber.

The present educational process has caused alienation from others. It fosters maximum gathering of information and competence. It is based on an antagonistic spirit of competition and fosters a random, casual, egoistic, happy-go-lucky approach to civic realities and responsibilities. Even Research and Training Programmes were neither developed adequately nor applied to qualitative improvements, which failed to materialize the institutional infrastructure to remain almost the same in form and functioning as was inherited from the neglect and inertia. Quality declined; only quantity exploded[2].

Education can achieve its ultimate purpose of making one an ideal human being only if it helps in fostering universal and eternal values in the minds of its entire people. And for this we must revolutionize our education, its means and ends, its tryst with destiny, so that our rising generation, rich in mental and creative intelligence, righteous in moral indignation against environmental, political, economic and other pollution and ready to die for human dignity and integrity.

What we need today is a large number of voluntary agencies wedded to Gandhian concept of education to work, independently or with government agencies to change the educational pattern and to make it worthy of a culture that India is. Of course, there is need for change in government policies and in many other things which will come if new avenues are opened up for the future.

Education is an integral part of the society and has to be correlated with one's concept of a good social order. Similar character building is a part and parcel of the social system as it exists and as is visualized for the future.

Our democracy, our socialism, our secular values, our republic's sovereignty depend on universal education. Centuries back, Martin Luther told us what today we need to remember:

"The prosperity of a country depends, not on the abundance of its revenues, nor on the strength of its fortifications, nor on the beauty of its public buildings; but consists in the number of its cultivated citizens, in its men of education, enlightenment and character".

John Ruskin, a most refined soul of his time, wrote:

> *"Education does not mean teaching people what they do not know. It means teaching them to behave as they do not behave. It is not teaching the youth the shapes of letters and the tricks of*

> *number, and leaving them to turn their arithmetic to roguery and their literature to lust. It means, on the contrary, training them into the perfect exercise and kingly continual of their bodies and souls. It is painful, continual, and difficult work to be done by kindness, by watching, by working by percept, and by praise, but above all by example".*

Gandhi on Education

Gandhi wrote: "By education I mean an all-round drawing out of the best in the child and man—body, mind and spirit". For Gandhi education is an instrument of socio-economic progress material advancement, political evaluation and moral development for individuals in the society. To him, literacy in itself is no education. Gandhi's concept of education stresses the four-fold development in human personality, namely, body, mind, heart and spirit with integration of three H's (Head, Heart and Hand) rather than 3 R's (Reading, Writing and Arithmetic). True education stimulate the spiritual, intellectual and physical faculties of the individual. To Gandhi the clear implication is that meaningful education must not overlook any area of human development. So the goal of education is not merely to produce good individuals, but to turn out individuals who understand their social responsibilities as integral elements of the society in which they live.

Gandhi was a staunch advocate of discipline, which is an important aspect of a sound system of education. Education without discipline is like a boat without sailor. Discipline is a quality which comes from within one's self leading to the regulation of one's intellectual, moral and social behaviour. To him, goals of education include character building through development of such values as courage under all circumstances, strength and force of personality, the virtue of compassion, magnanimity and fair-mindedness and the ability to give all that one has while working towards a noble objective. Gandhi is of the view that education is not an end in itself but a powerful instrument which creates men and women of strength and sterling character. Without the qualities of firmness, truthfulness, patience, etc., education generates like a fully blossomed flower without any fragrance. For Gandhi, true education is a life-long process. So here he comes very close to Plato.

Gandhi's concept of education involves the making of education self-supporting. Gandhi believes that the student must be trained to become an earning unit after the competition of his studies. His idea is to make education need-based so that the problem of unemployment could be eradicated at the earliest opportunity. So the real education to Gandhi means economise self-sufficiency. He very rightly says that "you have to start with conviction that looking to needs of the villages of India our rural education ought to be made self-supporting if it is to be made compulsory".

Modern education is a process of learning from real life and from the pulsating, dynamic society around us. So there is a need of fundamental change in the total education system in India and it must be replaced by taking Gandhian nation of education so that the goal of *Swaraj* can be fulfilled not in theory but in practice.

Gandhism in University

The main purpose to Gandhism in university is to develop an individual and through him the society. For this, the Gandhian concept of Trusteeship, Non-violence, Bread-labour, *Satyagraha*, Religion, God and Truth, became very important.

Many universities have opened the specialized subject on Gandhi and inclusion of Gandhian philosophy in the syllabus of modern Indian political thought. In some university even at B.A. stage Gandhism is taught in different subject like Political Science, Sociology, Economics and Philosophy. Universities like Delhi, have a separate optional paper on Gandhi titled "Gandhian Thought and Action". Bhagalpur and Punjab University have already started M.A. in Gandhian Studies.

In the case of Gandhigram Rural University, it has a combination of both Gandhian thought and Social work. Also it offers a two credit audit course in a Gandhian thought for all

UG and PG programmes under the auspices of the Department of Gandhian Thought and Peace Science in the above university.

There are some universities which have Gandhi Bhawans. These Bhawans were started for the specific purpose of promoting Gandhian studies, peace-research, national integration, harmony between man and nature and between man and man, etc. Many of these Bhawans lost their identities and became non-functional. The Gandhian institution virtually became the place of dirty politics and their activities itself became anti-Gandhian and shelter place for old so called Gandhian. So there is a great need to revive the Gandhian institution throughout the country.

To revive the Gandhian institution and convert Gandhian principle into action, there is no need of establishment of new or separate university or department. But the need of the time is to strengthen the existing institution, and for that these existing Institutions must start action-oriented programmes and greater importance should be given to incorporate youth.

Conclusion

One may conclude by saying that if education in India is to serve any meaningful purpose, the entire education system at every level should be over-hauled and re-structured. I suggest that the educationists and intellectuals (not so called intellectuals) should come forward and should give up the power politics of manipulation and evolve a sound, ethical and rational system of education, which trains both the body and mind enriching the society and lessening unemployment, which causes frustration. Education should be value lead and not only academic oriented.

NOTES

1. Haralambas, Michael and Healed, R.M., *Sociology: Themes and Perspectives*, Delhi, Oxford University Press, 1980, p. 173.
2. Kiripal, Prem, "How to Plan Education of the Future", *Yojana*, Vol. 33, No. 14 and 15 August, 1989, p. 82.

9

Satyagraha and World Crisis

Satyagraha was not originally coined by Gandhiji. Even before him, the idea of *Satyagraha* was found in religious books, like the *Upanishads*, the *Ramayana*, the *Mahabharata*, the *Gita*, the *Quran* and many others. It was also practiced by Indians as well as Westerners like Prahlad, Raja Harishchandra, Socrates, Plato, Jesus, King Ashoka, and many others. Prahlad, the first individual *Satyagrahi*, offered *Satyagraha* against the tyranny of his cruel father. It was not known then that it was what *Satyagraha* meant.[1] According to Gandhiji, "the principle called *Satyagraha* came into being before that name was invented. Indeed when it was born, I myself could not say what it was."[2] Some of the westerners believe that Gandhiji derived the idea of *Satyagraha* from Christ's New Testament, specially the Sermon on the Mount. Some others believe that he got this idea from the writings of Tolstoy, though Tolstoy himself deduced it from the New Testament. In fact Gandhi derived his idea of *Satyagraha* neither from Christ nor from Tolstoy, but from his own Vaishnavite faith.[3]

Satyagraha—Meaning and Genesis

The word *Satyagraha* is Sanskrit in origin. It is a compound word formed of *Satya*, meaning truth and *Agraha*, meaning clinging, holding fast, adherence, and insistence. In other words, *Satyagraha* means clinging to truth, holding fast to truth, insistence on truth or firm adherence to truth come what may. Defining the term *Satyagraha*, Gandhi once wrote:[4]

> *Truth (Satya) implies love and firmness (agraha) engenders and therefore serves as a synonym for force. I thus began to call the Indian movement Satyagraha, i.e. the force which is born of truth and love or non-violence and gave up the phrase passive-resistance in connection with it.*

Gandhiji described *Satyagraha* as "firmness in a good cause"[5] in Indian opinion. In *Young India*, he pointed out that *Satyagraha* was just a new name for "the law of self-suffering."[6] And in *Hind Swaraj*, he proclaimed that "sacrifice of self is infinitely superior to sacrifice of others," and that a self sufferer does not make others suffer for his mistakes.[7]

Satyagraha, which was Gandhi's supreme invention, discovery or creation, stands for a ceaseless and relentless pursuit of truth without resorting to hatred, rancour, ill-will or animosity. His concept does not imply passivity, weakness, helplessness or expediency. It is essentially an attitude of mind and a way of life based on the firm desire for vindicating just causes, correcting wrongs and converting wrong-doers by voluntary self-suffering and by patient and active use of the means which are non-violent and intrinsically just. In J.B. Kripalani's words, "*Satyagraha* is strike plus something more. This something makes for better morals amongst those who carry on the fight. It also means greater loss of morals for the opponent. A *Satyagrahi* is better non-co-operator than a striker."[8] In fact *Satyagraha* is action-oriented search for and adherence to truth and a non-violent fight against untruth.

Satyagraha also implies an assertion of the power of the human soul against political and economic domination, because domination amounts to a denial of truth since it takes resource to falsehood and manipulation for maintaining itself. Thus, *Satyagraha* is the vindication of the glory of the human conscience. The latter (conscience) reinforces the non-violent battle for the victory of truth.[9]

Satyagraha is utter self-effacement, greatest humiliation, greatest patience and brightest faith. It is its own reward.[10] *Satyagraha* is a relentless search for truth and a determination to reach truth.[11] It is a force that works silently and apparently slowly. In reality, there is no force in the world that is so direct or so swift in working.[12] It implies the exercise of the purest soul-force against all injustice, oppression and exploitation. Literally, it means "truth pressure" and denotes the operation of the soul or spirit suffering, confidence, self-purification and trust are attributes of soul-force.

The theory of *Satyagraha* is not a new innovation. It is as old as Patanjali. Gandhiji emphatically asserted that its origin had deep linkage with the idea of purity. Calling *Satyagraha* as *Kamadhenu*, he believed that it was useful both for a *Satyagrahi* and his adversary.[13] *Satyagraha* has also been linked with yojna of Indo-Aryan days. Between the original form of human and animal sacrifice and its contemporary manifestation in *Satyagraha*, it has undergone the intellectual refinement of the *Upanishads* and humanistic transfusions from Jainism and Buddhism.[14]

Gandhi discovered this term during his endless non-violent resistance movement against racial discrimination in South Africa. In 1906 Gandhi organised the Indians in South Africa and led a new kind of resistance movement against the unjust laws under which they were then suffering. In the beginning, Gandhi used the term 'Passive Resistance', but as the time passed and his struggle for justice advanced, this phrase gave rise to confusion and was considered as the weapon of the weak. As a result, it appeared shameful to use an English word which could not be easily understood. He felt that the movement he had started was essentially different from what was ordinarily known as passive resistance. Gandhi, thus, felt the need for an appropriate word for the new kind of resistance and announced a small prize in his weekly, *Indian Opinion* for the best suggestion in this regard. One of the competitors, Shri Maganlal Gandhi, suggested the word *'Sadagraha'* meaning firmness in a good cause. Gandhi liked the word but he felt it did not represent the whole idea he wished it to connote, namely, 'truth-force' or the power of truth, force born of truth and love or non-violence. He, therefore, corrected it to *'Satyagraha'*, which literally means insistence or truth or the pursuit of truth.

Discussing the origins of *Satyagraha* with Joseph J. Doke, Gandhi is represented to have stated: "I remember," he said, "how one verse of a Gujarati poem, which, as a child, I learned at school, clung to me." In substance it was this:

> *'If a man gives you a drink of water and you give him a drink in return, that is nothing. Real beauty consists in doing good against evil.'*
> 'As a child, this verse had a powerful influence over me, and I tried to carry it into practice.' Then came the *'Sermon on the Mount'*.
> But, said, I, 'Surely the *Bhagavad Gita* came first?' 'No', he replied 'of course I knew the *Bhagavad Gita* in Sanskrit tolerably well, but I had not made its teaching in that particular a study. It was the New Testament which really awakened me to the rightness and value of passive resistance. When I read in the *'Sermon on the Mount'* such passages as *'resist not him that is evil but whosoever smiteth thee on thy right cheek turn to him the other also'*, and *'love your enemies and pray for them that persecute you, that ye may be sons of your Father which is in heave'*, I was simply overjoyed, and found my own opinion confirmed where I least expected it. The *Bhagvad Gita* deepened the impression, and Tolstoy's the Kingdom of God is within you gave it permanent form.'[15]

Satyagraha and Passive Resistance

Until the invention of this term *'Satyagraha'*, the South African movement was called 'Passive Resistance'. But so long as the phrase passive resistance was used, the *Satyagrahis* were mistaken to be a danger to person and property which the suffragists in England were, and the movement was regarded as a weapon of the weak. Gandhi apprehended the possible psychological effect of characterizing the South African movement as a weapon of the weak and the helpless and sharply contrasted *Satyagraha* to passive resistance:

> "The power of suggestion is such, that a man at last becomes what he believes himself to be. If we continue to believe ourselves and let others believe, that we are weak and helpless and therefore offer passive resistance, our resistance

> would never make us strong, and at the earliest opportunity we would give up passive resistance as a weapon of the weak... Again, while there is no scope for love in passive resistance, on the other hand, not only has hatred no place in *Satyagraha* but is a positive breach of its ruling principle. While in passive resistance there is a scope for the use of arms when a suitable occasion arrives, in *Satyagraha* physical force is forbidden even in the most favourable circumstances."[16]

Thus if a passive resister does not use violence, it is due to this incapacity or under the force of circumstances, whereas a *Satyagrahi* refrains from using violence even if he were in a position to use violence effectively. A *Satyagrahi* never seeks to take advantage of the opponents weakness. Passive resistance may, therefore, sometimes be looked upon as a preparation for the use of force while *Satyagraha* can never be utilized as such. It may also be offered side by side with the use of arms, *Satyagraha* and brute force, being each a negation of the other, can never go together.

Passive resistance is a new technique of fighting wrongs or a policy resorted to by the unarmed against superior force, while *Satyagraha*, as seen by Gandhi, is a matter of faith or creed. Hence, the latter is grounded in an integrated philosophy of the universe life and fundamental ethical principles.

In passive resistant, the aim is to embarrass and harass the adversary and eventually to defeat him; but in *Satyagraha* the effort is towards not causing the slightest harassment or injury to the other party. In passive resistance, the resister's aim is to gain a victory over the adversary, while terms like 'victory' or 'defeat' have no place in the *Satyagrahi's* vocabulary. The latter's aim is the moral and mental conversion of the other party.

Passive resistance may be undertaken against persons while *Satyagraha* is never directed against a person as such. It is directed only against institutions, systems, political and other vested interests, and wrongdoings (and not strictly against the wrong-doer).

Passive resistance may arise from hatred, anger or frustration and may thus be motivated by a feeling of retribution or retaliation, but not so with *Satyagraha* which is accompanied with love for the other party and possibly with a prayer that he may see reason without coming to personal harm.[17]

Satyagraha may be offered to one's nearest and dearest; passive resistance can never be offered to them unless, of course, they have ceased to be dear and become an object of hatred to us.

Satyagraha goes beyond passive resistance in the stress on a spiritual and moral teleology because the final source of hope and consolation for the *Satyagrahi* is God. Hence Gandhi wrote:

> *Satyagraha* differs from passive resistance as the North Pole from South. The latter has been conceived as a weapon of the weak and does not exclude the use of physical force or violence for the purpose of gaining one's end whereas the former has been conceived as a weapon of the strongest and excludes the use of violence in any shape or form."[18]

Thus passive resistance is, according to Gandhi, a 'negative' concept and has little in common with the 'active' principle of love on which *Satyagraha* is based.[19]

Basic Postulates of *Satyagraha*

There are some essentials or basic postulates of *Satyagraha* like truth, non-violence, faith in God, brotherhood of man, supremacy of moral law and purity of means.[20] These are discussed below:

Truth

Truth is the core of Gandhian philosophy of *Satyagraha*. *Satyagraha* minus truth or *satya* is zero. In fact, *Satyagraha* is based on truth or soul force. Inner voice is the voice of truth and justice. Howsoever man might be selfish or crooked the voice of truth, resides in his innermost depth and *Satyagraha* tries to appeal to that voice of reason and truth.

Truth is derived from the Sanskrit word *Sat* which means

being, existing living. Thus truth means 'that which exists'. Since the existence of nothing is more obvious than that of the various laws governing the universe, truth, according to Gandhi, is nothing but a law operating in the universe. "The world", he says, "rests upon the bedrock of *Satya* or Truth".[21]

For Gandhi, it was not mere perception of truth which mattered; what was more important for him was speaking the truth, acting the truth and realizing the truth in every breadth of life and action. Self-realisation was another name for realization and establishment of the truth of life and being.

Gandhi identified God with truth. Hence his famous proposition: "God is Truth". The reason for his identification, according to Gandhi, was that God alone is that law which governs all life. But in 1929, he reversed the earlier proposition and asserted that "Truth is God". This inversion of the proposition does not change its basic meaning yet there was a reason behind this change of formulation. Gandhi said "I found that the nearest approach to truth was through love. But love has many meanings in the English language. But I never found a double meaning in connection with truth and even the atheists had not demurred to the necessity or power of truth. And it was because of this reason that I saw that rather than say that 'God is Truth', I should say that 'Truth is God'. Accordingly, in our fight for social change, we must hold fast to truth and truth alone".[22]

Non-violence

To Gandhi, the path of truth is narrow as it is straight.[23] As a result, truth and non-violence are inseparable and it is impossible to realize perfect truth so long as we are imprisoned in the moral frame without non-violence, it is not possible to seek and find truth. Hence, non-violence and truth are so intertwined that it is practically impossible to disentangle and separate them. So, *Satyagraha* is impossible without non-violence.[24]

Non-violence literally means non-killing or non-injury. According to Gandhi, every act of injury to a living creature and endorsement of such act by refraining from non-violent effort, whenever possible.

Historically, or chronologically speaking, to prevent it, is a breach of ahimsa.[25] Gandhi's active non-violence emerged as a result of his experiences in South Africa especially his painful experience at Maritzburg. But, it also followed logically from his conception and quest for truth. Gandhi said, "Without non-violence it is not possible to seek and find truth.... They are like the two sides of a coin. Truth is the end".[26] The principle of non-violence is hurt by every evil thought, undue haste, lying, hatred and wishing ill-will to anybody. It is such a state of physical and mental discipline that can move the chord of human heart and bring a change of heart in the so-called enemies.

Supremacy of Moral Law

Satyagraha does not depend upon physical or brute force. It is based on moral force—the force of truth and justice, the force of self-purification and self-suffering, love and service, courage and discipline. Gandhi says, "Purity of means is based upon the recognition of the supremacy of moral law." Therefore, the entire gamut of the philosophy of *Satyagraha* is based on the fact that truth and morality alone can be victorious, and we cannot adopt immoral principles to create a moral society. Hence, Gandhi made *Satyagraha* "the moral equivalent of war". It is a way of life based on the laws of love and holiness.[27] However, insistence on moral means does not imply that evil, injustice, tyranny and exploitation are to be tolerated. On the other hand, he believed that evil must be resisted and eliminated but resisted through means that are in consonance with morality, not with hate, war, violence and ill-will.

Faith in God

Gandhi emphasizes that a *Satyagrahi* must be a believer in God. A *Satyagrahi* has no other stay but God, and one who has any other stay or depends on any other help, cannot offer *Satyagraha*, because he may be a passive resister, a non-co-operator and so on, but cannot be a true *Satyagrahi*.

Brotherhood of Man and Faith in the Goodness of Man

Gandhi believed in the principle of one universal soul. To Gandhi, brotherhood of man means, "that we are one of another". It means that you cannot injure your neighbour without injuring yourself or *vice-versa*. Hence the entire edifice of *Satyagraha* rests on the faith in the goodness of man. *Satyagraha* aims at change of heart through non-violent, noble and friendly action.

Gandhi mentions the following as the basic assumptions for successful *Satyagraha*.[28]

(a) There must be common honesty among *Satyagrahis*.
(b) They must render heart discipline to their commander. There should be no mental reservation.
(c) They must be prepared to lose all, not merely their personal liberty, not merely their possessions, land cash, etc., but also the liberty and possessions of their families, and they must be ready cheerfully to face bullets, bayonets, or even slow death by torture.
(d) They must not be violent in thought, word or deed towards the 'enemy' or among themselves.

Vows of *Satyagraha*

For the success of *Satyagraha* and in order to make the *Satyagrahis* intellectually, morally and spiritually strong enough to withstand enough all temptations, provocations and inflictions, Gandhi prescribed certain cardinal disciplines (eleven vows) a code of conduct, to be observed by them—more by the *Satyagrahi* leaders than by the *Satyagrahi* masses—in their daily life. The vows fall into two categories—principal and subsidiary.[29]

Principal Vows

Truth

Of all disciplines, the observance of the vow of truth comes first. The observance of the vow of truth is generally understood as merely confined to speaking the truth. But, according to Gandhi it really means that we must be truthful in thought, word and deed. Thus the observance of truth rules out the practice of secrecy, cunning and deception. Truth is to be realized by devoted constant practice and indifference to all other interests in life. It means ceaseless striving and complete detachment. The realization or *darshan* of truth, said Gandhi, "can only be attained by the man of pure detachment. Anger, greed, pride not fear, all these things draw a veil across the seeker's eyes".

Ahimsa (non-injury)

Ahimsa or non-violence literally means non-killing or non-injury. It is not enough not to take the life of any living being. The follower of this vow may not hurt physically or mentally even those whom he believes to be unjust; he may not be angry with them, he must love them; thus he would oppose the tyranny and injustice, whether of parents, governments or others, but will never hurt the tyrant. The follower of truth and *ahimsa* will conquer the tyrant by love; he will not carry the tyrant's will but he will suffer punishment even unto death for disobeying his will until the tyrant himself is conquered.

Celibacy or Brahmacharya

It is well-nigh impossible to observe the foregoing two vows unless celibacy is also observed; for this vow, it is not enough that one does not look upon any woman with a lustful eye; he has to control his animal passions so that they will not move him even in thought; if he is married, he will not have a carnal mind regarding his wife but will consider her as his life-long friend and will establish with her the relationship of perfect purity.

Control of the Palate

Until one has overcome the temptations of the palate, it is difficult to observe the foregoing vows, more especially that of celibacy. Control of the palate is the first essential in the observance of the vow of *brahmacharya*. Sex is indeed so tightly bound up with the palate that one who has not mastered taste cannot control animal passion either. An aspirant and striver for *brahmacharya* should, therefore, cultivate a feeling that he is eating not to satisfy the palate but just to keep body, mind and soul in perfect health.

Non-stealing

To take another person's property without his knowledge or permission or in the belief that it is an unclaimed property is, no doubt, an act of stealing. But stealing according to Gandhi, also includes taking of something from another without really needing and working for it, or taking it in larger quantity than is required for the immediate use, or to use it for a purpose different from one intended by the leader or to use it for a period longer than fixed with him, needless multiplication of wants, needless accumulation and hoarding for future use while others are in need of it at the moment, etc. In his opinion all amassing of wealth, above and beyond one's legitimate requirements, is theft.

Non-possession or Aparigraha

It is not enough not to possess and keep much, but it is necessary not to keep anything which may not be absolutely necessary for our bodily wants; thus if one can do without chairs, one should do so. The follower of this vow will, therefore, by constant reflection simplify his life.

Subsidiary Vows

Social and Religious Equimindedness

A *Satyagrahi*, according to Gandhi, should be convinced believer in social and religious equality and in the equality of sexes. He should cultivate perfect equimindedness towards all people irrespective of their caste, colour, occupation, sex, religion, birth-place and habitation and should cultivate equal reverence for all the principle religions of the world. He should try to eradicate all kinds of unreasonable distinctions and discriminations, including untouchability, from the society; should try to establish communal harmony and to elevate the position of the fallen sections of the society, including those of the untouchables, the aboriginals and the women.

Bread-Labour

The vow of bread-labour means that everybody, especially a *Satyagrahi*, must earn his bread and other primary needs of life by labouring with his hands, since production of every essential article involves bodily labour. "Bread-labour is a veritable blessing to one who would observe non-violence, worship truth, and make the observance of *brahmacharya* a natural act". It develops habits of obedience, self-respect and reliance, tenacity of will, sense of unity with others, endurance of hardships, sense of order and cooperation, energy, courage, equanimity, and practice in handling moral equivalents of weapons. Gandhi recommended hand-spinning as only universal form of bread-labour. But he never ceased to regard agriculture to be the ideal. In addition to spinning, everybody must, according to Gandhi, be his own scavenger. He felt that "there must be something radically wrong where scavenging has been made the concern of a separate class in society". Every one should therefore, commence bread-labour as a scavenger. Scavenging thus intelligently taken up, will help one to a true appreciation of the equality of man.

Swadeshi

It is inconsistent with truth to use articles about which or about whose makers there is a possibility of deception. Therefore, for instance, a votary of truth will not use articles manufactured in the mills of Manchester, Germany, or even in his own country, for he does not know that there is no deception about them. The vow of *Swadeshi* requires the use of simple and simply made clothing of the exclusion of even fancy buttons, foreign cuts, etc., and so will *Swadeshi* be applied to every department of life.

Fearlessness

Truth and non-violence or love are the principal keystones of *Satyagraha* and these require sufficient fearlessness. One who fears cannot seek and follow truth. *Satyagrahis* will, therefore, endeavour to be free from the fear of kings, people, caste, families, thieves, robbers, ferocious animals such as tigers and even death. Cultivation of courage and preparedness for sacrifice and sufferings which are necessary for a non-violent fighter also demand fearlessness. "He who has not overcome all fear cannot practise *ahimsa* to perfection".[30] A truly fearless man will defend himself against others by truth force or soul force.

Humility

Arrogance, egotism, self-importance, anger, and the pride of achievement—all these draw a veil across a truthseeker's eyes. Detachment, openness and tranquillity of mind, absence of prejudice and of the idea of doership in action, mildness, sublimity, forgiveness, fortitude—these are the real attributes of dispassionate seeker after truth and follower of non-violence. All these qualities taken together are called humility. Hence Gandhi writes in his *Autobiography*: "The instruments for the quest of truth are as simple as they are difficult. They may appear quite impossible to an arrogant person, and quite possible to an innocent child. The seeker after truth should be humbler than the dust."[31]

Code of *Satyagraha*

After discussing vows of *Satyagraha*, in detail, in the preceding pages, we now take up the code of *Satyagraha*.

A *Satyagrahi* bids good-bye to fear. He is, therefore, never afraid of trusting the opponent. Even if the opponent plays him false twenty times, the *Satyagrahi* is ready to trust him the twenty-first time, for an implicit trust in human nature is the very essence of his creed.[32]

A *Satyagrahi* is nothing if not instinctively law-abiding, and it is his law-abiding nature which exacts from him implicit obedience to the highest law, that is the voice of conscience which overrides all other laws.[33]

Since *Satyagraha* is one of the most powerful methods of direct action, a *Satyagrahi* exhausts all other means before he resorts to *Satyagraha*. He will, therefore, constantly and continually, approach the constituted authority, he will appeal to public opinion, educate public opinion, state his case calmly and coolly before everybody who wants to listen to him, and only after he has exhausted all these avenues will he resort to *Satyagraha*. But when he has found the impelling call of the inner voice within him and launches out upon *Satyagraha*, he has burnt his boats and there is no receding.[34]

The *Satyagrahi*, whilst he is ever ready for fight, must be equally eager for peace. He must welcome any honourable opportunity for peace.[35]

My advice is *Satyagraha* first and *Satyagraha* last. There is no other or better road to freedom.[36]

In the code of the *Satyagrahi* there is no such thing as surrender to brute force. Or the surrender then is the surrender of suffering and not to the wielder of the bayonet.[37]

As a *Satyagrahi* I must always allow my cards to be examined and re-examined at all times and make reparation of an error is discovered.[38]

Qualifications of a *Satyagrahi*

The following are the qualifications. I held as essential for every *Satyagrahi* in India:

1. He must have a living faith in God for He is his only rock.
2. He must believe in truth and non-violence as his creed and therefore have faith in the inherent goodness of human nature which he expects to evoke by his truth and love expressed through his suffering.
3. He must be leading a castle life and be ready and willing for the sake of his cause to give up his life and his possessions.
4. He must be a habitual *khadi*-weaver and spinner. This is essential for India.
5. He must be a teetotaller and be free from the use of other intoxicants in order that his reason may be always unclouded and his mind steady.
6. He must carry out with a willing heart all the rules of discipline as may be laid down from time-to-time.
7. He should carry out the jail rules unless they are specially devised to hurt his self-respect.

The qualifications are not to be regarded as exhaustive. They are illustrative only.[39]

Forms and Techniques of *Satyagraha*

The technique of *Satyagraha* admits of various methods to be used in successive stages, and many of them simultaneously, the most important being basic education and other items of the Constructive Programme, persuasion through reason, persuasion through change of heart by self-suffering and persuasion through non-violent direct action or non-violent non-co-operation which may take the forms of strike, picketing, boycott, and hijrat, ultimately culminating in civil disobedience.

Basic Education

Gandhi wanted every individual to be a full-blooded, fully developed member of society and aimed at the all round development of man's personality, that is, his physical, mental, moral and spiritual faculties. He knew that "man is neither mere intellect, nor the grass animal body, nor the heart or soul alone. A proper and harmonious combination of all the three is required for the making of the whole man."[40] Thus, he devised a scheme of basic education, which aimed at "an all-round drawing out of the best in child and man—body, mind and spirit. He aimed at a perfect, well-balanced, all-round education in which the body, the intellect and the heart have all simultaneous and full development into a natural harmonious whole. He described the system of basic education as "the spearhead of a silent social revolution fought with the most far-reaching consequences"[41] which will lay the foundation of a more just social order in which there is no unnatural division between the haves and the have-nots.

Constructive Programme

Constructive programme was an integral and positive aspect of Gandhi's post-1920 *Satyagraha* movements. It was adopted for the achievement of economic self-sufficiency and inculcation of the *swadeshi* spirit amongst the masses. It was employed for the promotion of communal harmony and removal of social evils like untouchability, unemployment and illiteracy.

Constructive programme according to Gandhi is designed to build up the nation from the very bottom. It must mean complete independence in every sense of the expression. Indeed his claim that civil disobedience is not absolutely necessary to win freedom through pure non-violent effort if the cooperation of the whole nation is secured in the constructive programme. For Gandhi constructive work was the heart of the matter. He described it as the permanent part of the non-violent effort. Handling of *Satyagraha* without the constructive programme will be, in his words, "like a paralysed hand attempting to lift a person."[42]

Gandhi adopted constructive programme as a method of *Satyagraha* for the first time during his Non-violent Non-co-operation Movement of 1920. In the course of this movement, national schools and institutions were started, arbitration courts and panchayats were established, and spinning on *charkha* began with the sole object of replacing government schools and colleges, law courts, and foreign goods which were to be completely boycotted.

Spinning and social welfare activities were continued throughout the Bardoli *Satyagraha* of 1928 with an emphasis upon the entire *khadi* programme. Even during his Salt *Satyagraha* of 1930, the wearing of hand-spun cloth was imperative for all *Satyagrahis*, and welfare and self-sufficiency work was undertaken as a way of achieving *swaraj*. However, the constructive programme as a definite method of achieving complete Independence found its clear and full exposition only in the post-individual *Satyagraha* period of December 1941.

Constructive programme was not conceived by Gandhi in a single day. It took several years to give shape and form to the programme. It was during the post-individual *Satyagraha* period that Gandhi expounded his whole philosophy of constructive programme and published a 25-page booklet entitled *Constructive Programme*. In 1941, Gandhi had listed the following thirteen items:

1. Communal Unity
2. Removal of Untouchability
3. Prohibition
4. *Khadi*
5. Other Village Industries
6. Village Sanitation
7. New or Basic Education
8. Adult Education
9. Uplift of Women
10. Education in Health and Hygiene
11. Provincial Languages

12. Propagation of *Rashtra Bhasa*
13. Promotion of Economic Equality

On February 15, 1945, Gandhi addressed Kasturba Nidhi workers. The booklet on constructive programme was revised with some more items added to the already existing thirteen. The items added were:

14. Kisans
15. Labour
16. *Adivasis*
17. Lepers
18. Students[43]

After Gandhi's death, the following items were added by his followers to strengthen the movement:

19. Cow Protection
20. Nature Cure
21. *Bhoodan*
22. *Gramdan*
23. *Shanti Sena*[44]

Conversion through Persuasive Argumentation

Simultaneous with mass education and other constructive activities, it is necessary in order to bring about any lasting revolution or radical change, first to change the attachment of individuals and groups to certain ideas, sentiments and assumptions. This is possible only by conversion through rational and gentle persuasion, not by coercion and compulsion.

In *Satyagraha*, persuasion takes two forms, to be applied in successive stages. The first stage is largely characterized by rational argumentation. The opponent is sought to be convinced by reason. Gandhi said: "I have no desire to carry a single soul with me if I can not appeal to his or her reason. My conventionality I carry to the point of rejecting the divinity of the oldest *Shashtras* if they cannot convince my reason."[45] In his opinion, one of the greatest qualities of a *Satyagrahi*, particularly a *Satyagrahi* leader, is to possess the capacity for independent thinking and convincing others by reason. Thus a *Satyagrahi* has first of all to try to convince his opponent by reason and mobilize public opinion against the evil which he is out to eradicate. When public opinion is sufficiently roused against an evil the strongest will not dare to practise or openly to lend support to it. An awakened and intelligent public opinion is the most potent weapon of a *Satyagrahi*.[46]

Conversion through Self-suffering

According to Gandhi, the next step that the *Satyagrahi* has to take in the direction of weaning the evil-doer from the evil is, to appeal to his heart by patient self-suffering, sympathy, sincerity, chivalry and humility. "You cannot inject new ideas into a man's head by chopping it off; neither will you infuse a new spirit into his heart by piercing it with a dagger."[47] Voluntary self-suffering opens the eyes of the evil-doer which are otherwise shut to the voice of reason. Thus a *Satyagrahi* has to appeal continuously to the evil-doer's head and heart combined.[48] Having failed to convince the evil-doer merely by reason or in case he refuses even to listen to his arguments, the *Satyagrahi* seeks, by means of self-suffering, to get through to his unprejudiced judgment so that he may willingly come again onto a level where he may be persuaded through reason "...the hardest metal yields to sufficient heat. Even so must the hardest heart melt before sufficiency of the heat of non-violence. And there is no limit to the capacity of non-violence to generate heat."[49]

Fasting

The most delicate form of *Satyagraha* is fasting. Unlike some other forms of *Satyagraha*, Gandhi was himself the author of fasting. Fasting is chiefly, a way of personal cleansing and penance.[50] It is a potent "infallible weapon in the armoury of *Satyagraha*." It is a fiery-weapon.

Gandhi enunciated certain general principles and conditions under which a *Satyagrahi* could resort to fasting: "A *Satyagrahi* should fast only as a last resort when all other avenues of redress have been explored and have failed. Suffering even unto death and, therefore, even through a perpetual fast is the last weapon of a *Satyagrahi*. That is the last duty which is open to him to perform.[51] He was of the considered view that fasting should be undertaken only by an "expert" and by him, too, only according to his capacity to fast. Fasting should be undertaken either for self-purification or self-restraint, or for appealing to the better nature of the opposite party, in order to make him reconsider his stand and realize his wrong. It may be undertaken to check acts of violence, to remove bitterness or even purify political atmosphere. It should, however, be employed only as "a species of tyaga," and never as a method of exercising undue pressure on the opposite party.

As an expert in *Satyagraha* Gandhi himself undertook fasts on as many as seventeen different occasions during his life, but he warned his friends and followers against imitating him blindly or out of false or hysterical sympathy. Of these facts, his three fasts were against official injustice, four against the institution and practice of untouchability, three against Hindu-Muslim riots, and four against other acts of violence. Further, three of his fasts were for self-purification and penance,[52] and, one to encourage the Ahmedabad Mill workers in the strike which they were continuing on his advice in order to secure increase in their wages.[53]

Non-violent Non-cooperation

Gandhi admittedly learnt the technique of non-violent non-cooperation from Leo Tolstoy. Non-violent non-cooperation is a sacred duty and an alternative to anarchy. It is the most expeditious method known to the world of winning over opponents. Non-cooperation with the evil-doer is a mild form but can be an immensely potent technique when undertaken on a mass scale. It is the activisation of love for the redress of wrongs. There can be non-cooperation between a father and his sons as well between an imperial oppressor and the citizens. Non-cooperation indeed means renunciation of the benefits of a system with which we non-cooperate. A non-cooperator has therefore, to renounce the benefits of schools, corporations, courts, titles, legislatures and other institutions set up under an evil system.

Gandhi's scheme of non-cooperation presupposed ability on the part of *Satyagrahi* masses to control all the forces of evil. His scheme also presupposed suffering and losses to the non-cooperator. According to Gandhi, non-cooperation is a "measure of discipline and self-sacrifice, without which no nation can make real progress."[54]

Gandhi started his first Non-cooperation Movement in India in 1920. It aimed to redress the wrongs of the Khilafat and the Punjab massacres and for the attainment of *swaraj*. The items of the programme were as follows:[55]

(a) Surrender of titles and honorary offices and resignation of nominated posts in local bodies.
(b) Refusal to attend government levies, durbars and other official and semi-official functions held by government officials or in their honour.
(c) Gradual withdrawal of children from schools and colleges in the various provinces.
(d) Gradual boycott of British Courts by lawyers and litigants and establishment of private arbitration courts by them for settlement of private disputes.
(e) Refusal on the part of the military, clerical and labouring classes to offer themselves as recruits for service in Mesopotamia.
(f) Withdrawal by the candidates from election to the reformed councils and refusal on the part of the voters to vote for any candidate who may despite the congress advice, offer himself for election.
(g) Boycott of foreign goods.
(h) Laying down of arms and the suspension of taxes were the two last stages of non-cooperation.

Non-violent non-cooperation may take the form of strike, picketing, boycott, *hartal* and *hijrat*, ultimately culminating, in Civil Disobedience.

Strikes

According to K.L. Shridharani, the strike as such "is labour's instrument for the acquisition of a desired standard of treatment and living from the employer."[56] Strikes may be employed directly and openly to achieve political ends. For example, during his South-African *Satyagraha* Movement, he advised and himself conducted a strike of Indian coalmine workers and railway-men in the months of October-November, 1913, for the singular object of persuading the Government to repeal £-3 tax.[57]

However, whether the strike method is employed to achieve economic ends, or to secure political betterment, it must fulfil certain preliminary requisite in order to find a definite place in the *Satyagraha* scheme. *Firstly*, a peaceful strike must be limited to the actual sufferers and must, at the same time, be justifiable on its own merits. *Secondly*, it should be spontaneous and not manipulated. During his Ahmedabad *Satyagraha*, Gandhi laid down the other conditions of a successful strike. These were: [58]

1. Never to resort to violence,
2. Never to molest black-legs,[59]
3. Never to depend upon aims, and
4. To remain firm, no matter how long the strike continued, and to earn bread, during the strike by any other honest labour.

Gandhi, however, warned against the use of strikes in the public utility services and thought that the strike or abstention from work in essential services was against the spirit of *Satyagraha* for it puts the community or at least a substantial section of it, to loss, harassment or inconvenience. He thought that "dislocation of these would dislocate public life."[60]

Hartal

Hartal or peaceful stoppage of work is another form of *Satyagraha*. *Hartal* means voluntary suspension of business in protest against some evil authority. It is a way of signifying protest, and its purpose is to strike the imagination of all—the people as well as the government. According to Gandhi, it is an "act of self-purification".[61] It is the best method of making our strong disapproval of the action of the government. It is a means more powerful than monster meetings expressing national opinion.[62] *Hartals*, however, should be absolutely voluntary; otherwise they would cease to be non-violent. *Hartal* forcibly brought about cannot be considered *Satyagrahi hartal*. They should be brought about by persuasion, gentle argument and propaganda. In any case, there should be no element of compulsion or force in it. Besides, *hartals* should not be organised too frequently, for then they would be hardly effective.

Boycott

Another *Satyagraha* method advocated by Gandhi was the boycott of economic, social, political, educational, legal and other institutions with the object of lodging protest against, and putting pressure on, the opposite party in order ultimately to seek redress of grievances. It is a sort of punishment and is conceived in a vindictive spirit.

Economic boycott is implied in the vow of *Swadeshi*. It implies the boycott of commodities of universal use, for they must always be locally produced. According to Gandhi, foreign cloth is such a commodity. Hence in 1920-22, he went so far as to urge the destruction of foreign cloth in India. Gandhi himself inaugurated the bonfires of foreign cloth in Bombay in July 1921.

In the social sphere, boycott takes the form of non-violent social ostracism. But Gandhi tells us that in the complex conditions of the modern world, social ostracism is of a very limited application. It may be employed only in extreme cases "when a defiant minority refused to bend to the majority, not out of any regard for principle, but from sheer defiance or worse."[63] Social boycott should be applied only in such a way that it is not felt as a punishment by the object of boycott. "It must cause pain to the party using it, if it causes inconvenience to its object."[64]

In the political sphere, boycott takes the form of civil disobedience. It includes resignation of offices and titles and refraining from making use of the services of those who do not represent popular will and flout public opinion. Voters "must ratify their verdict by complete abstention from any encouragement of the so-called representatives. The public will be bound, if they are non-cooperationists, to refrain from giving these representatives any prestige by attending their political functions or parties."[65]

The boycott of educational, legal and other institutions means setting up of such parallel institutions on the non-violent model in the light of the ideal.

Picketing

Peaceful picketing is also a valid and useful form of *Satyagraha*. Picketing, like *hartal*, should also be persuasive and coercive. Both during the Non-cooperation Movement and the Civil Disobedience Movement of 1930-34, Gandhi urged picketing, preferably by women, of foreign as well as country liquor shops and foreign cloth shops. However, Gandhi does not favour *dharna* as a method of picketing. He considered *dharna* as a form of barbarity, a crude and cowardly way of using coercion. Picketing as a species of *Satyagraha* has to be entirely non-violent.

Hijrat

Hijrat or *deshatyaga* is an age-old technique—individual as well as corporate—of meeting wrongs. It means voluntary emigration by people from the land they have hitherto believed to be theirs,[66] when they are grievously oppressed and terrorized and when they have no other recourse. But in Gandhi's opinion, in the purest form of *Satyagraha*, there is no need for doing hijrat. But in case of incapacity of offering non-violent or even violent resistance to the oppressor, Gandhiji's alternative to cowardly submission to oppression and demoralization was hijrat. "It is wisdom to vacate houses or places that are plague infected. Tyranny is a kind of plague and when it is likely to make us angry or weak it is wisdom to leave the scene of such temptation."[67]

Gandhi advised hijrat to the Hindus of Sindh province during communal riots in 1939-40.[68] He also advised hijrat to the city women of India during World War II to escape criminal assaults and violation by foreign soldiers stationed in India.[69] Earlier he had commended hijrat to the *Satyagrahis* of Bardoli in 1928, and those of Junagadh and Vitthalgad in 1939.[70]

Hijrat, however, should be resorted to in extreme cases. It should be a planned, and not a cowardly fight. But "planned hijrat requires courage and forethought".[71]

All these various species of non-cooperation culminate in civil disobedience which is the next logical weapon.

Civil Disobedience

It is an active, strong and extreme form of *Satyagraha*. According to Gandhiji, civil disobedience is a necessary part of non-cooperation.[72] Gandhi conceived it as "a substitute for violence or armed rebellion. It is a non-coercive method which any law-abiding citizen can adopt, provided he is saturated with the spirit of non-violence and is ready for the utmost sacrifices.[73]

According to Gandhi, complete civil disobedience implying a refusal to render obedience to every single state made law can be a very powerful movement.[74] In Gandhiji's opinion, civil disobedience should be "so complete that if an order was issued on us by the government saying 'Go to the right', we must not hesitate to move leftward." It is a complete, effective and bloodless substitute of armed revolt.

Civil disobedience can be undertaken for the deliberate breach of certain unmoral statutory enactments, or as the symbolic non-violent revolt against the state. In either case, it does not reflect want of respect for the constituted authority. Its ultimate aim is to substitute voluntary cooperation for involuntary cooperation and willing obedience for forced obedience. This underlying objective alone can make the *Satyagrahis* adhere to their inner voice.[75] Civil disobedience can be practiced "only as a last resort and by a selected few in the first instance at any rate."[76]

Civil disobedience is primarily of two types—offensive or assertive and defensive. Either of the two types may be offered by single individuals as completely independent units or by masses collectively. But whereas individual civil disobedience is self-led, mass civil disobedience needs a leadership. Gandhi considered civil disobedience as essentially an individual affair and he regarded individual civil disobedience as more effective, almost irresistible. According to him, offensive compromise is based on give and take, but in *Satyagraha* "there can be no give and take in fundamentals. Any compromise on fundamentals is a surrender because it is all give and no take."[77]

However, this list like any other list, cannot be said to be complete and exhaustive. There can be as many forms and techniques of *Satyagraha* as there are forms of injustices, their different grades of intensity, different nature of the agents and their relations with others. It is through the advocacy and use of these techniques that Gandhi delivered his supreme message of substituting willing obedience to forced obedience and voluntary cooperation for involuntary cooperation. In the words of Diwakar, "It is not Gandhiji who made *Satyagraha* but *Satyagraha* which has made Gandhiji.... If it is a matter of obligation between two, it is *Satyagraha* which has obliged Gandhiji rather than its reverse.[78]

Conclusion

Satyagraha is, in fact, a growing science. Gandhi has demonstrated the efficiency and efficacy of *Satyagraha* not only in getting political freedom but against exploitation, oppression, social injustice and social evils in his life time. *Satyagraha*, moreover, is not the weapon of the weak or coward, rather it is a weapon of the strong or brave which demands for a new real civilization and culture for the humanity as a whole.

In fact, *Satyagraha* is the most powerful and permanent weapon to solve political, social and economic as well as religious problems. It holds good even today in our democratic setup against any perpetrated evil. Gandhi claimed that the sarvodaya social order would be free from moral degradation, economic exploitation, and political subjugation.

NOTES

1. Gouri Kant Thakur, *Mahatma Gandhi's Philosophy of Satyagraha*, Kishore Vidya Niketan, Varanasi, 1988, p. 3.
2. M.K. Gandhi, *An Autobiography or the Story of My Experiments with Truth*, Navajivan, Ahmedabad, 1956, p. 239.
3. Gouri Kant Thakur, *op. cit.*, p. 3.
4. M.K. Gandhi, *Satyagraha in South Africa*, I Edition, S. Ganesan, Madras, 1928, p. 173.
5. *The Collected Works of Mahatma Gandhi*, Vol. VIII, The Publications Division, Ministry of Information and Broadcasting, Government of India, Delhi, 1962, pp. 22-23.
6. *Ibid.*, Vol. XVIII, 1965, p. 133.
7. M.K. Gandhi, *Hind Swaraj or Indian Home Rule*, II Edition, III Imprint, Navajivan, Ahmedabad, 1958, p. 79.
8. J.B. Kripalani, *Gandhian Terminology* (unpublished MSS), AICC Papers, File No. 15, 1936, p. 27.
9. V.P. Varma, *The Political Philosophy of Mahatma Gandhi and Sarvodaya*, Lakshmi Narain Agarwal, IV Edition, 1980-81, p. 162.
10. *Young India*, 26-2-1925, p. 73.
11. *Young India*, 19-3-1925, p. 95.
12. *Young India*, 4-6-1925, p. 189.
13. *The Collected Works of Mahatma Gandhi*, Vol. XIII, p. 522.
14. K.L. Shridharani, *War Without Violence*, Bombay, 1962, p. 162.
15. V.P. Varma, *op. cit.*, pp. 163-64.
16. M.K. Gandhi, *Satyagraha in South Africa*, *op. cit.*, p. 114.
17. S.C. Gangal, *Gandhian Thought and Techniques in the Modern World*, Criterion Publications, New Delhi, 1988, pp. 154-55.
18. V.P. Varma, *op. cit.*, p. 168.
19. *Harijan*, 14.5.1938, p. 111.

20. Ramjee Singh, *Gandhi and the Modern World*, Classical Publishing Company, New Delhi, 1988, p. 79.
21. M.K. Gandhi, *Satyagraha in South Africa, op. cit.*, p. 433.
22. Anil Dutta Mishra, *Fundamentals of Gandhism*, Mittal Publications, New Delhi, 1955, p. 22.
23. M.K. Gandhi, *Satyagraha*, Navajivan, Ahmedabad, 1954, p. 40.
24. M.L. Sharma, "Mahatma Gandhi's View of Satyagraha", *Gandhi Bhavan News Letter*, University of Delhi, Vol. II, No. 1, January 1989, p. 52.
25. *Young India*, 11-8-1920.
26. S.C. Gangal, *op. cit.*, p. 152.
27. Ramjee Singh, *op. cit.*, pp. 82-83.
28. *Harijan*, 1-9-1940.
29. R.R. Diwakar, *Saga of Satyagraha*, Gandhi Peace Foundation, New Delhi, 1969, p. 225.
30. *Harijan*, 1-9-1940.
31. M.K. Gandhi, *Autobiography, op. cit.*, p. XV.
32. M.K. Gandhi, *Satyagraha in South Africa*, 1950 Edition, *op. cit.*, p. 159.
33. *Speeches and Writings of Mahatma Gandhi*, G.A. Natesan and Company, Madras, 1933, 4th Edition, p. 465.
34. *Young India*, 20-10-1927, p. 353.
35. *Young India*, 19-3-1931, p. 40.
36. *Harijan*, 15-9-1946, p. 312.
37. *Young India*, 30-4-1931, p. 93.
38. *Harijan*, 11-3-1939, p. 44.
39. *Harijan*, 25-3-1939, p. 64.
40. *Harijan*, 8-5-1937.
41. *Harijan*, 9-10-1937.
42. M.K. Gandhi, *Constructive Programme*, 1941, p. 29.
43. *Ibid.*, p. 3.
44. Anil Dutta Mishra, *op. cit.*, p. 77.
45. *Young India*, 14-7-1920.
46. *Young India*, 8-8-1929.
47. Louis Fischer, *The Life of Mahatma Gandhi*, (Bhavan's Library), Vol. I, p. 93.
48. Quoted in D.G. Tendulkar, *Mahatma*, Vol. II, p. 265.
49. *Harijan*, 7-1-1939.
50. M.K. Gandhi, *Autobiography, op. cit.*, p. 419.
51. *Harijan*, 18-2-1933.
52. For details see Ram Rattan, *Gandhi's Thought and Action*, Kalinga Publications, Delhi, 1991, pp. 289-92.

53. *The Collected Works of Mahatma Gandhi*, Vol. XIV, *op. cit.*, 1965, pp. 254 and 268.
54. D.G. Tendulkar, *op. cit.*, p. 13.
55. *Ibid.*, p. 12.
56. K.L. Shridharani, *War Without Violence: A Study of Gandhi's Method and Its Accomplishments*, I Edition, Victor Gollancz Ltd., London, 1939, p. 36.
57. *The Collected Works of Mahatma Gandhi*, *op. cit.*, Vol. XII, 1964, pp. 658-68.
58. M.K. Gandhi, *Autobiography*, *op. cit.*, p. 427.
59. Black-leg is a person who offers to work when the regular workers are on strike.
60. *Harijan*, 10-8-1947, p. 274.
61. M.K. Gandhi, *Autobiography*, *op. cit.*, p. 562.
62. D.G. Tendulkar, *op. cit.*, Vol. I, p. 312.
63. *Young India*, 8-12-1920, p. 298.
64. *Young India*, 16-2-1921.
65. *Young India*, 8-12-1920, p. 298.
66. *Young India*, 31-5-1928.
67. M.K. Gandhi, "Bardoli on Trial", *Young India*, 31-5-1928.
68. *Non-violence in Peace and War*, Vol. I, Navajivan Publishing House, Ahmedabad, 1948, pp. 253-54.
69. *Ibid.*, Vol. II, p. 377.
70. *Harijan*, 20-5-1939.
71. *Non-violence in Peace and War*, *op. cit.*, p. 253.
72. *Young India*, 27-3-1920.
73. *Harijan*, 24-6-1939, pp. 159-160.
74. *Young India*, 4-8-1921.
75. *Harijan*, 15-10-1938, p. 290.
76. *Young India*, 23-3-1921.
77. *Harijan*, 30-4-1940.
78. R.R. Diwakar, *Satyagraha: Its Technique and History*, Hind Kitabs, Bombay, 1946, p. 91.

10

Panchayati Raj: A Gandhian Perspective

Panchayats have been in existence in India right from ancient times. It is a proven fact that almost every village in ancient times had a self-governing body of its own. They were, an integral part of Indian polity and enjoyed considerable prestige and autonomy. In the midst of conquest and the rise and fall of empires, the village Panchayats continued to survive, and thus gave a continuity to Indian tradition. Therefore, recognizing the village Panchayats as a part of ancient Indian tradition that deserved to be preserved, the Constitution laid down as a directive principle of state policy that "the state shall take steps to organize village Panchayats and to endow them with such powers and authority as may be necessary to enable them to function as units of self-government" (Article 40). In fact, the founding fathers of Indian Constitution included the Panchayats under Article 40 after timely intervention of Mahatma Gandhi at the draft stage of the Constitution.

The Panchayati Raj Institutions (PRIs) in India are the prime instruments of decentralization at the grass-roots level[1]. It is essentially an institutionalized mechanism for empowering the people. They assume importance due to the need to contain the relentless demographic pressures and optimum use of scarce resources for development. They act as a vehicle in carrying back to the people the power that really belongs to them[2]. India lives in villages. There are over 2,17,300 village Panchayats in the country covering over 96 per cent of about 5.79 lakh inhabited villages and 92 per cent of the rural population of the country. Unless the socio-economic and political situations are changed, democracy can not flourish.

Gandhian Perspectives

Mahatma Gandhi's basic concept of Panchayat may be given in his own inimitable style: "My idea of village *swaraj* is that it is a compete republic independent of its neighbours for its vital wants and yet interdependent for many others in which independence is necessary. The Government of the village will be conducted by the Panchayat of five persons, annually elected by the adult villagers, male and female, possessing prescribed qualifications. These will have all the authority and jurisdiction required.... here there is perfect democracy based upon individual judgement"[3]. He (Gandhi) conceived of the entire hierarchy of administration in terms of Panchayats. Gandhi wanted that the village republics should be basic units of *Swaraj* Government enjoying maximum autonomy in social, economic and political affairs. The village should be properly co-ordinated at the Taluka, the District, the Province and the All India Centre through the Taluka and District Panchayats, Provincial Assemblies and Federal Parliament.

To Gandhi perfect Panchayat democracy was synonymous with *Ram Rajya* which he defined as follows:

> "It can be religiously translated as kingdom of God on earth. Politically translated, it is perfect democracy in which inequalities based on possession and non-possession, colour, race or creed or sex vanish. In it land and state belong to the people. Justice is prompt, perfect and cheap and, therefore, there is freedom of worship and of speech and the press-all this because of the reign of the self-imposed law of moral self-contained village and communities"[4].

Gandhi placed rural development at the core of India's future destiny; not rural development visualized macrocosmically but in terms of the development of each of its numerous villages to full potential. From time immemorial the people of India have mostly lived in villages. Gandhi not only expected most of them to continue living in villages but wanted them to do so, for thereby, the country would preserve the more wholesome features of its culture and traditions, without being deflected by the values and attractions of modern urban life as in the rest of the world.

Gandhi in his various speeches and in his articles written through out the freedom struggle spoke highly of democratic decentralization. He said, "India's independence must begin at the bottom"[5]. In fact, the people for greater autonomy to the rural bodies received conceptual strength with the advent of Mahatma Gandhi on the national scene. But Dr. Ambedkar, who was primarily responsible for the draft Constitution, gave no place in it to the Panchayats. He (Ambedkar) spoken clearly and unequivocally condemning the village Panchayats[6]. He observed: "I hold the view that these village republics have been the ruination of India. I am therefore, surprised that those who condemn provincialism and communalism should come forward as champions of the village. What is the village but a sink of localism, a den of ignorance, narrow mindedness and communalism? I am glad that the draft Constitution has discarded the village and adopted the individual as its unit"[7].

After a prolonged debate storm and protest the Article 40 incorporated in the Constitution, which legitimizes rural self-Government as a high objective of legislative and executive endeavour of the state is not just one article out of whole Constitution. It is rather an embodiment of the most cherished dream of Constitution makers and an objectification of the most widely held consensus. So long as the minds of the citizens is respected by their leaders, this would continue to guide the course of Panchayati Raj in this country and endow every step in the progressive realization of the idea with the necessary sanctity and sanction[8].

In the present scenario, the concept of Panchayati Raj has come to be accepted as an extension of democracy up to the village, and has found favour amongst politicians. It is often said that mere exercise of the right to elect representatives to the Central and State legislatures is not enough for the ordinary citizen. In other words, the concept of participation of the people should be considered as an ideological commitment and therefore what is needed is legislative and structural measures to give legitimacy to people's participation[9].

The PRIs in India have travelled a long road to acquire a constitutional status from a mere mentioning of it in the Constitution in the form of Directive Principles (Article 40). Before they could get constitutional status, several exercises were carried out in this direction viz., Balwant Rai Mehta Committee (1957), Ashok Metha Committee (1977), Committee on Administrative Arrangements for Rural Development (1985), L.M. Shinghvi Committee (1987), 64th Constitutional Amendment Bill (1989) and 74th Constitutional Amendment Bill (1990) etc.[10].

The 73rd Constitutional Amendment Act, 1992 has added a new dimension to the concept of Panchayati Raj by providing enough scope for direct elections and for political parties to contest elections and to play effective role, and by giving it a constitutional status[11].

The Panchayati Raj has been established in all states on a legal footing. "An effective democracy", says W.J. Sheprad, "demands something more than that the qualified voters shall occasionally cast their ballots for national or state representatives"[12].

The over all pattern of Panchayati Raj represents an earnest at decentralization and devolution of power and authority on the rural communities so as to "usher in Poorman's *Swaraj* in accord with genius of our race"[13]. *Swaraj* at one time meant independence, but it also included the elimination of poverty and hunger, equality between classes and sexes, freedom from fear and hope for a better future. Sadly, the *Swaraj* of Gandhi's dream remains a dream unfulfilled[14].

Panchayati Raj is a means to the revival of the village the life-spring of India. Revival of the village is indeed the key to the regeneration of India and the fulfillment of her mission in the world. "I want villages to live", says the architect of modern India Pandit Jawahar Lal Nehru," and I do not care what happens to the towns because I am convinced that if villages live, towns will live automatically, but if villages die, there can be no hope for towns. If village the prosper India is also bound to prosper"[15].

In fact the road to the village is the road to the haven of India's soul, the road to the cradle of our civilization, the road to real yagna. The village will be barometer of India's progress and prosperity. "Going back to villages", says Dr. Radhakrishnan, "is not to become primitive. It is the only way to keep with us a mode of existence that is instructive to India, that supplied her once with purpose, a faith and meaning. It is the only way to keep our species civilized"[16].

The idea of Panchayati Raj essentially is based on the principle of involving the people themselves directly in the management of their affairs because it is the people who know best what their problems are, what their priorities are and what could be the best solutions to suit their requirements. The 73rd Constitutional Amendment Act 1992 which came into force with effect from April 24, 1993 has paved the way for decentralization of power, both political and economic, to the grassroots level. It is eagerly hoped that this long awaited measure will speedily usher in Gandhi's dream into reality of bringing *Swaraj* to every village, treating it as a republic or Panchayat having full powers to shape its own destiny. The 73rd Constitutional Amendment Act provides for a uniform three-tier system of Panchayat at the village level, the intermediate level, and the district level, throughout the country, with elections mandatory every five years. The Act also provides reservation for SCs and STs at all levels in proportion to their percentage in the total population of the area. One-third of the seats are to be reserved for women. Apart from reservation in membership, there is reservation in posts of chairpersons in PRIs at all levels. The Act also empowers the Panchayats to levy taxes/duties, fees, etc. And envisages setting up of a Finance Commission every five years to review the financial position of Panchayat and make recommendations to the State Governments.

In fact, it can be said that India is on the threshold of a historic transition of political power to the grassroots with all the States completing the process of enacting fresh legislation on strengthening the PRAs on April 23, 1994. As many as eleven States pushed through fresh legislation in 72 hours, some of them even in the early hours of April 23, 1994 to beat the stipulated deadline of April 23, 1994; the day Panchayats became part of the Indian Constitution. However, the 73rd Constitutional Amendment Act is not applicable to Jammu and Kashmir, Mizoram, Nagaland and certain scheduled areas of the country[17]. But mere enactment of laws does not ensure results. The success of PRIs will depend on the administrative and financial powers delegated to them by individual State Governments. What is more important in their operationalisation?[18]

The essential prerequisites for the Panchayati Raj Institutions to function as institutions of self-government according to Prof. S.N. Mishra are: (i) clearly demarcated jurisdiction, (ii) commensurating with responsibilities adequate power and authority, (iii) to manage the affairs of PRIs necessary human and financial resources, and (iv) within the federal structures functional autonomy[19]. The New Panchayati Raj must be seen as "third tier of government" as the Constitutional Amendment Act opens possibilities for fulfilling these conditions[20]. Even then there is a major lacuna in the Act i.e., the Act is contradictory and inconsistent in its approach to the idea of Panchayati Raj being the institution of self-government. The bill had rightly defined the Panchayats as an institution of self-government but later, in defining the functions of these institutions, had narrowed them down to developmental functions. Without law and order (police) functions of each level, no institution self-government is effective[21].

There are certain prerequisites for the survival of PRIs. These are:

1. There should be commitment of the PR as a political value and the consequent political will to establish it.
2. It should not be forgotten that the effort to revitalize PR, in fact, is an attempt to reconstruct Indian polity by way of bringing so far deprived sections into the mainstream.

3. PRIs should be treated as the single agency for development of the rural area.[22]

Summing Up

One may conclude that a time will come when the Panchayati Raj Institution will fulfil the people's aspirations. And it is expected that by the end of 2015 A.D. the PRIs will be deeply rooted in the rural community and become the real vehicle of change and development[23]. In fact, the Panchayati Raj system would usher India into the 21st century to fulfil the new hope and aspirations of the people by incorporating the Gandhian model of development with new science and technology. No model is immutable and valid for all times to come. What is, therefore needed is a trade-off between the pristine purity of Gandhian village model and the modern worldwide economic paradigm preserving some parts and not all of the Gandhian model.

NOTES

1. S.N. Mishra, "Panchayati Raj and Peoples Aspirations" in M. Wadhwani and S.N. Mishra (ed.), *Dreams and Realities: Expectations from Panchayati Raj*, Indian Institute of Public Administration, New Delhi, 1996, p. 1.
2. *Ibid.*
3. Mahatma Gandhi, *Harijan*, 26.7.1942.
4. *The Hindu*, 22.6.1944.
5. Mahatma Gandhi, *Harijan*, 22.7.1946.
6. S.N. Mishra, *op. cit.*, p. 2.
7. Sweta Mishra, *Democratic Decentralisation in India*, Mittal Publications, New Delhi, 1994, p. 20.
8. *Ibid.*, p. 22.
9. Ali, Ashraf and S.N. Mishra, *Public Administration: A New Paradigm*, Cadplan Publisher and Distributor, New Delhi, 1996, pp. 313-14.
10. *Ibid.*, p. 314.
11. S.N. Mishra, *op. cit.*, pp. 2-3.
12. R.L. Khanna, *Panchayati Raj in India*, The English Book Shop, Chandigarh, 1956, p. 14.

13. *Ibid.*, p. 15.
14. Kamla Choudhary, "What are we Celebrating Today?", *The Hindustan Times*, New Delhi, August 15, 1996, p. 16.
15. R.L. Khanna, *op. cit.*, p. 15.
16. *Ibid.*
17. S.N. Mishra, *op. cit.*, p. 5.
18. *Ibid.*
19. Ali, Ashraf and S.N. Mishra, *op. cit.*, p. 316.
20. S.N. Mishra, *op. cit.*, p. 5.
21. Ali, Ashraf and S.N. Mishra, *op. cit.*, pp. 316-17.
22. *Ibid.*, pp. 319-320.
23. *Ibid.*, pp. 320-21.

11

Disability Management: A Gandhian Perspective

As charity begins at home, management also begins at home. All the more, disability management emerges from the heart. Where there is a commitment, devotion and dedication, there could be an effective divine management. I use the word "divine" as a pre-fix to the management because man has all the three qualities—animal, human and divine. Every individual has a divine spark of truth and everybody is a mobile temple as Mahatma Gandhi said. Hence, it is justified to use the concept of Divine Management.

Under any management system, three things need to be stressed. (1) Divinity, (2) Purity, and (3) Unity. Disability management is possible only when there is divinity. Recently I have come across a book titled "*Management Leadership through Bhagwad Gita*" by Arun Kumar (2000) published by Shubhi Publications, FK 30, Shastri Nagar, Delhi. I hope there will be such books like "*Management through Bible*" as well as "*Management through Quran*". It will be inspiring to draw lessons from spiritual literature for disability management.

When in the scientific era, management experts have seriously started probing the importance of spiritualising management, I feel "disability management" ought to be oriented towards spirituality. Disabled are otherwise known as "differentially abled". Everybody has some capacity and ability whether disabled or not. They ought to have equal opportunities. Disability management requires extra care and attention as experienced by the disabled homes. Management based on love towards disabled will become a model.

In the Indian context, many families feel unlucky and feel the burden of having a disabled. In Philippines, I was told that a family blessed with a disabled child is considered lucky. For the kind attention of the readers, I say it with authentic reports and field based experience that there are families which go to the extent of killing disabled child which is serious in nature. However, it is a hidden process which may be explored for research.

There are centres where disabled serve the disabled. Amar Seva Sangam, Ayakudi, Tenkasi has been actively serving for the cause of physically challenged. One Mr. Ramakrishnan, founder of the said sangam, is disabled and quadriplegic and he has been serving the disabled. Irulam Oliyagum—St. Joseph Centre for the Blind at Thomaiyarpuram, Dindigul is headed by a blind person, Mr. Machakalai, committed in serving the visually challenged, who has bagged national award.

Such centres for the disabled stand as a living model and individual disabled persons prove to be efficient managers under the management system. Besides, there are businessmen being disabled but economically abled and stable. It is high time we bring out a workable model to manage the disabilities. In this context, I suggest a Gandhian model to manage the disabilities. For example, all of us are aware of the fact that Gandhi himself treated and helped a leper called Parchur Shastri. He said, "Leprosy is curable" and I say that disability can be prevented and managed by individuals under any circumstances.

Another Gandhian Dr. Baba Amte, winner of the Gandhi Peace Prize for the year 1999, was actively engaged in "disability management"—by way of serving the lepers, physically challenged, deaf and dumb etc. His own son a medical Doctor by profession, Mr. Vikas Amte is serving the disabled at Anandwan, Maharashtra. Kasturba Hospital at Gandhigram Tamil Nadu headed by Dr. Kousalya Devi has an Artificial Limb Centre (ALC) serving the man-made disability. Besides, Avvai Ashram, Sivasailam under Gandhigram Trust is running a school for deaf and dumb. Hence, they all provide a Gandhian model to manage disabilities.

Under the University system, there is a course called "Gandhian Way of Management" as part of the curriculum in the UG programme in Rural Reconstruction and post-graduate programme in Gandhian Studies offered by Madurai Kamaraj University, Madurai. All that Gandhi desired was "management based on truth and non-violence". "Supreme consideration for the humans in the management" ought to be given. Humanism is Gandhism and it is Gandhism which holds key to solve the problems in the humanity as African Gandhi Nelson Mandela said.

Under the umbrella of disability management, "To remove every tear from every eye of the disabled" should be the goal of disability management in tune with the main object of Gandhian philosophy. Further, Gandhi said, "India's hunger is my hunger" similarly, hunger among the disabled must be tackled. Moreover, disability and poverty are like twins in the community, which need to be attacked. Also we should feel that pain of the disabled as the pain of our own self.

I have come across a lot of children with disability living in utter poverty. Disability management is also linked with socio-economic problems of the disabled. However, 'zero poverty' is to be achieved in the world of disabled.

It may be noted that love of non-violence is the key for disability management. It requires a lot of patience and tolerance. We have also celebrated an international year of tolerance (1995). But it is to be practiced in everyday life. The parents of the disabled children are very much worried about their family condition and they also loose patience with their own disabled children and adults. However, they should learn to treat them as Divine Children. Otherwise, there is no joy of life. Disability is nothing but a play of the Divine as the writer thinks.

The book in Tamil titled *Tiruvilaiyadal Puranam* in prose by T. Namasivayam highlights Divine sports of the Lord. Tiruvilaiyadal literally means the sacred sports of Lord which could be interpreted as Divine sports of the disabled. There are both national and international olympics conducted for the disabled. What a courage with which disabled manage to participate in such olympics. It is nothing but sports of the Lord-Divine. The writer is also proud to record the fact that he has experience in organising sports for disabled in collaboration with a local NGO headed by Dr. P.M. Kanagasabapathy who is also a wheel chaired person since his childhood.

In the *Tiruvilaiyadal Puranam* of Paranjothi Munivar (1700 A.D.), 64 selective divine sports of Lord Siva are presented in 3363 Viruttam verses, studded with enchanting natural descriptions, imageries, rhetorical beauties, melodious diction, ethical excellence and above all devotional fervour. Folk-motifs are many in this *Purana*.

All the sports, which reveal the Lord's compassion took place in and around Madurai, the capital of the Pandyan kingdom. Siva, His Consort, Parvati and Divine Child, Muruga, manifested themselves respectively as Sundara Pandya, Tadatakai Piratti (Meenakshi) and Ukkira Kumara to protect the people, establish righteousness and to patronise the Tamil Sangam.

Many episodes are related to the Sangam poets. Nakkirar's undaunted arguments with the Lord regarding the real sense of a poem, *Konguther Vaazhkai* is picturesquely portrayed. The miracles of transforming jackals into horses and *vice versa*, for the sake of Manickavasagar, the author of the Tiruvasagam and Sambandar's encounter with the Jain ascetics in religious debate, are wonderfully narrated.

Such a miracle may also happen to transform the disabled into normal. It has been proved through world's first hospital on wheels conducted by the Impact India Foundation and Rajiv Gandhi Foundation for which the writer served as the project coordinator during the year 1994. There are disabled who have seen miracles in their life about which the writer has heard and also the evidences are available.

Disability Management is an art and a process. Man's life is also an art which has been part of management. The more man grows, the more he can learn to manage the affairs. As part of training for the executives of disability management, I suggest a spiritual training programme for managers of disability. Training in conflict management is also suggested. Conflicts do take place in our daily life and it should be resolved amicably for the smooth functioning of disability management.

There are two different areas of management. (1) Private sector or NGO based disability management. (2) Government based disability management. There are some voluntary organisations which provide a better model for disability management.

The earlier National Youth Policy was formulated in 1988 and the latest youth policy document 2003 is designed to galvanize the youth to rise upto the challenges, keeping in view the global scenario, and aims at motivating them to be dynamically active and committed participants in the exciting task of National Development. This policy accorded priority to the following groups of young people including Disabled.

(a) Rural youth,
(b) Urban youth,
(c) Student youth,
(d) Non Student youth,
(e) Disabled youth.

Disability can also be seen in the above groups. Hence, disability management training may be imparted for such categories. All the more, it is necessary that all of us, in particular youth, should be disabled-friendly at all levels and try to light a candle in the world of disability. If everyone has a deep feeling, we can see the almighty at the feet of the disabled and better future for the disability management.

Let me close my thoughts on the subject with the following words of Machiavelli :

I was hungry and you formed a committee to investigate my hunger,

I was homeless and you filed a report on my plight,

I was sick and you held a seminar on the situation of the underprivileged,

You have investigated all aspects of my plight

And yet I am still hungry, homeless and sick.

This is exactly what is happening in the world of disabled as well as rural India for which we have to devote our time and work for the cause of disabled.

12

Ecology: A Gandhian Perspective

Forty-four years after his assassination, Mahatma Gandhi remains an elusive figure, discomforting and difficult to comprehend. While acknowledged as one of the architects of the twentieth Century, his image has been reduced in books and films to a simplistic archetype of the emaciated figure in loincloth, spectacles and sandals confronting the might of the British Empire. But a careful analysis of his ideas and emotions reveals a man whose actions followed honourably from his convictions. Gandhi's spiritual experimentation reflected the moment rather than provided a historical blue print for the future of an India which has departed painfully from his aspirations.

The purpose of this article is to look at modernisation from the stand point of eternal varieties or as has been called by Alodous Huxly "The perennial philosophy" in which the Mahatma had faith and which he described as "Truth as old as the hills". I must confess that the chosen topic of the article has an element of disenchantment with the increasingly centralised social, political and economic system that has come to us along with the modernisation process that the world has undertaken. One does not have to look far in order to feel the consequences. Man had led by a combination of passion and reason. At various times one has dominated the other and influenced the process of modernisation which in turn effects the economic development and therefore Industrialisation. Industrialisation has led to increasing centralisation of economic activities and therefore, polity too cannot be looked at separately.

"Modernisation has led to rapid industrialisation of the nation, which in turn caused exploitation of natural resources thus posing a great threat to human survival". Today, environmental hazards pose a greater danger to our survival than even the nuclear holocaust. Even two decades back the Stockholm Conference (1972) had proclaimed that 'the protection of the environment is a major issue which effects the well-being of peoples and economic development throughout the world'. The growth of population and its growing urban ratio taking away good agricultural land, severe degradation of the Earth's soil, the destruction of tropical forests, dramatic rise in transport having extensive environmental impact, pressure of human numbers on agricultural land, non-availability of clean water and waste disposal system, growing under-nourishment and malnutrition in developing countries, less of productive capacity of soil, worsening drought, increasing magnitude of floods, and such man made hazards as the nuclear explosions damaging ozone layer etc. have indeed posed the worst threats to the existence of all the living beings. No technological advancement, however so brilliant, no socio-economic reform however profound will be able to save us from this catastrophe which we are facing not only in developed countries but also in developing countries" (Ramjee Singh: Gandhi and the environmental challenge).

The need to revalidate Mahatma Gandhi's thoughts in contemporary India is felt because so much that Gandhi strove to change in order to achieve real *Swaraj* has remained or indeed has developed in directions alien to Gandhi's thinking. Although he accepted that a Western style of democratic state was probably necessary in India, at least in the short-term; his ideal was the diffusion of power down to the local level so that village communities could organise their own affairs as far as possible. In modern India the State has increased massively in power since the days of imperial rule. The British Raj was a light-handed, amateur affair compared to the Indian state of the later twentieth century, with its greatly increased numbers of employees and functionaries, its bigger revenues, higher expenditure on the army and the police, its economic planning and control of the economy through directives and a pervasive system of licenses. It is also far more intrusive into personal life with its policies for development, education, welfare and family planning. Even the new structures of village-based local government bear no resemblance to Gandhi's ideals, but are the instruments of government control and often the arenas for local factional struggle and the exercise of power rather than service of the community. In any case the whole attempt at the 'Democratic Decentralization' can at best be called half-hearted.

Gandhi's economic ideals have similarly been shelved. Whereas he had envisaged a very small role for modern style industry and a dominant place in the economy for small scale, rural industry complementing agriculture, India has become one of the world's most highly industrialised nations, its range of products and its development of a consumer-oriented economy, a far cry from the austere economy of sufficiency advocated by Gandhi. Handicrafts are an aspect of tourism and interior decor, rather than a local supplying of basic needs of clothing, and domestic and agricultural equipment; these village-based industries that have developed have tended to eliminate jobs and line the pockets of those who have the capital to invest in plant and machinery, whereas he had advocated them as a means of alleviating rural unemployment and giving the poorest an additional source of income to ensure their dignity of life. India is still a land of villages and villagers—only about 20 per cent of Indians live in towns. Yet percentages belie numbers. Because the population has risen so steeply in the last half of the century, as a result of greatly improved health and nutrition, and a falling death rate, millions more Indians now actually experience what Gandhi felt were the degrading and de-Indianizing influences of urban life than over did in his day.

Contemporary and later observers criticised Gandhi's asceticism, his attitude to sexuality, his negation of the tensions within his own personality. There is considerable truth in this. His was not a personality at peace with itself. Often he was tormented with self-questioning, anger and frustration; yet it is only out of tension, stress and conflict that lasting solutions of fundamental problems are born. Further, against the harshness and self-distrust, against the demands he made on others and himself, must be set the evidence of humour and tenderness which did so much to attract men and women to him, the personal concern for the individual which made so many feel at his death a personal bereavement and the extinguishing of a guiding light. Gandhi's experiments with simple, communal living and with health or villagers which did not rely on expensive drugs, even led him to consideration of mankind's relations with the environment, human obligations towards animals, and use of air, water and soil. Unlike most politicians of his day, his breadth of concern again led him to ask fundamental questions about life. They make him sound distinctly modern as his ideals of simplicity and smallness of scale echo the fears of people in the later part of the century who have glimpsed some of the darker aspects and unsuspected repercussion of industrialisation, the driving force of the western civilization he so condemned.

Issues

With a view to making a holistic research in Gandhian thinking I have tried to bring out the Gandhian corpus in its totality with particular attention to Gandhian world-view and philosophy of life. This is of utmost importance so that each aspect and sphere of Gandhian thinking could be located within it and thus be seen in its proper perspective. The justification for such an attempt comes from three quarters, first, the developed capitalist world has reached a point of crisis precisely because its massive technological and economic growth has created a gap between this growth on the one hand and the organisational and value system on the other. Besides, the crisis of pollution of the environment has spotlighted the dangers of the destruction of the balance between man and his ecological system.

Secondly, in erstwhile communist countries the massive accumulation of political and economic power in the hands of the state-indeed in the hands of a small minority—has reduced vast populations to sub-human levels.

Thirdly, it is the gross poverty, absence of development, external threats to their independence, decline in domestic spirit and total frustration of 'third world' the so called 'under developed' countries which have contributed most to the revival of interest in Gandhi.

Modernisation and Ecology

Modernisation process has brought up many effects on our lives. Here I have tried to analyse modernisation keeping in view changes is our life style. Modernisation involves a variety of aspects, namely economic specialisation, political secularisation, urbanisation, opening of mobility particularly through widespread formal education, development of a highly differentiated political structure, differentiation of cultural and value systems and growth of a widespread communication network. But actually it is a complex process in which there is an interaction between social factor, on the one hand, and economic, political, cultural, technological and other factors, on the other. While Gandhi has not totally rejected the various values for which modernization stands, he saw danger in the blind pursuit of these values and in an over-zealous adoption of modernisation tendency.

The way I have tried to bring out Gandhi's concern and relevance finds reflection in the prestigious club of Rome, formed by discerning sociologists, social psychologists and a large group of economists, which predicts the following pattern for the collapse of civilization. As industrialisation grows, it voraciously consumes enormous amount of resources. Resources become scarcer, forcing more and more capital to be spent on procuring raw materials which leaves less and less money for investment in new plants and facilities. Population outstrips food and supplies. Industrial base begins to collapse carrying along with it the service and agricultural activities. '*The Ecologist*' magazine from Britain in an article endorsed by 33 most distinguished scientists also projects disaster and argues for quick action to end exponential growth. Unrestricted industrial and pollution expansion, it warns, must lead to the breakdown of society and the life support systems on this plant. The Gandhian way of life finds adequate relevance in any society of the world-western, socialist or underdeveloped. So modernisation must be linked with ecological problems. Ecological consciousness in development planning may be described as the exercise of caution in development planning to ensure, firstly, that the natural resources, including air, are protected for safe and adequate use by future generations and, secondly, that development projects do not jeopardize the lives of people working on them or living near them.

Modernisation involves rapid industrialisation in every sphere. This development activity in India has proceeded on a resource-intensive path rejecting the concept of "small is beautiful". It has seriously disrupted ecological stability of life support systems which has been maintained through centuries. Resource demands of the process have undermined the production potential of natural resources and have created severe ecological instability. It is in this context that ecological movements have emerged and are throwing up indicators to assess the impact of development process on natural resources, their uses and how the costs and benefits they carry are distributed among different societal groups.

Clearly, the need for such ecological consciousness exists under all socio-economic systems. The need, however, is the greatest in highly inegalitarian and oppressive systems because under such systems a relatively small number of individuals (or commercial organisations) acquire highly concentrated power to use natural resources to maximize their profits, irrespective of the havoc this pursuit may cause to a large number of people in this and the next generation. Such ruthless plunder of natural resources, apart from the destruction and pauperisation it causes immediately, will leave the country so exhausted of the base of prosperity that the welfare tasks of a people's government that may emerge at a future date would become extremely hard to achieve.

In fact it is clear that environmental consciousness in

modernisation process is extremely important in India today. Unfortunately, despite all the talk about environment that one hears, it cannot be said that consciousness exists in bureaucratic circles of the government, the experts, the press etc. What exists is merely the pretence of such consciousness, often surfacing in totally distorted views on environmental protection.

The Alternative

The relevance of Gandhian view has to be brought forth through his concept of decentralization which does not stand in isolation but is shaped by other concepts and ideas. Gandhi's *Hind Swaraj* or Indian Home Rule had raised lively debate, not only among the Westerners but also among the Indians. His *Hind Swaraj* is a warning against a mad race after the so-called civilization equated with modernization, materialism and a wrong model of development for rapid industrialisation. The solution lies in Gandhian model of development based on cottage Industries. In his model every village is self-sufficient interacting in a concentric circle pattern. Gandhi preached non-violence, stressed on the moral aspects of life and limiting human wants and fought for freedom and equality for the poor, opposed state control over individuals, pleaded for *Swaraj*, explained the concept of 'trusteeship' for the welfare of all, opposed big industries to save cottage and *Khadi*. All these concepts, directly or indirectly, flow from the theme of Decentralization. It is also necessary to establish a clear-cut linkage between various Gandhian concepts and the themes of Ecology and Decentralization to find the solution of crisis which we are facing today.

The various movements for better environment have at best relied on adhoc measures to check pollution and other ecological problems. There is a need for a comprehensive look at the relationship between man and nature. Gandhi's answer to this is to look inwards for an answer and not the way the present demands for preservation are being set. For Gandhi, it is important that individuals exercise self-rule (i.e., self-control) attainable through spiritual self-development. This is needed because the primary impetus to economic growth is the natural condition of man as the subject of needs.

Conclusion

One may conclude by saying that environmental challenges provide a turning point in the sphere of human vision of development and modernization, and have raised a basic question "whether we need development at the cost of ecological imbalances?" The simplistic explanation or suggestion is that we need sustainable development. In fact there is a need to shift from the mechanistic to the holistic concept of development, and mass production to home production. Simple living and high thinking can solve many more problems relating to environment than a fire fighter's attitude to preservation. Many ecological movements in America and Europe, notably the Green movement, are coming to realize that it is not possible to fight ecological problems in isolation with each other. The result has been the gathering of conservationists in a summit like the "RIO MEET". But again, while mankind is faced with the question whether resolutions like the "Agenda 21" are sufficient to ensure a clean earth for the coming generations, Gandhiji has provided many answers to today's questions in his suggestions about proper usage of air, water and soil. The need is to reflect on his ideas and exercise control of the 'self' in order to keep the Earth cleaner and ensure sustainable development.

13

Rural Development: The Gandhi Way

Introduction

The tragedy of modern India is that the important aspects of the Gandhian philosophy are not given serious attention. The ruling elite never realized that Gandhi was much ahead of his time. The quest of humanity for social justice and sustainability will remain a dream until and unless humanity realizes what Gandhi meant when he said, that economics is untrue which ignores and disregards moral values. Gandhi in his various speeches and in his articles written throughout the freedom struggle spoke highly of democratic decentralization and rural development. In the July 22, 1946 issue of *Harijan*, Gandhi stated that 'Independence must begin at the bottom'[1].

From the time he (Gandhi) arrived in India from South Africa in 1914 till his death on 30 January 1948, Gandhi had two objectives. One was the perfection of the technique of *Sarvodaya* in its individual, group and mass forms and to persuade the people of India and through them, the whole world, to accept it as the only method for resolving political, economic, social and religious conflicts. The other was the reconstruction of the Indian village on a self-governing, self-sufficient, egalitarian, self-contained and spiritually oriented basis as the foundation for the political, economic, cultural and spiritual growth of the country[2]. Gandhi held that by serving the villages, *swaraj* could be established. The country's prosperity and progress depends upon the villages. He maintained that if the village perishes, India will perish too. The importance of rural development should be obvious in a country where four out of every five citizens live in the countryside. India lives in villages, unless the socio-economic and political situation of rural India changed, India cannot progress.

Rural development as a concept has a long history and has gained popularity in recent years, particularly since the 1970s. It is an elastic concept and everyone interprets it in his own way. But, the broad consensus is that rural development implies all round development of rural areas. It implies a process of economic, political and social transformation of an agrarian rural society[3].

In the context of the developing countries, rural development is viewed as an attempt of improving the living conditions of the rural people. The development policies of the third world during 1950s and early 1960s, centered on growth maximization and the poor were expected to gain from the 'trickle down' of the benefits resulting from overall rapid growth[4]. However, despite an impressive economic growth in most of the developing countries during this period, problems of rural poverty and unemployment remain all pervasive, intense and intricate[5].

This called for a change in the concept and strategy of rural development. As a result, since early 1970s such terms as 'redistribution with growth', and 'growth with social justice' became very popular and the concept of people's participation in the process of development began to be emphasized. The change of emphasis made rural development more broad-based.[6]

Rural development has emerged as a distinctive field of policy and practice and of research, in the last decade and a half. As a strategy it is defined by its concern with equity objectives of various kinds especially the reduction of inequalities in income and provision of employment, access to public goods and services and alleviation of poverty. It is this distributional issue which has marked out 'Rural Development' as a district field, because an overwhelming majority of poor people in the developing countries of Asia and Africa live in rural areas[7].

In view of the enormity, nature, complexities and urgency of the rural development problems most of the developing nations initiated development programmes which led to the creation of a number of new institutions—political, economic, social and administrative. While creating these institutions, greater attention was paid to people's institutions. The reason behind this was that the programmes of development were to be carried out not only by the state bureaucracy, but also through active and effective people's participation. Besides, effective people's institutions have to be created to promote political development and social justice. Thus, local institution is a necessary, if not sufficient, condition for accelerated rural development[8].

The element of participation is central to rural development. It responds to the need to mobilize and use more effectively all the resources available or potentiality available in rural areas of labour, skills, saving, land, fisheries, forests, livestock and water. Even with substantially increased help from government, most of the resources required for broad based rural development will have to be found in rural areas[9]. Rural development is not merely the agricultural development but rural transformation as a whole, which includes development of all facets of human resources like social, economic, cultural, spiritual, etc. Therefore, rural development has to be viewed in its totality rather than it's being a fragmented approach[10].

Importance of Rural Development

Development of rural areas and rural people has been the central concern of development planning in India. Rural India which encompasses three-fourths of the country's population is characterized, by low-income levels, not even adequate to ensure a quality of life compatible with physical well-being[11]. Rural development, therefore, occupies an important place in the agenda for national development. It is, in fact, a strategy to improve the economic and social life of a specific group of people—the rural poor[12].

The politico-economic and socio-cultural structural

disabilities threaten the development of rural poor. This has aggravated the problem of poverty, which has manifested itself in various forms, i.e., unemployment, inequality, malnutrition, growth of slums and ignorance. The growing poverty, which undermines planned development is much more severe in rural than urban areas and has become the biggest bottleneck in national development.[13]

The importance of rural development was also felt by the World Bank. The World Bank has popularized the problem of rural poverty and the concept of rural development and encouraged its introduction into the official development plan documents of almost all developing countries which are members of the World Bank. Other international agencies like the Food and Agriculture Organization (FAO), the International Labour Office of the United Nations and other agencies, have also highlighted the need for rural development.[14]

Since rural development holds the key to nation building, it can transform rural society from traditional isolation to integration with a mainstream of national life. It will evolve a new society with a built-in value system by raising the social, economic and cultural values of rural people through basic infrastructural amenities.

Finally, due to lack of resources and little or no bargaining power, the owners of small, scattered and unorganized rural enterprises are exploited to the hilt vis-à-vis those to whom they sell their products and from whom they purchase raw materials, etc. These small rural entrepreneurs can be protected from exploitation and their financial conditions can be improved only through rural development in the form of price support, credit facilities, insurance, etc.

Conceptual Analysis of Rural Development

The concept of rural development was born in the context of agriculture and it remained, for a long time, co-terminus with agricultural development in India. For example, the Royal Commission on Agriculture (1928) gave the interpretation to rural development in the following words:

"We cannot too strongly state our conviction that the directorship of agriculture is one of the key posts in rural development and that agricultural advance must in a very great degree depend upon the suitability of the officer appointed."[15]

Another Committee after 50 years took a more or less similar view of rural development. In 1972, the Planning Commission's Task Force on Integrated Rural Development observed that:

"After careful consideration, we have belatedly decided to take what might be considered a rather restricted view of the expression rural development. We have chosen to equate it with agricultural development in the widest sense so as to embrace, besides crop husbandry, all the allied activities."[16]

Since the 1970s the concept of rural development has undergone a change and has become more comprehensive. The World Bank defines rural development as a strategy designed to improve the economic and social life of a specific group of people, that is the rural poor. It involves the extending of the benefits of development to the poorest among those who are living in the rural areas. This group includes small-scale farmers, tenants and landless. Rural development should include a mix of activities including projects to raise agricultural output, create new employment, improve, health and education, expand communication and improve housing[17]. Thus, the World Bank defines rural development in terms of an improvement of the economic and social life of the rural poor[18].

Besides the above concepts, various other concepts of rural development have been propounded by various authors. The former Union Finance Minister, Shri C. Subramanian, who put forward the thesis of rural development at the All India Science Congress, Waltair 1976, viewed it as a "systematic and scientific use of all our natural resources and as a part of this process enabling every person to engage himself in a productive and socially useful occupation and earn an income that would meet at least the basic needs"[19]. Uma Lele defines rural development as "improving living standards of the masses of the low income population residing in rural areas and making the process of rural development self-sustaining"[20].

Thus, rural development is, of late, viewed as a strategy to bring about improvement in the economic and social life of the rural poor. It implies both economic betterment of people as well as greater social transformation. It encompasses a spectrum of activities and human mobilization to make people stand on their own feet and break away from all structural disabilities which claim them to condition in which they may live in[21].

Rural Development: Gandhian Approach

To Gandhi salvation of India could come only through rural development. The soul of India lives in villages. Gandhi's approach to rural development, occupies a significant place. As against the localized village uplift movements of Tagore and Braynes, Gandhi attracted the attention of the entire country. His first experiment in rural reconstruction was at Champaran in 1916. People at Champaran lived in utter poverty and ignorance. The root cause of poverty according to Gandhi was the ignorance of the people. So, he started the mass education programme with the help of some devoted workers. Champaran was the first laboratory where Gandhi forged not only his political weapon but also his rural reconstruction programme. From 1918 onwards, Gandhi rose to new heights and became the uncrowned king of India. He launched the *Swadeshi* movement to save the decaying indigenous products. Gandhi was not an idle preacher. He was an example. He himself settled in a village called Segaon near Wardha in April 1936. There he taught to the people the spirit of self-help. The Gandhian programme of rural reconstruction included the following points:

Use of *khadi*, development of village industries, socio-economic equality, communal unit, removal of untouchability, prohibition, equal status for women and adoption of basic education.

Gandhi, 'the born democrat', wanted to build the structure of the pure democracy 'inch by inch' directly from below. He wanted to make each village "a complete republic, independent of its neighbours for its vital wants, and yet interdependent for many others in which dependence is necessity". He was convinced that "if all Indian villages could come up to the ideal, India would be free from most of its worries".

Today, everyone is talking in terms of rural development. Gandhiji did not approve of the Western civilization which is urban for the entire world. He said that "a big country with a teeming population with an ancient rural tradition which has hitherto answered its purpose, need not, must not copy the western model. What is good for one nation situated in one condition is not necessarily good enough for another differently situated". So he advocated a rural style of life and culture based on neighbourliness and sharing. His mission was to build a non-violent culture and civilization which could only be built on self-reliant and self-contained villages[22].

According to Gandhiji rural development is the natural development and rural development of better human relations, is different from city development which results in alienation of the individual from his surroundings, ultimately leading to frustration and destruction[23].

Gandhi therefore determined to work for small rural communities wherein people will cooperate with one another and give aid to those who lack the resources for growth and development. He spoke and wrote about village *swaraj*. He says, "The *swaraj* of my dreams is the poor man's *swaraj*. The necessaries of life should be enjoyed by you in common with those enjoyed by the princes and the moneyed men. But that does not mean that you should have palaces like theirs. They are not necessary for happiness. You or I would be lost in them. But you ought to get all the ordinary amenities of life that a rich man enjoys. I have not the slightest dought that *swaraj* is not *Poorn Swaraj* until these amenities are guaranteed to you under it"[24].

Gandhiji found the picture of his free India in its essentials embodied in a song that was sung at one of his evening prayers in Banghi Colony, New Delhi. What emerged was a picture of the India of his dreams. It was as follows:

> We are inhabitants of a country
> Where there is no sorrow and no suffering,
> Where there is no illusion nor anguish,
> no delusion nor desire,
> Where flows the Ganges of love?
> and the whole creation is full of joy,
> Where all minds flow in one direction,
> and where there is no occasion for sense of time,
> All there wants satisfied;
> Here all barter is just,
> Here all are cast in same mould,
> Here is no lack nor care,
> No selfishness in any shape or form,
> No high no low, no master no slave;
> All is light, yet no burning heat,
> That country is within you-
> It is *Swaraj, Swadeshi,*
> The home within you-
> Victory! Victory! Victory!
> He realizes it who longs for it[25].

Gandhiji concept of rural development emerge out from what he said in '*India of My Dreams.*' It follows:

'I shall strive for a Constitution, which will release India from all thraldom and patronage, and give her, if need be the right to sin. I shall work for an India, in which the poorest shall feel that it is their country in whose making they have an effective voice; an India in which there shall be no high class and low class of people, an India in which all communities shall live in perfect harmony. There can be no room in such an India for the curse of untouchability or the curse of the intoxicating drinks and drugs. Women will enjoy the same right as men. Since we shall be at peace with all the rest of the world, neither exploiting, nor being exploited, we should have the smallest army imaginable. All interests not in conflict with the interests of the dumb millions will be scrupulously respected, whether foreign or indigenous. Personally, I hate distinction between foreign and indigenous. This is the India of my dreams.... I shall be satisfied with nothing less.'[26]

Gandhi placed rural development at the core of India's future destiny—not rural development visualized microcosmically but in terms of the development of each of its numerous villages to full potential. Gandhi not only expected most of them to continue living in villages but wanted them to do so for to give legitimacy to people's participation[27].

Revival of the village is indeed the key to the regeneration of India and the fulfillment of the mission in the world, "I want villages to live", says the architect of modern India Pandit Jawahar Lal Nehru, "and I do not care what happens to the towns because I am convinced that if villages die, there can be no hope for towns. If villages prosper India is also bound to prosper"[28]. In fact, the road to the village is the road to the Heaven of India's soul, the road to the cradle of our civilization, the road to real *Yojna*. The village will be barometer of India's progress and prosperity. "Going back to villages", says Dr. Radhakrishnan, "is not to become primitive". It is the only way to keep us in the mode of existence that is instructive to India, that supplied him once with purpose, a faith and meaning. It is the only way to keep our species civilized"[29].

The Gandhian perspectives on rural development is based on the following values and premises:

1. Real Indian is found not in its cities, but in its villages.
2. The revival of villages is possible only when the villagers are no more exploited. Exploitation of villagers by city dwellers was 'violence', in Gandhi's opinion.
3. Simple living and high thinking, employing voluntary reduction of materialistic wants, and pursuit of moral and spiritual principles of life.
4. Dignity of labour, every one must earn his bread by

physical labour and one who labours must necessarily get his subsistence.

5. Preference to the use of indigenous (*swadeshi*) products, services and institutions.
6. Balance between the needs and the means—Gandhiji believed that non-violence and truth could not be sustained unless a balance between the needs and the means was maintained.[30]

R.K. Patil tried to summarize how village development was envisaged by Gandhi in the last phase of his life. The cities and towns today are exploiting the countryside. The interests of the town and country and of industry and agriculture are divergent and cannot be reconciled. The only efficient, least expensive and surest way of ensuing a decent standard to the people at large in the immediate present in the system of economy recommended by Gandhi. The salient features of this system may be summarized as follows:

(i) Intensive small scale, individual and diversified farming supported by a cooperative effort as opposed to mechanized, large-scale or collective farming;
(ii) Development of cottage industries as ancillary to agriculture;
(iii) A cattle-based economy with strict enforcement of the "law of return";
(iv) A proper balance animal, human and plant life; and
(v) Voluntary protection of both man and animal against the competition of machinery as the price of social insurance.

According to Gandhi village development should be carried on through means and resources of the village without government help. Gandhi also believed in the overall development of the village people including moral, material and social development keeping their natural requirements and circumstances in mind. Participation of the local people in the development process is necessary and unavoidable.

Summing Up

Rural development has become a buzzword in the era of liberalization, privatization and globalisation (LPG) can succeed only when we take care of rural people and their needs. In other words rural economy must be integrated with global economy and *vice-versa*. The Gandhian concept of rural development must be analysed in the light of LPG. In fact Gandhi was the first to focus attention on the development of a new approach to the rural development. No one can claim to have the last word or to set an absolutely perfect model there may have been drawbacks or defects in the scheme; but it is undeniable that it was Gandhi who made by far greatest contribution to the cause of rural development in India.

Rural development is not as simple as it looks on paper. Capabilities have to be built up, suitable structures have to be valued, and changes have to be brought about in the administrative, technical and political arena. Equally important is kindling the zeal and enthusiasm of the people. But the most important agents to make rural development a success are the political and administrative will to decentralize decision-making powers to the lower level on Gandhian line with a clear policy enunciation, full political support, and needed administrative infrastructure, it is expected that the goals of real *swaraj* will be achieved by fulfilling the dream of the father of the Nation. It is high time for both our policy makers and the people, to turn the torch within so that they may be inspired to adopt the Gandhian way, if not for any other consideration, but for its pragmatic strength to solve our present day maladies of rural India. There is need to reiterate Gandhian values, and instead of merely garlanding the portraits of Gandhiji, India must translate his ideals into real life and make Rural India free from hunger, poverty and exploitation.

NOTES

1. Mishra, Anil Dutta (2002), *Panchayati Raj: Gandhian Perspective*, Mittal Publications, New Delhi, p. 1.

2. Santhanam, K. (1974), Gandhi and Rural Construction, *Gandhi Marg*, Vol. 18, No. 3, July, p. 188.
3. Sau, Sachinandan (1998), "Approaches to Rural Development Problems: A Review with Special Reference to India" in *Rural Development Theories and Experiences* (eds. Sachinandan Sau), Allied Publishers, New Delhi, p. 10.
4. Dutta, Prabhat (1998), *Major Issues in the Development Debate Lessons in Empowerment from India*, Kanishka Publishers, p. 119.
5. Mishra, S.N. and Mishra, Sweta (2002), *Decentralized Governance*, Shipra, New Delhi, p. 1.
6. Datta, Prabhat, *Ibid.*
7. Sau, Sachinandan, *op. cit.*, p. 11.
8. Bajpai, Ashok (1997), *Panchayati Raj and Rural Development*, Sahitya Prakashan, Delhi, 1997, p. 5.
9. Mishra, S.N. and Sharma, Kushal (1983), *Problems and Prospects of Rural Development in India*, Uppal Publishing House, New Delhi, pp. 3-4.
10. Jha, L.K. (1998), "Planning for Rural Transformation in Eastern India: An Integrated Approach" in *Rural Development in India: Problems and Prospects* (ed. Ugra Mohan Jha), Anmol Publications, New Delhi, p. 105.
11. Dasgupta, K.R. (1997), Rural Development Programmes in India—Concepts and Strategies in *Kurukshetra*, Vol. XLV, No. 11, August, p. 29.
12. Mishra, S.N. and Mishra, Sweta, *op. cit.*, p. 63.
13. *Ibid.*
14. *Ibid.*, p. 64.
15. *Report of the Royal Commission on Agriculture in India* (1926), Government Central Press, Bombay, p. 631.
16. Government of India (1972), *Interim Report on Integrated Agricultural Development Projects in Canal Irrigated Areas by the Task Force on Integrated Rural Development*, Planning Commission, New Delhi, p. 4.
17. *World Bank* (1975), Rural Development and Sector Policy Paper, Washington D.C., pp. 28-29.
18. Maheshwari, S.R. (1985), *Rural Development in India*, Sage Publications, New Delhi, p. 18.
19. Dasgupta, K.R., *op. cit.*, p. 29.
20. *Ibid.*
21. Mishra, S.N. and Mishra, Sweta, *op. cit.*, p. 66.
22. Arunachalam, K. (1981), *Gandhian Approach to Rural Development*, Sarvodaya Ilakkiya Pannai, Madurai, Prefare.

23. *Ibid.*, pp. 16-17.
24. *Ibid.*, p. 17.
25. Gandhi, M.K. (1996), *Village Swaraj*, Navajivan Publishing House, Ahmedabad, p. 9.
26. Gandhi, M.K. (1962), *India of My Dreams*, Navajivan Publishing House, Ahmedabad, p. 6.
27. Ali, Ashraf and Mishra, S.N. (1996), *Public Administration: A New Paradigm*, Cadplan Publisher and Distributor, New Delhi, pp. 313-14.
28. Khanna, R.L. (1956), *Panchayati Raj in India*, The English Book Shop, Chandigarh, p. 15.
29. *Ibid.*
30. Singh, Kartar (1999), *Rural Development: Principles, Policies and Management*, Sage, New Delhi, pp. 85-86.

14

People's Participation and Sustainable Development

Introduction

Indian culture and civilization have been built up from ancient times on rural communities. The national life is sustained by the villages. It is wrong to ignore the interests of the villages or allow them to decay. Villages are the places where the spiritual knowledge comes easier to man and takes deeper roots.[1] The village is the heart of the town. Without it, the town becomes lifeless. This ancient culture rooted in the villages, spread over the years to the cities. Today the situation is reversed. Practices of the cities are spreading to the villages. Modern education and modern ways of living cannot serve to improve the quality of life. The sustainability as an indicator of well-being of the village determines the well-being of the nation. By providing the essential amenities for the people in the villages, promoting mutual cooperation as well as participation amongst them and developing fraternal feelings among them, the progress of the village has to be ensured. Entertain the sacred feeling that the nation's welfare is your welfare.[2]

Problems of Today

The following are the problems experienced in the world today:

- One-sixth of the human family goes hungry and malnourished.

- One billion people live on less than a dollar a day, most of them lack security to access to food, the most basic needs.
- About 800 million people are food insecure.
- One billion people do not have access to clean water.
- 1.7 billion have no access to sanitation.
- Those last two figures together result in 2 to 3 million eminently avoidable infant deaths a year.
- 185 million children under the age of six are seriously underweight.
- The gap between rich and poor continues to widen. The share of global income obtained by the world's poorest 20 per cent has dropped from 2.5 per cent in 1960 to 1.3 per cent in 1990.
- Hundreds of millions of poor farmers have difficulty in maintaining the fertility of the soils from which they eke out a meagre living.[3]

Identify the Need and Problems of Villagers

Youth should go to villages and identify the need and problems of villagers and serve them honestly and sincerely to satisfy their wants. If people purify their hearts, they begin to feel pain witnessing the problems of helpless people. This motivates them to undertake service activities that benefit the poor and needy. Such selfless, dedicated, dynamic and hard-working youths become role models for simple villagers. People engaged in *rural development and sustainable development* should be free from exploitation, jealousy, hatred and anger so that love sprouts in their hearts. Thus they become sensitive to the problems of rural people and respond to their demands with genuine concern.[4]

I

Participation: what it is and what it is not

Not everybody is agreed on what participation means. The fact is that participation has come to mean different things to different people. The real purpose of participation is to develop human capabilities for development decision-making and action. Participation means a kind of local autonomy in which people discover the possibilities of exercising choice and, thereby, becoming capable of managing their own development.[5]

Participation, as defined in a UNESCO document, is "collective sustained activity for the purpose of achieving some common objectives, especially a more equitable distribution of the benefits of development."[6] Although participation is defined in different ways, the dominant view is to regard it as a strategy to improve the development process.

A Philippine study identifies six modes of participation:

The *first mode* involved only the educated and moneyed people in the community without the participation of the 'grassroots' or the beneficiaries. The *second mode* is one in which the people or beneficiaries are asked to legitimize or ratify projects identified as formulated by the government. In the *third mode* of participation, the people are consulted about the project but they do not actually participate in the planning and management of project. In the *fourth mode,* the people are consulted from the very start and they actively participate in the planning and management of projects. In the *fifth mode,* the people or the beneficiaries are represented in the highest policy making body of the agency. Finally, in the *sixth mode,* the representatives of the people control the highest policy making body of the agency.[7]

Emrich clarifies the meaning of participation through his six axioms. The axioms of participation are:

First, participation must begin at they very lowest level. There must be real opportunities for participative decision-making for the poorest, and those decisions must relate to the aspirations of the poor more than to the wispy musings of those who will not identify with them. *Second,* participation must take place at all stages of the development process, from the earliest pre-planning exercises, to the development of plans, the design of implementing mechanisms, and the actual implementation. *Third,* it must be recognized that a solitary vote is not participation. If people do not participate as members of relatively powerful groups, which serve their interests, then they participate only for the benefit of their masters. *Fourth,* participation must have substance and usually political clubs and cooperatives do not have substance. 'Participative processes' must deal with the allocation and control of goods and services related to the production process. *Fifth,* participation must somehow deal with existing loyalties. If the result is merely to strengthen existing inter-class groupings it will just strengthen existing leadership. *Sixth,* it must be accepted that the development of effective participation will cause conflict in some form.[8]

Real People's Participation

Real people's participation can be explained by citing an example. A village panchayat desires to make a road or a tank contributes out of its balances some amount to an adhoc body to get the work done more cheaply than through normal channels. It is not the panchayat's contribution which constitute public participation, but it is the margin of sacrifice which the participants in the adhoc effort have suffered. That is entitled to be counted as public participation. The central theme of people's participation is voluntarism and it is something more than a tax in cash or kind.

Why Participation?

Even more than the people affected, it is the development planners who now favour participation. They want people to participate not only in sharing the fruits of development, but also in contributing to the process of development at every stage from planning to evaluation through implementation and monitoring. Experience suggests that development plans have a greater chance of success with the involvement of target groups. On the contrary, planners are quite certain in their minds that without the cooperation of the people there is every likelihood of projects not proceeding along their planned course. The reasons why planners seek participation are thus purely of a practical kind, and they have made no secret of their real intentions. In the context of a pioneering World Bank participatory programme (PIDER) in Mexico, Michael M. Cernea recently noted that 'Participation of beneficiaries was the only avenue to pursue—not for just political or ideological reasons, but primarily for more efficiency and for reasons of an economic and technical nature.[9]

Obstacles to Participation

The following are the obstacles encountered while eliciting people's participation:

1. *Structural*
   - Political environment
   - Centralised systems
2. *Administrative/Bureaucratic*
   - Centralised administration
   - External donor agencies
   - Inappropriate attitude and skills of project staff
   - Request transfer of personnel
3. *Social/Cultural*
   - Dependence on leaders (Informal and formal)
   - Lack of leadership and organizational skills
   - Survival needs—Immediate results
   - Rural people not homogeneous, economic and social units hence: the poor are marginalized as to
     — Caste — Class
     — Religion — Geographical differences

Further, Frances F. Korton, in her study on participation, has classified obstacles to participation into three broad categories:

(a) Obstacles within the agency

(b) Obstacles within the community
(c) Obstacles within the society[10]

Emerging Participatory Organisations

Organisations that seek involvement of the poor from rural areas in programmes designed to further their development have now sprung up in many Third World countries. Their forms range from cooperatives to water users' associations to women's organizations.

Broadly speaking, rural organizations are of two kinds. One kind is that which the government generally sets up to elicit participation of the people in its development programmes. Panchayati Raj Institutions in India fall in this category. Such governmental organizations are sometimes referred to as standard rural organizations.

The other kind of organization arises primarily from the initiative of the people themselves. Mutual aid societies, workers' associations, etc., are organizations that fall in this broad category. Such rural organizations are commonly referred to as non-governmental organizations (NGOs). In order to distinguish these organizations from standard rural organizations, they are often referred to as participatory rural organizations. Another common name for them is voluntary organizations. Table 14.1 lists organizations of both the standard and the participatory kind which commonly exist in rural areas of Third World countries.[11]

Table 14.1: Standard and Participatory Rural Organisations

Standard Organizations	*Participatory Organizations*
1. Cooperatives 2. Village development committees 3. Government sponsored farmers' organizations 4. Trade unions 5. Women's organizations	1. Special organizations of rural disadvantaged groups, such as tenants' associations and organizations of agricultural labourers and landless workers

(Contd.)

Table 14.1 (*Contd.*)

Standard Organizations	*Participatory Organizations*
6. Youth clubs 7. Political party branches 8. Development committees in new settlements 9. Other voluntary organizations represented by the government	2. Village-based ad hoc organizations formed for a specific and immediate local need 3. Village welfare associations 4. Village funeral societies 5. Kinship associations 6. Caste associations 7. Ethnic associations 8. Irrigation associations 9. Mutual aid work groups 10. Rotating credit associations 11. Religious associations

Source: Adapted from G. Shabbir Cheema (1983). The Role of Voluntary Organisations. *In* G. Shabbir Cheema and Dennis, A. Rondinelli (eds.). 1983. *Decentralisation and Development.* Beverly Hills: Sage, p. 210.

II

What is Development?

- Development is a daily concern according to United Nations.
- Development means growth with structural change.
- A process of socio-economic change for broadening the economic base.
- Development by definition disturbs the existing milieu of subsistence systems.
- Development introduces conflicts, inequality and instability.
- The great clash between ecology and economy had been discovered in the 1980s. This was the idea of "Sustainable Development."[12]

What is Sustainable Development?

The concept of sustainable development has been a central theme in development strategies since the late 1980's. Sustainability combines the improvement in living standards of the poor with a concern for the long-term viability of development programmes, the health of the environment and people's control over processes that affect them.

But the idea of sustainable development is not new. An early proponent of this idea was the Chinese scholar and renowned social activist, Dr. Y.C. James Yen. From his highly successful literacy campaigns in China in the 1920's grew *rural reconstruction*, a *sustainable development approach* that aims to release the power of poor rural people to change their own lives.[13]

According to the Philippine Rural Reconstruction Movement (PRRM), "Sustainable development means the institutionalization of a new development model that promotes ecological sustainability, social equity, community ownership and management of resources, gender equality, and equality among nations."

Further, the International Institute of Rural Reconstruction (IIRR) has defined sustainable development as "Development that needs of the present without compromising the ability of future generations to meet their own needs, and that which the people are able to effectively control and manage by themselves."

- Integration of words 'conservation and development' gave rise to the concept of *sustainable development*.
- A multi-dimensional concept and a human-centred philosophy.
- It integrates the environmental, economic and social dimensions
    - Assessment of carrying capacity of land (Environmental Dimension)
    - Compilation of economic aggregate in per capita terms (Economic Dimension)

- Definition of an overall human development index (Social Dimension)

- Sustainable development refers to capacity of a system to maintain its productivity at a stable rate without compromising integrity of the eco-system.[14]

Sustainable Development Paradigm

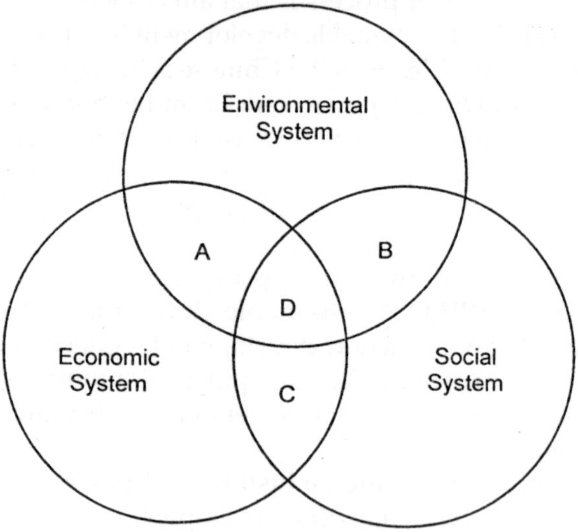

Fig. 14.1: The space represented by 'D' in the diagram constitutes the sustainable development core

- Sustainability is a dynamic phenomenon—inherent past, present and future.
- It has to be made compatible with development goals.
- Natural systems remain in equilibrium with their surrounding.
- Technological innovations could change very tapestry of nature.[15]

Six Advisors for Sustainable Development

Today in the villages under block development scheme, houses are constructed unto the roof stage and stalled there. To change this scenario, educated *youth should have as vow, the sustainable development of villages.*

Youths today who undertake the responsibility of rural development and sustainable development should have good health and commitment. They should also be assisted by six advisors viz., WHO, WHEN, WHAT, WHY, WHERE, and HOW, which will facilitate the successful implementation of various plans pertaining to rural development based on sustainability. One should ask the following questions: What should be done? Why it should be done? How it should be done? Where it should be done?[16] Above all, one should analyse whether it has sustainability?

Moral Values for Sustainability

Human development has no meaning without values. True education should promote morality, character and spirituality. Science and technology are undoubtedly necessary for comfortable living. But there is an unseen power, which underlies the physical world. Today students should acquire both physical knowledge for living and spiritual knowledge for understanding that *which sustains life*. The two together help to make humanness blossom. It is morality that imparts value to human life. Man has progressed in science and technology. But morality and integrity are going down from day-to-day.[17] The immediate task is to promote *moral values for development* in particular sustainable development as the years roll by.

Global Sustainable Development

Voicing concern over the fragile state of the world's environment, Secretary General Kofi Annan on 14 May, 2002 called for new ethic of global stewardship to promote sustainable development across the planet.

"Together, we can and must write a new and more hopeful chapter in natural and human history," the Secretary-General said in a speech entitles "Towards a Sustainable Future" which was delivered on his behalf by his wife, Nane Annan at the American Museum of Natural History in New York.

The Secretary General said countries have been slow to deliver on promises made at the UN's Earth Summit held in 1992 in Rio De Janeiro. Looking to the future he said this September's World Summit on Sustainable Development, set to convene in Johannesburg, offered "a chance to restore the momentum that had been felt so palpably after the Earth Summit." While lauding the fact that preparations for the Summit have brought renewed attention to environmental issues, he cautioned that there remained a "need for greater clarity on what Johannesburg is about and what it can achieve."

Offering his own perspective, Mr. Annan called for action in five areas where "concrete results are both essential and achievable: water, energy, agriculture, biodiversity and health." Specifically, he urged measures to widen access to clean drinking water, improve energy efficiency, fight land degradation, preserve the world's ecosystems, and tackle the environmental causes of disease.

"Progress (in those five areas) would offer all human beings a chance of achieving prosperity that will not only last their own lifetime, but can be enjoyed by their children and grand children too," he said.[18]

A Global Framework for Sustainability (See Fig. 14.2)

III

People-Centred Development

Planners are now beginning to perceive their task differently. 'Putting people first' in development projects has emerged as a major concern of planners in recent years. There is a growing awareness of the fact that people cannot be ignored any more if their development is what the plans aim to promote. On the goals of development, the consensus which is emerging favours

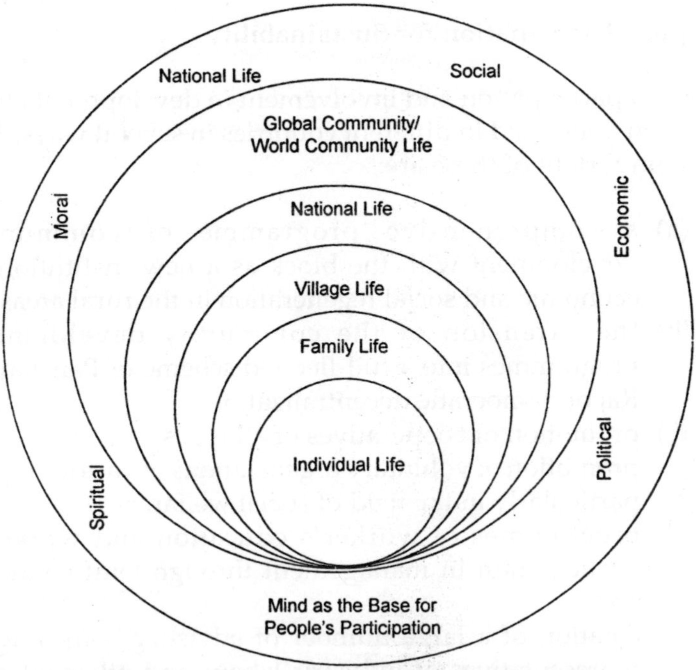

Fig. 14.2: Global Framework for Sustainability

Individual life is sustained by the mind.
Family life is sustained by the individuals.
Village life is sustained by the families.
National life is sustained by the villages.
World community life is sustained by nations.

Source: The Diagram is developed based on the readings of the book "*Grama Seva is Rama Seva*," (2000), Sri Sathya Sai Books and Publications Trust, Prasanthi Nilayam, Andhra Pradesh.

for the people a central place in the whole scheme of things. Statements such as the one which Cocoyoc participants adopted are readily evoking acceptance almost universally. 'The goal of development should be not to develop things, but to develop man' beautifully sums up what planners now think should be the real aim of development.[19]

People's Participation for Sustainability

People's participation and involvement in development effort has been attempted in different countries in several ways. The more important of these are:

(a) a comprehensive programme of community development with the block as a new institution of economic and social regeneration in the rural areas;
(b) the extension of the community development programmes into a full-fledged scheme of Panchayati Raj or democratic decentralization;
(c) promotion of cooperatives of all types;
(d) promotion of voluntary organizations of various types, particularly in the field of social welfare;
(e) programmes of worker's education and worker's participation in management through joint councils; and,
(f) creation of a large number of advisory bodies, with representatives of industry, labour and other interest groups, for advising and helping the government both in the formulation of policies and programmes and in implementing them.[20]

According to Vinoba, *Loka-sakthi*-civil power means the non-violent and self-reliant power of the people. It is a power which is opposed to *Himsa-sakthi* or *the military power* and different from *Danda-Sakthi or the legal power* of the state. The difference between civil power and state power is illustrated by Vinoba thus: "A zero in combination with unity yields ten. The zero has its great utility but without unity it is of no use. So unity represents the self-reliant power of the people, while zero represents the power of a government circular. The students of mathematics know that vast researches are conducted to investigate the qualities of the zero. Yet, it cannot be gainsaid that it has no independent strength of its own. Likewise, the state power can be effective only if it is based on the people's initiative or *Loka-Sakthi*.[21] However, the enormous task of social and economic revolution can be carried forward successfully only with the involvement and participation of the people said the late Prime Minister of India Shri Lal Bahadur Shastri."

Popular participation in the development process first appeared in more developed societies. Its emergence coincided with the growth in education, the rise of democratic institutions, and the spread of communications. The opening sentence of an important study focused on political dimensions of the participation process in developing countries reads: "Broadening *political participation* is a hallmark of political modernization." Traditional society, wrote Daniel Lerner half a century ago, is *non-participant*...modern society is *participant*.

There is a growing consensus that people everywhere have a basic human right to take part in decisions that affect their lives. Consequently, participation in third world countries is being promoted by the United Nations agencies and the governments themselves. China, Tanzania and Guyana are among the developing countries where participation has proceeded quite far. This experience suggests and encourages the hope—that participation is possible even in societies that are not yet part of the developed world. Following the success of these efforts, participation in some form or the other is being included as an important element in development strategies of most third world countries.[22]

Involvement of People for Sustainability

Sustainability cannot be achieved through a mere approach of concepts. It can be accomplished only if people were also involved in the programmes being implemented, the Governor, P.S. Ramamohan Rao, said. The real problem in most organizations was ensuring sustainability.

Mr. Rao said one should not be dogmatic to approaches to rural development. A combination of approaches was necessary. He said even in economic development any particular approach could not be standardized and claimed to be the best. In modern management, more than standard packages, standard practices were thought of.[23]

Sustainable Development Depends on Unity

Humanity is one. If you strive to serve the country unitedly, the nation will make enviable progress. If all the one hundred crores of people in the country act as one, India will stand forth as an ideal nation.[24]

Unity is essential for achieving anything, as has been declared in the 'vedic' saying: Let us live together, strive together, impart to others what we have learnt and lead a life of harmony and unity. There must be unity and harmony among the villagers in the reconstruction of their social life.[25]

People's Participation and Prevention of Clashes

It is argued that development introduces conflicts, inequality and instability. The great *clash between ecology and economy* had been discovered in the 1980s. This was the idea of 'Sustainable Development'.[26] However, we need to involve people so as to prevent clashes and conflicts in the areas affecting sustainable development. Also we may take efforts to inspire youths for sustainable development.

Participation in Sustainable and Eco-friendly Tourism

Through its impressive record of devoted leadership and outstanding voluntarism, Pacific Asia Travel Association (PATA), in the last half century, has also accomplished more than any other travel organization in educating the tourists, as well as in improving the tourist destinations—environmentally, socially and culturally. As we all know, the United Nations has declared the year 2002 as the International Year of Eco-Tourism and Mountains. Prime Minister Shri Atal Bihari Vajpayee applauded PATA for this concern for *sustainable and eco-friendly tourism*, which has to be at the very core of all our activities in promoting tourism. This responsibility can be handled only by creating a well-regulated, and often self-regulated, *partnership* between the Government, private sector players in the infrastructure and hospitality business, mass media, voluntary organizations, and, last but not the least, tourists themselves.

India is now all geared up to reach its true potential in tourism. We fully recognize that the Asia Pacific region is extremely important for us if this potential is to be fully tapped. We offer both the ancient and the modern. We are investing large sums for expanding and modernizing our infrastructure in airports and airlines, railways, national highways, hotels and transport, development of tourism circuits, preservation and maintenance of monuments, human resource development information technology and all things related to tourism.[27] In order to promote sustainable and eco-friendly tourism, we need people's participation at all levels.

People's Participation and Sustainable Development

The impact of people's participation and sustainability is expressed in a 1985 document from the World Bank's Operation Evaluation Department (OED), *Sustainability of Bank Projects: First Review of Experience*. The report was based on impact evaluations of 25 projects five to 10 years after project completion. The conclusion: 12 of the 25 which had achieved long-term sustainability exhibited beneficiary participation. Said the OED report: "A major contribution to sustainability came from the development grassroots organizations, whereby project beneficiaries gradually assumed increasing responsibility for project activities during implementation and particularly following completion.... Where grassroots organizations thrived there were certain distinct qualities inherent in their growth and in their relationship to project activities. These included some form of decision-autonomy and self-reliance, a measure of beneficiary control over management of continuing alignment of the project activities with the needs of beneficiaries."

Interpreting Participation

The meaning of participation has evolved over the years. Since the 1970s an enormous amount of literature have come out which helped broaden our understanding of the concept of participation and at the same time have challenged all efforts to package it neatly within a single statement. Among the interpretations are:

Participation as Contribution: Participation is the voluntary contribution by people in one of the public programmes—but people are not expected to shape the programme or critic its content (1973—Economic Commission for Latin America). Contribution is also called people's counterpart to pre-determined programmes/projects.

Participation as Involvement: Cohen and Uphoff (1977) described four kinds of participation as distinct from one another. These are:

(a) participation in *decision-making*, in identifying problems, formulating alternatives, planning activities, allocating resources;
(b) participation in *implementation* in carrying out activities, managing and operating programmes, partaking of services;
(c) participation in economic, social, political, cultural, or other *benefits* individually or collectively; and
(d) participation in the *evaluation* of the activity and its outcomes.

A major contribution of Cohen and Uphoff is the development of a framework for describing and analyzing participation in rural development.

Participation as Organization: Participation is concerned with organized efforts to increase control over resources and regulative institutions in given social situations on the part of those excluded from such control (1979—Stifel).

Participation as Empowerment: Community participation is an active process whereby beneficiaries set the direction and the execution of a development project with a view of enhancing well-being in terms of income, personal growth, self-reliance or other values they cherish (Paul, 1987).

Another useful contribution by Paul (1987) is his conceptualization of different objectives of people participation to ensure sustainability: (a) empowerment; (b) building beneficiary capacity; (c) increasing project effectiveness; (d) improving project efficiency; and (e) project cost sharing.[28]

A Model Village for Participation and Sustainable Development

Development is a process. Development to be stable and sustainable requires multi-dimensional strategy. Several strategies and approaches have been designed and tested in development practice. During the visit of the author to Cuddalore District, he came across a village Koonankuruchi, where a member of the Village Water Sanitation Committee (VWSC) claims that his own village is a model village for Tamil Nadu. He says, "Ours is a resettlement story. Our roots were elsewhere. We were rather replanted here. This place was bare of facilities when we first set our feet in, with our bags and baggage on. Now, we can proudly say that almost every house has latrine facility, there is no problem of safe water for drinking, the road has also become jeepable/motorable. We feel dignified to think that we have made it—a model village for Tamil Nadu."[29] It is obvious that people's participation is very encouraging in the village.

Koonankurichi is located close to Neyveli Lignite Corporation mines. It was originally an agriculture-based village. In 1975, when the agriculture land was taken over by the Neyveli Lignites, the village was turned out to be an industrial labour oriented village. About 80 per cent workers are seasonal industrial daily wage labourers.

Today, it stands out as a model village panchayat for village based Management System. Mr. S. Thangasamy, I.A.S., the Collector Cuddalore district and Dr. Lennart Nilsson, Chief Project Adviser declared Koonankurichi as a model for village based Management System on February 16, 2002 in the presence of Dr. Govindasamy, MLA.

Result of Community Participation

Before the Project Intervention	*After the Project Intervention*
Water Supply	
The problem of inadequate and unequal water services persisted till 1999. Sometimes, women had to walk 1-2 km.	All households get adequate and safe water supply close to their houses.
Two water sources and 2 pump sets went defunct beyond servicing. One of the 2 Over Head Tanks, was not working. There were 18 stand-posts without proper tap and platforms.	One OHT, pump room and D' system were rejuvenated. One new bore well (120 m) and one 10 hp pump set were installed. The number of stand-posts were increased to 55 with proper platform. All are in good working conditions and are well maintained for the past two years.
Pit taps and illegal connections caused many problems. Neyveli Lignites delivered water to the existing OHT which was inadequate.	
Lack of funds in the panchayat.	
Sanitation	
School did not have latrine facility.	School got 2 units of latrines and are well used.
All water collection points were slushy. No road facilities. Waste water stagnation, garbage were lying on the streets. Bushes around the villages and streets were used for open defecation, which made the village ugly and unhealthy.	The demand for household latrines increased. Nearly 60 per cent of the households are covered and many more latrines are under construction. The notable aspect is that 99 per cent of the latrines are in use and well maintained. A group of 2-3 families share one latrine. At present, about 111 families share 50 latrines. Village cleanliness is well maintained by the community.

Village Based Management System

To sustain the established facilities without financial and technical constraints, the Project established VMS in 2001. To strengthen the capacity of Panchayati Raj Institutions, the Village Water and Sanitation Committee (VWSC) formed Water User Groups (WUG), Environmental Protection Group (EPG) and Quality Assurance Group (QAG) in a participatory approach. The members took oath and sworn in the Committee/Groups during a Gram Sabha meeting held on 11th February 2002 after the new Panchayat Raj election.[30] However, we should appreciate the efforts of DANIDA, in particular for having taken efforts to guide and create Koonankurichi village as a model village for Tamil Nadu.

Conclusion

It may be emphatically said that the people themselves must have some voice in making the final choices that will most directly impact on their lives and planning systems must be designed to be responsive to their voice, not only because their involvement is essential to gaining their commitment, but also because they have relevant information which otherwise may be unavailable to the planner. However, the idea of people's involvement in development is by no means new. Further, it may be summarized in the following credo of the Rural Reconstruction Movement for Sustainable Development:

> Go to the people
> Live among the people
> Learn from the people
> Plan with the people
> Work with the people

In particular, "Work with Youth" for Sustainable Development.

NOTES

1. Sanatana, Sarathi S.S., 26.05.1985, p. 7.
2. *Ibid.*, p. 138.
3. N. Mohanan (2002). Sustainable Development—Concepts and Indicators, NIRD, Hyderabad, Unpublished Paper, p. 1.
4. Sri Satya Sai Siscourses (2002). *Gram Seva is Rama Seva*, Sai Publications, Prasanthi Nilayam, Andhra Pradesh, p. 4.
5. Hari Mohan Mathur (1986). *Administering Development in the Third World*, Sage Publications, New Delhi, p. 19.
6. UNESCO (1979). *Meeting of Experts on the Institutional Problems of Participation in the Strategies of Integrated Rural Development*, Lima, Peru 4-8 Sept., p. 15.
7. Mary, R. Hollnsteiner (1976). People Power: Community Participation, *Philippines Studies*, Vol. 24, p. 8.
8. Keith, R. Emrich, Participation: Cure or White wash? In Inayatulleh (ed.). (1979). *Approaches to Rural Development: Some Asian Experiences*, Kuala Lumpur, p. 360.
9. Hari Mohan Mathur (1986) *op. cit.*, p. 15.
10. *Ibid.*, p. 31.
11. *Ibid.*, p. 23.
12. N. Mohanan (2002). *op. cit.*, p. 1.
13. International Institute of Rural Reconstruction (IIRR), (1998) Vision of Sustainable Development Since 1920's, Course on Rural Development Management, April 20-May 15, *Study Materials*, p. 17.
14. N. Mohanan (2002). *op. cit.*, p. 4.
15. *Ibid.*, p. 5.
16. *Ibid.*, p. 27.
17. *Satya Sai Speaks*, dated 23.11.1991.
18. *UN Newsletter*, May (2002). Vol. 57, No. 20. p. 4.
19. Hari Mohan Mathur (1986). *op. cit.*, p. 14.
20. S.K. Chatterjee (1981). *Development Administration in India*, Surjeet Publications, Delhi, p. 308.
21. Vinoba (1957). *From Bhoodan to Gramdan*, Sarvodaya Prachuralaya, Tanjore, pp. 20-28.
22. Hari Mohan Mathur (1986). *op. cit.*, pp. 1-2.
23. *The Hindu*, Madurai, 23.9.2002, p. 5.
24. *Satya Sai Speaks*, dated 2.2.1985.

25. Sanatana, Sarathi, 20.05.1995, p. 4.
26. N. Mohanan, (2002). *op. cit.*, p. 1.
27. *Text of the Prime Minister, Shri Atal Bihari Vajpayee's Speech While Inaugurating the 51st Pacific Asia Travel Association (PATA) Annual Conference* in New Delhi on April 15, 2002.
28. *IIRR*, 1998, *op. cit.*, p. 37.
29. Visit to Cuddalore on 26.7.2002.
30. DANIDA Document code: WS/DTFC/BR/E/07, March 2002.

15

Voluntary Organizations and Reconstruction of India

Introduction

Voluntary organization has been a long tradition in India and occupies a pride of place, especially in the field of welfare and social services to people of different strata. The role of voluntary organizations is well-recognised and the policy-makers and administrators also recognize its contribution. The responsibility of society towards individuals in distress and the groups in need was shared equally by the community and the rulers. Devotion and service towards one's fellow-men, love for charity and brotherhood existed even in the feudal times. According to *Bhagvad Gita*[1], charity is valid, if it takes into account, *Desh* (place), *Kal* (time) and *Patra* (recipient). The forms of charity were *Artha* (money), *Vidya* (education) and *Abhaya* (courage)[2]. Kautalaya has mentioned in his *Arthashastra* that the responsibility for the care of the poor, the aged, infirm, destitute, etc. was that of the ruler. The stories preserved in Jatakas provide some reference to the ideals of social work[3].

The great boost and inspiration for voluntarism in Modern India must be traced to the advent and impact of Gandhi in our national life. While leading a mass movement for political freedom, he drew on the religious value system and insisted that political liberation must go hand in hand with a sense of social responsibility. Gandhi was never tired of reminding the people that the heart of India lies in the poor masses, for whom he created a countrywide network of voluntary organizations devoted to the cause of the downtrodden and raised a widely spread corps of social workers working for them.

The post-Independence era has witnessed a phenomenal increase in the number of voluntary organizations. About 11,000 voluntary organizations[4] working in different parts of the country are presently registered with the Home Ministry. The planners recognized their role in the First Five Year Plan document itself in the field of social welfare. The Third Plan characterized the voluntary action as an aspect of public cooperation. The Sixth Plan noted the voluntary agencies with a rise in grant-in-aid. Planning Commission raised in the Approach paper for the Seventh Plan a crucial issue of an alternative monitoring machinery to lend a hand to the development bureaucracy for meeting the problem at hand to reach aid with faster pace to the poor, and thus hit the 20-point programme target designed for the weaker sections[5]. The commission itself identified voluntary agencies as the alternative mechanism for the purpose because voluntary organizations are supposed to be potentially superior to official agencies in three respects:

1. their workers can be more sincerely devoted to the task of reducing the sufferings of the poor than government staff;
2. they can have a better rapport with the rural poor than government employees; and
3. since they are not bound by ridig bureaucratic rules and procedures, they can operate with greater flexibility, they can readjust their activities quickly and continuously as they learn from experience[6]. In an other way we can say that voluntary agencies' efforts are more economical than the government departments and they can motivate more public participation in development efforts than the government departments.

Meaning and Typology

The term 'voluntarism' is derived from Latin word 'voluntas' which means 'will'. The will assumes various forms of impulses, passions, appetites or desires, it is prior to or superior to the intellect or reason. All theories of voluntarism, whether psychological, ethical, theological or metaphysical which interpret various aspects of experience and nature in the light of the concept of the will, subscribe to the thesis[7].

It is very difficult to define voluntary organizations. Caste and communal organizations, educational and philanthropic associations, missionary and religious organizations—all these known forms are present in all parts of India and their activities over a wide range. Even then the social scientist have tried their best to define the voluntary organization. A voluntary organization properly speaking is an organization which, whether its worker are paid or unpaid, is initiated and governed by its own numbers without external control[8]. David L. Sills[9], a sociologist, identified it as a group of persons, organized on the basis of voluntary membership without state control, for the furtherance of some common interest of its members.

There are so many types of voluntary organizations working for the people. These voluntary organizations have been classified on a variety of basis:

(i) their size,
(ii) their internal political structure,
(iii) their independence or dependence on outside control,
(iv) their societal functions,
(v) source of their support,
(vi) their location,
(vii) the class and characteristics of their members,
(viii) intimacy of contact among members,
(ix) bases of the incentives—material, soldiery or purposive, and
(x) beneficiary of the association's activities—prime beneficiary may be the membership, the client, the public or the owners[10].

On the other hand some writers have employed either structure or function as basis of classification. For instance,

Sherwood Fix[11] based his classification after examining five thousand associations upon the distinction between major[12], minoral[13] and medial[14] organisations.

Prof. N.R. Inamdar[15] has outlined a typology of voluntary organizations in simple terms, applicable to Indian conditions, as follows:

1. (a) Allied with the state; and
   (b) Purely voluntary;
2. (a) Idealistic Organizations;
   (b) Economically-Oriented; and
   (c) Clienteless, own;
3. (a) Urban; and
   (b) Rural;
4. (a) Women's; and
   (b) Non-female;
5. Function-wise:
   (a) Economic;
   (b) Social;
   (c) Cultural;
   (d) Educational;
   (e) Health and Medical; and
   (f) Miscellaneous;
6. (a) Local;
   (b) Regional; and
   (c) Federal; and
7. (a) Single-function; and
   (b) Multi-functional.

Gandhian Perspective

Gandhi in his political career showed a deep understanding of Indian social problems concerning all aspects of life, such as social, political, economic, cultural and spiritual. He combined constructive work and social reforms with his political programmes. His main emphasis was for the development of the poor masses through government effort as well as voluntary effort. His concept of *Swadeshi*, Sarvodaya, and Trusteeship was based on voluntarism. In fact, political activities and social work were two sides of the same shield. He took up the cause of the Harijans and women. Whenever he could not achieve social or economic betterment for certain sections at the hands of the British Government, he resorted to *Satyagraha*. He throughout his life campaigned for constructive work for the down-trodden people. He laid a foundation of the voluntary organization like Harijan Sewak Sang and Sewagram (Wardha) as part of his constructive programme. Thus, he combined in his work social reform economic betterment and political upliftment.

During the freedom struggle, a large band of dedicated workers inspired and influenced by Gandhi took to constructive work and made it their life's mission and spread it throughout the country. He founded several organizations to consolidate and carry forward various programmes. For example, he founded Harijan Sevak Sangh, Gramodyog Sangh and Hindustan Talim Sang. These organizations have still retained their existence and have continued to work to build India of Gandhi's dream.

National reconstruction on the basis of Gandhian concept of voluntarism have secured a fresh base in the recent times. Gandhi based a voluntarism on the philosophy of spiritualism, of the soul-force or love force. In brief Gandhi through voluntary organization favoured building of a society which offered equal opportunities to all individuals for educational economic and social development. In fact the basic aim of Gandhian voluntary organization is to provide a model of society based on value of non-violence, justice and freedom.

Role of Voluntary Organization

Voluntary organizations are playing a significant role in development of the poor, oppress and rural people, for centuries in India. Of course, their role has changed from time-to-time, depending on the need of the people and society. For instance, in pre-independent India, voluntary organizations had set up educational institutions, Ashram Shalas, and build hospitals to meet the needs of remote rural people. They had also built a network of institutions catering to the needs of the society and its disadvantaged groups. Apart from that, they mobilized resources for creating common facilities for all types of people. On the other hand the Gandhian workers had spread through the length and breadth of the country to organize what was called 'constructive work' for all-round development of the people. But this role has substantially changed, in the post-independent India, with government directly assuming lot of responsibility of initiating, organizing and managing welfare and development programmes.

One can realize the importance of voluntary organization in each and every field with increase of their number. In fact, there has been enormous increase in the number of voluntary organizations all over the country since Independence. They have registered five-fold increase from 1,739 in 1953 to 8,052 in 1980 and at present it is estimated that there are more than 11,000 voluntary organizations engaged in various welfare and developmental works[16].

Historically speaking, voluntary organizations have proliferated and have actively taken part in various fields of social action. The existence of a number of organizations were exclusively for promotion of social, educational, literary and cultural advancement. Role of voluntary organizations in our country can be broadly classified into the following categories: charity, welfare, relief, rehabilitation, services, development of socio-economic environment around human beings and development of human beings[17]. These roles cover women, children, handicapped, the aged, the youth, scheduled castes and scheduled tribes, and other backward classes, landless and small farmers, artisans, etc.

. Voluntary organizations can play following role for reconstruction of modern India:

1. Voluntary organizations can play a useful role in planning, implementation and evaluation of various development plans which has been endorsed by the government. The voluntary organization could be used to plan the programme on the basis of real local needs

and resources at the local level and entrusted with execution of programmes.

2. Voluntary organizations can supplement government efforts in each and every field.
3. Voluntary organization can play a role of eye opener of the people as well as an agency to act as a reliable feedback so that government policies and programmes could be designed taking real problems of the people into account.
4. Voluntary organization can set up an example for the other organization for the benefit of the people.
5. Voluntary organization must take up the task to activise the people and the system and make it responsible.
6. Voluntary organization must act as an agent of providing the information to the people about the governmental programmes.
7. Voluntary organization must illustrate how local resources would be used for their own development.
8. Voluntary organization must train a cadre of dedicated workers, who can meet the challenges coming out in the modernization process.
9. Voluntary organization must take a task of spreading of secular values and communal harmony among the people.
10. Voluntary organization must act as a catalysts in the transformation of the society to meet the new challenge.

Conclusion

Regarding the performance of voluntary organizations we have two diametrically opposed views. On the one hand, Mohit Sen[18] views, "It is wrong and even harmful to rely on voluntary agencies even partially for the implementation of plan projects, especially directed at poor millions". Prof. K.N. Kabra[19] has the same opinion. He opines, "like so many false alternatives being propagated to so many genuine issues, the officially recognized, financed and co-opted voluntary agencies will provide another anarchanism and false alternative". On the other hand, we have a long list of politicians, activist, academics and social workers who have lauded their role for development of the weaker section particularly and society as a whole. Planning Commission members, C.H. Hanumantha Rao[20], and Raj Krishna[21] and social workers, like Mahasveta Devi[22], and many others have made a full some praise in favour of voluntary organization. No doubt, there are good and bad voluntary agencies.

One may conclude by saying that voluntary organizations are doing commendable work in the reconstruction of Modern India. If the ultimate goal is self-reliance of communities and every section of the society, there is a significant role that voluntary organization can play and usher India into the twenty-first century free from casteism, untouchability, communalism and other social problems.

NOTES

1. D. Paul Chaudhary, *Voluntary Social Welfare in India*, New Delhi, Sterling, 1971, p. 9.
2. *Ibid.*
3. *Ibid.*, pp. 9-10.
4. Shriram Maheswari, "Voluntary Action in Rural Development in India", *IJPA*, Vol. XXXIII, No. 3, July-September, 1987, p. 566.
5. M.A. Muttalib, "Voluntarism and Development—Theoretical Perspectives", *IJPA*, Vol. XXXIII, No. 3, July-September 1987, p. 413.
6. Raj Krishna, "It would just be a Futile Exercise", *Yojana*, Vol. 28, Nos. 20 and 21, November 1984, p. 7.
7. Richard Taylor, *The Encyclopaedia of Philosophy*, Vol. 8, p. 270.
8. D. Paul Chaudhary, *op. cit.*, p. 36.
9. David, L. Sills (ed.), *International Encyclopaedia of Social Science*, Vol. 16, pp. 362-63.
10. Constance Smith and Ann Freedman, *Voluntary Associations: Perspective on the Literature*, Cambridge, Harvard University Press, 1972, p. 2.
11. David, L. Sills, *op. cit.*, p. 336.
12. *Majoral associations* are those which serve the interest of the majority institutions of society, such as business, professional, scientific and agricultural associations.

13. *Minoral associations* serve the interest of significant minority in the population, such as women's club, church organizations, hobby clubs and above all, ethnics.
14. *Medial associations* mediate between major segments or institutions in the society. For example, a parent-teacher association mediates between the family and the school system.
15. N.R. Inamdar, Ole of Voluntarism in Development, *IJPA*, Vol. XXXIII, No. 3, July-September 1987, pp. 428-29.
16. N.V. Lalitha and Madhu Kohli, *Status of Voluntary Effort in Social Welfare*, New Delhi, NIPCCD, 1982, pp. 18-19.
17. J.B. Singh, "Testing Voluntary Agencies—Let's First Understand Them", *Yojana*, Vol. 28, Nos. 20 and 21, Nov. 1984, pp. 45-47.
18. Mohit Sen, "No, No Nothing Doing with them", *Yojana*, Vol. 28, Nos. 20 and 21, November 1984, pp. 45-47.
19. Mohit Sen, "No, No Nothing Doing with them", *Yojana*, Vol. 28, Nos. 20 and 21, November 1984, p. 23.
20. C.H. Hanumantha Rao, "Ás the Planning Commission Views the Concept", *Yojana*, Vol. 28, Nos. 20 and 21, November 1984, pp. 5-6.
21. Raj Krishna, *op. cit.*, pp. 7-8.
22. Mahasveta Devi, "You Just Can't Do without Them", *Yojana*, Vol. 28, Nos. 20 and 21, November 1984, pp. 52-54.

16

Gandhian Concepts of Social Work and its Application

Introduction

The concept and practice of social work is as old as the human race itself whereas Gandhian concepts of social work are the creation of 20th century. Community living is the pattern. Naturally to help the needy, sick and the unfortunate has been the responsibility of the society. Some had an aptitude to take up such work. Buddha and Jesus emphasised the necessity of taking care of the sick and destitutes. Mahatma Gandhi equally emphasised the welfare of all through Sarvodaya being the rise of all or awakening of all. Religious institutions developed social work as part of religion. The idea grew that service rendered to the community is service rendered to God.[1]

Gandhian Movement is becoming stronger in the world today. We cannot conceive of the modern world without Gandhi and his thought. To say that, "All his ideas are right but he is two hundred years ahead of his time" is to denigrate both Gandhi and his Sarvodaya. In fact, Gandhi is more relevant today than ever before. We have to choose between Atom and *Ahimsa*, Non-violence and Non-existence, Sarvodaya and Sarvanasa (total annihilation). More than ever before, that too at a time when humanity is involved in a serious reappraisal in view of the new challenges, there is a growing awareness all over the world that Gandhi's work, teachings and his thought have greater relevance. This is what Dr. Nelson Mandela said: "Gandhi holds the key to human progress."[2] It would be no exaggeration to say that constructive programme is the key to the construction of *Poorna Swaraj* or complete Independence by truthful and honest means and it has greater relevance today. One of the best ways to express our gratitude to the Father of our Nation is to carry out constructive programme in our day-to-day life and to remember as often as possible the relevance of his thought in our life today. The constructive programme is almost half a century old and therefore, in my view the relevance of Gandhian Thought is as old as the constructive programme.

Nelson Mandela's prophetic words that the twenty first century belongs to Gandhi appear to be more than a mere ripple among today's intelligentsia. Gandhi gave to the world new and revolutionary concepts such as *Satyagraha* i.e. truth force, Sarvodaya i.e. Welfare of all and *Shanti Sena* i.e. peace brigade. Besides, there are some key concepts of Mahatma Gandhi. They are, namely Truth, Non-violence (*Ahimsa*), Ends and Means, Non-possession, Trusteeship, Vows and Life Style, Constructive Work, Basic Education, *Swadeshi* and *Gram Swaraj*. All these concepts are bound to gain greater relevance and currency as years roll by.[3] Gandhi borrowed the word "Sarvodaya" from a Jain text by Acharya Samantabadra, who lived about two thousand years ago.[4] The basis of Sarvodaya according to Vinoba, rests on the three-fold programmes—*Gramdan, Khadi* and *Shanti Sena*. They are indivisible, and the three would revolutionise the life of man and build a new world, believed Vinoba.

Based on the two basic principles of Truth and Non-violence, Gandhi developed the Concept of Constructive Work/ Programme in early 1930's. The constructive programme resulted in the eighteen-fold activities and reforms. After the assassination of Gandhi in 1948, Vinoba took the mantle of Gandhian Movement. In 1951, he discovered *Bhoodan* (land gift) developed it into *Gramdan* (village gift) and the movement began to manifest new dimensions. Vinoba's charismatic leadership constituted a potential strength for the movement. Jayaprakash Narayan undoubtedly had his own personal charisma and it has been shown on many occasions, particularly on the occasion of his grand declaration of *Jeevandan* i.e., life gift, meant the dedication of one's whole life and energy to the cause of the movement.

With the appearance of Mahatma Gandhi on the Indian public scene, in 1920, the gulf between the social reformers and critical rebels was bridged. The foundations of Voluntary Work had already been laid and Mahatma Gandhi helped in setting up Harijan Sevak Sangh, All India Village Industries Association, etc. at Sevagram, Wardha; as part of Constructive Work/ Programme, which was a movement for economic betterment and improvement in the social life of the people.[5]

Gandhian Concept of Social Action

Gandhian social work is basically concerned with the reconstruction of society based on truth and non-violence and with welfare of all—the last and the lowliest as its end. Hence it cannot ignore the problems relating to social adjustment and maladjustment, to catastrophic situations such as fires, floods, epidemics, famine and even wars, to social welfare needs of the people, as also the problems relating to social injustice, economic exploitation and political subjugation as it recognises the inter-relatedness of the problems. The effort of Gandhian social work would naturally be to find out the basic causes and conditions out of which arise all such problems. The method of social action will then be directed towards the removal of those causes and conditions so that truth, non-violence and social justice could be given a practical shape in the reconstruction of the society.

This would make it imperative to bring about basic and fundamental changes in the institutional framework and value system of the society. Even those laws which may be bad in themselves or obedience to which would be inconsistent with the self-respect of the individual or human dignity the respect of which is the ultimate value of the profession of social work, will have to be opposed or disobeyed if necessary.

The aim of social action is, therefore, to combat problems and their causes which require a group and collective effort and which are necessary to be resolved for the reconstruction of the society. Whenever group and collective energies are directed towards combating certain problems for meeting certain emergency situations or for obtaining long-term results, we have social action.[6]

Relevance of Gandhian Thought to Social Work

Gandhi is usually called a political leader and a social reformer. It is because most of his life he was actively engaged in the struggle for independence of India from the foreign rule and in the crusades against some of the social evils e.g. untouchability, low status of women etc. Ammu, M. Muzumdar says, "In the course of many of his activities of a social welfare nature, Gandhiji had developed certain principles, practices and procedures which harmonize remarkably with the principles and techniques of pre-professional social work as it has developed in the western world—settlement-houses, social group work, social case work, community welfare organisation, social legislation, social action."[7]

But Gandhi was not a social worker in the strict sense of the term as it is understood. A social worker is one who enables the individuals in distress, singly or in groups, to adjust to their situation by helping them to help themselves, to overcome their difficulties through the well defined techniques of case work, group work and community organisation. But Gandhi never practised social work in this spirit. His concern with the specific techniques of social work as such was little. But he combined the social work spirit with his activities in the fields of politics, social reform and social welfare.

Dr. Frances M. Yasas has made an interesting study: whether or not the professional social work values are compatible with Gandhian values? Commenting on this study S.K. Khinduka says, "She...finds that Gandhi's work is something of a reaffirmation of the basic tenet of social work philosophy that 'Man is an object of infinite worth' Dr. Yasas does not lose sight of the few dissimilarities that exist between Gandhian values and social work values, but,... she shows the essential compatibility, and hence, the similarity between the philosophy of Mahatma Gandhi and the values underlying social work."[8]

Social work, today, is something more than a method. It is a "social institution" as Witmer calls it and it should be understood as such. This means that it should be understood in terms of present day needs and the social and cultural forces of the society as well as in terms of its purpose. The present day India is largely of Gandhi's making as he held and shaped the destiny of India for over a period of thirty crucial years of her history more than any body else. He introduced basic changes in the mode of thinking and living of the people. He also made people think fundamentally about many problems that confront the country even today. He has left a profound impress on the thoughts and actions of the people. It is, therefore, necessary to examine his contribution to theory and practice of social work. Frances M. Yasas also says, "Indian students could learn the basic values of professional social work more easily, if they could see them as different ways of saying some of the things that have been taught by their own philosophers, saints, social thinkers and social reformers, especially a person of the stature of Mahatma Gandhi.[9]

Realisation of the Concept of Truth and Non-violence

Gandhi has often expressed his own spiritual aspiration in his autobiography thus: "What I want to achieve, what I have been striving and pining to achieve is self-realisation, to see God face to face, to attain *'moksha'*. I live and move and have my being in pursuance of this goal. All that I do by way of speaking and writing, and all my ventures (even) in the political field, are directed to this end."[10]

When Gandhi speaks of self-realisation, he is obviously speaking about the realisation of the higher self which for him coincides with the ultimate reality better known to him as truth. He considers non-violence as the manifestation of truth. Self-realisation by implication is the attainment of perfect non-violence. Negatively speaking, it is freedom from the deadly coil of violence. Violence is the brute force belonging to the lower self which, according to Gandhi, should be reduced to zero in order to realise the higher self. He realised that violence and untruth were the greatest obstacles in man's progress.

When Gandhi refers to his motive as attainment of '*moksha*', he means the attainment of perfect non-violence which is the essence of spiritual freedom. He says, "*Moksha* is liberation from impure thoughts."[11] These impure thoughts are manifested in the violent behaviour of man. To realise non-violence in life one has to gradually free himself from the evil propensities in him. The animal in man must die in order that man may live as human.

Gandhian Concept of Constructive Work

'Constructive work' signifies a programme that would lead to the reconstruction of both men and society by correcting the faults of private and public life. Gandhi regarded constructive work to be 'the fulfillment of *swaraj*' and the present Sarvodaya thinkers attach to it no less importance.[12] An important question in connection with constructive work, concerns the place and type of organization necessary for it. Vinoba argued that non-violence needs no external machinery to propagate itself. What are required are self-purification, service of living beings, an all-embracing love and fearlessness. What he permitted is a kind of brotherhood. The organization of the Sarva Seva Sangh corresponds to his ideas. A constructive worker is expected to keep aloof from power politics which is also observed in our day-to-day life. The above lack of faith in party or parliamentary politics does not imply any non-cooperation with the government in such schemes as are conductive to the good of the people. It may be stated that the Sarvodaya thinkers are still experimenting to discover a programme of work as would create enthusiasm in the people and would lead society towards the realization of Sarvodaya.[13]

The 18 item-constructive programme [(1) Communal Unity, (2) Removal of Untouchability, (3) Prohibition, (4) *Khadi*, (5) Village Industries, (6) Village Sanitation, (7) New or Basic Education, (8) Adult Education, (9) Women, (10) Education in

Health and Hygiene, (11) Provincial languages, (12) National language, (13) Economic equality, (14) Kisans, (15) Labour, (16) Adivasis, (17) Lepers, (18) Students] provides a picture of Gandhian concept of social order. Gandhi says, "The constructive programme may otherwise, and more fittingly, be called construction of *Poorna Swaraj* or complete Independence, by truthful and non-violent means."[14] Through the constructive programme, on the one hand, Gandhi attempted to establish certain moral and spiritual values like truth, non-violence, bread labour, unity of all men without any distinction, social justice, self-reliance and so on in the life of the individual and society. On the other hand he pointed out certain social problems spreading in Indian society which should be fought and eradicated in order to bring about a social order which he called 'Sarvodaya Samaj'—a society in which the greatest good of all, the last and the lowliest, is the end and which is free from moral degeneration, social injustice, economic exploitation and political subjugation. Gandhi has avoided giving a graphic picture of the social order of his conception. Nevertheless he has a definite concept of a classless, casteless and stateless society based on the principles of truth in thought, word and action, non-violence in human behaviour, non-cooperation with evil, decentralisation of power and production, and the principle of bread labour for living. Social Action in Gandhian social work is directed to the realisation of such a social order.[15]

Social Work and Constructive Work

The principal element of Gandhiji's significance lies in his constructive programme, which aimed at changing the very basis of the whole social and economic order.

The constructive programme is not the same as traditional social work. Social work has been recently developed to help in solving social problems of modern society. It is something like a curative approach, whereas the constructive programme acts in the preventive approach in social behaviour and with minimised wants leading to a healthy cooperative endeavour.

The constructive programme based on non-violence and equality, eliminating violence, domination and inequality which are the causes of all the fundamental problems of mankind.[16]

Table 16.1: Social Work and Constructive Work

Social Work	*Constructive Work*
1. The relationship of social worker with client forms two separate entities.	Constructive worker is the member of the same society.
2. Trained professional practice but attached to no code of conduct.	Voluntary worker trained in non-violence.
3. To help others to help themselves.	To help his own society to grow from strength to strength.
4. Expects aid from external agency.	Generate sources from within.
5. Mostly urban-oriented.	Focussed on rural development.
6. Provides a healing touch but does not provide a permanent solution.	Creates preventive measures so as to form a foundation of permanent solution against ills of society.

Source: Gandhian Constructive Programme Museum, Gandhigram, Panel-I (1997).

Constructive Work and its Application— Gandhigram Model

Gandhigram was born in 1947. A team of dedicated disciples and contemporaries of Gandhiji, Dr. T.S. Soundram and Dr. G. Ramachandran, developed Gandhigram, the home of constructive work and rural development programmes. The Gandhigram Rural Institute (GRI) was founded in 1956. With undying faith and deep devotion to Mahatma Gandhi's revolutionary concept of *'Nai Talim'* system of education, GRI has developed academic programmes in Rural Development, Rural Reconstruction, Gandhian Studies, Peace Science, Gandhian Social Work, Rural Economics and Extension Education, Rural Oriented Sciences, Cooperation, Development Administration, Rural Sociology, English and

Communicative Studies, and, Tamil and Indian Languages. Students who emerge from its portals tend to meet the personnel needs for rural development under various governmental and non-governmental schemes. To teaching, was added the dimensions of research and extension in course of time. This three-dimensional approach became a pioneering model which earned appreciation from all over the country. The work of the Institute invited national attention and the Government of India (Ministry of Education), on the recommendation of the University Grants Commission, conferred the status of a Deemed University on the Institute under Section (3) of the UGC Act of 1956, on August 3, 1976. Today, it has become a nationally and internationally recognised Institute for its contribution to rural education, so much so that the New Education Policy of the nation reflects the principles evolved here in developing the rural university concept.

Starting in a small way, the Institute has developed into a big educational complex, comprising seven different faculties, offering in all about fifty different programmes. It awards Doctoral, Master's and Bachelor's Degrees, Diplomas and Certificates through its seven academic faculties: Rural Development, Rural Social Sciences, Rural Oriented Sciences, English and Foreign Languages, Tamil, Indian Languages and Rural Arts, Rural Health & Sanitation, and Agriculture and Animal Husbandry. It has, at present, about 2300 students and 125 teaching and 250 non-teaching staff.

A museum on Constructive Work at Gandhigram is worth mentioning.

The broad objectives of the Institute are:

(a) to provide for instruction and training in such branches of learning as will promote a classless and casteless society;
(b) to provide for research and advancement and dissemination of knowledge; and
(c) to function as a centre for extension work leading to integrated rural development.[17]

Gandhigram is a temple of Constructive Work.[18]

The following are the action programmes carried out by Gandhigram[19] under the umbrella of Gandhian Constructive Work:

Communal Unity

Maintenance of *Shanti Sena* and formation of youth peace brigades in the villages, promotion of religious harmony, removal of prejudices against other religious and caste groups, organising conflict resolution sessions/sittings in the villages, conducting peace marches, cycle rallies for peace, rushing to the riot-hit areas in the neighbouring districts, conducting inter-religious prayers at all times, bringing all religious groups in different forums, working for the unity of various religious and ethnic groups by various means form the hub of activities.

Removal of Untouchability

Campaigns against the practice of untouchability, encouraging inter-caste marriages, creating awareness among the villagers, discouraging tea stalls practicing untouchability, undertaking family visits, bridging the gap between Harijans and non-Harijans, attending weddings invited by the victims of untouchability, founder members of Gandhigram and workers setting an example to others, undertaking pledges, community dining, pledge taking, organising processions, arranging public meetings and screening films highlighting the removal of untouchability, conducting research studies on untouchability, staging dramas, songs are paramount programmes for removal of untouchability.[20]

Prohibition

Working for zero alcohol villages around Gandhigram, supporting the government in implementing prohibition, anti-liquor campaigns, organising *Padayatra* for prohibition in support of the local voluntary and sarvodaya organisations, highlighting the evils of drugs, displaying wall posters, distributing leaflets by procuring sponsorship from business houses, organising training programme for the transport crew of whom many are drug addicts, drug-deaddiction and rehabilitation programmes for addicts, prevention of drug abuse and alcoholism, organising cultural programmes and street plays on prohibition, organising village level conferences and meetings which fall under the category of constructive work.

Khadi

Khadi is the backbone of Gandhigram Institutions. Gandhigram has been encouraging *Khadi* and Village Industries and it promotes khadi production in the villages. Propagating the use of khadi and its philosophy, organising *khadi* exhibitions, encouraging every individual to wear *khadi*, conducting training programmes in *khadi's* village industries, offering a short term training courses in *khadi* and handloom technology, helping the individual to become entrepreneur under the self-employment programme, running a spinning unit each in the adopted villages are the activities carried out under this programme.[21] It would be no exaggeration to say that Gandhigram Trust is the father figure of this important constructive work.

Village Industries

Gandhigram has a separate complex called 'Village Industries Court' and it has several production units such as hand-pounding, soap-making, match making, footwear unit, hand-made furniture unit, ayurveda and siddha unit, weaving unit, food products unit, tailoring and embroidery unit, dairy unit, bee-keeping unit, oil ghony, dyeing unit, *papad* making and pickle making etc.[22]

Village Sanitation

As a remedy for villages around Gandhigram, there is a faculty of Rural Sanitation to advise and assist the villagers for the improvement of proper sanitation. Helping to construct low cost toilets, regulating drainages, preparation of soak pits, organising *shramdan* in the villages, road construction, campaign for village sanitation are the important activities.

Basic Education

Basically the educational system in Gandhigram is based on Gandhian pattern of education—new or basic education. Although there are certain changes in the system, the mettle of basic education is still kept alive. It would be no exaggeration to say that right from elementary education to higher education in Gandhigram is indeed with a difference and it is also unique in the country.[23] During her visit to Gandhigram, former Prime Minister Mrs. Indira Gandhi observed the following: "One of the major challenges is the restructuring of our educational system. The experience of Gandhigram will be useful in this."

Adult Education

Illiteracy and ignorance are the twins which are being attacked by Gandhigram ever since its inception. It has been trying to achieve cent per cent literacy through Adult Education Centres in the adopted villages. At present, Gandhigram is engaged in the 'Arivoli Iyyakkam' supporting the district officials in carrying out the work.

Women

Organising anti-dowry campaigns, highlighting the atrocities committed against women, creating awareness among women, encouraging women's participation at all levels, conducting periodical women's mela, free legal aid to the affected women, family counselling, taking care of the destitutes and home for the widows, celebrating the International Women's Day and Kasturba Day, organising seminars on Gandhi and women etc., are the important action programmes which enable to wipe out every tear from every woman.[24]

Health and Hygiene

Villagers are educated in health and hygiene and in particular personal hygiene of a villager and the child are insisted upon. The mind of the villager is partly getting purified through community prayers in the balwadi centres of the adopted villages and the *Bhajans* organised by the villagers themselves. In the village schools, health and hygiene activities are promoted by distributing prizes to the best participants of these contests.

Provincial and National Languages

Gandhigram gives equal importance to all languages for which the Faculty of Indian and Foreign Languages takes care. Although there is a controversy over the language issue elsewhere, Gandhigram follows the three language formula.

Economic Equality

One of the objectives of Gandhigram is to create a classless and casteless society and to work for the sarvodaya social order. It is a slow process, as we know, to achieve economic equality, but Gandhigram is striving its best to achieve it.

Kisans

Gandhigram is in touch with the *kisans* and it knows the pulse of the peasantry from time-to-time. Organising a forum for kisans, distributing saplings and seedlings, demonstrations, farm visits, soil testing, cattle protection, diary and poultry maintenance, preparation of compost manure are the activities for the *kisans*. There is a Faculty of Agriculture and Krishi Vigyan Kendra which provide guidance and counselling services to the *kisans*.

Labour

Gandhigram has been fully utilizing manpower and it has labourers working in different production centres. It has not come across any such major labour problems and has been maintaining brotherhood relationship. It also helps labourers working in the neighbouring mills in all the possible ways. Necessary efforts are being taken to organise training programmes in Gandhian ideology for the benefit of the mill workers.

Lepers

Gandhigram has an active contact with the institutions working for lepers. It jointly organises action programmes for lepers, awareness creation is given priority. It is in touch with the National Institute for Leprosy Control at Wardha and the local centre Damien at Nilakkottai. Organising anti-leprosy campaigns, processions highlighting the misconception about leprosy, film shows, conducting exhibitions, preventive measures are all such activities for the welfare of lepers.[25]

Adivasis: Several voluntary organizations are collaborating with Gandhigram for promoting the welfare of tribal people. The author of the book has also involved in some of the constructive programmes for the benefit of *Adivasis* including medical camp, etc. Ideas are generated through seminars and workshops high lighting issues relating to tribal areas.

Students

Gandhigram has the experience of working with both students and non-student youth. The future of students is shaped by way of organising suitable training programmes. Training programme in constructive work for the benefit of students, training in non-violence and peace for village youth, *shramdan* by students, Gurukula system for students are all such activities promoted for the welfare of students.[26]

New Items in the New Millennium

The list is not final and new items can be added as and when necessary.[27] The items may require equal attention in our march towards the twenty first century: (1) Population control,

(2) Resource exhaustion, (3) Pollution and Environmental Issues, (4) Afforestation, (5) Restoration of Ecology, (6) Prevention of profiteering, (7) Prevention of hoarding, (8) Prevention of black markets, (9) Prevention of smuggling, (10) Prevention of corruption, (11) Electoral reform[28], (12) Prevention of AIDS, (13) Moral spiritual education, (14) Home for the homeless, (15) Prevention of Disability and Welfare of the Disabled, (16) Removal of hunger, (17) Service to refugees, (18) Rehabilitation of prisoners, (19) Child and bonded labour, (20) Family welfare, (21) Prevention of female infanticide, (22) Care for the aged, (23) Prevention of beggary, (24) Protection for the victims of inter-caste marriage, (25) Prevention of suicides, (26) Uplift of slum dwellers, (27) Rain water harvesting.[29] Sarvodaya Movement should keep on experimenting with new items of constructive programme of a new generation in the New Millennium.

Conclusion

In conclusion it may be said that constructive work is the mother of all the development works including social work and they complement each other. In the process of the indigenization and Indianization of social work, we may replace (MSW) Master of Social Work into (MCW) Master of Constructive Work. In the Indian context, all the departments and schools of social work may include constructive work as one of the wings of the academic work in the New Millennium. Further, it could be said that the more we do Gandhian Constructive Work and Social Work, the more prosperous will be the community at large. Both Constructive Work and Social Work are the noble works which can be carried out by the individual and organisations wedded for the welfare of all being the creation of Sarvodaya Society and Sarvodaya Social Order.[30]

In order to promote both Social Work and Constructive Work and to prepare the younger generation in the new millennium, the modern social workers and constructive workers are Sarvodayites. They are otherwise known as Anna —"Brother" and Akka—"Sister" a common form of address among Sarvodaya/Constructive Workers in Tamil Nadu could easily follow the secret of Gandhiji's power:

A clear heart,
A clear conscience,
A cool head,
A regular communion with God,
Abstention from carnal food and pleasure,
No alcohol, smoking and condiment,
A strict vegetarian diet, and
Love for all our fellow men.
It is a new life and a new concept of
Social Work everyday!
I would end my paper stating the slogan:
"No social work today, No humanity tomorrow.
No new constructive work today, No community life
in the New Millennium."

NOTES

1. Paul Chowdhry, D. (1992). *Introduction to Social Work*, Atma Ram & Sons, Delhi, (Foreword) p. 1.
2. Quoted in the Foreword, Radhakrishnan, N. (1993). *Gandhi's Challenge to Religious Intolerance*, Peace Publishers (India), New Delhi.
3. Narayanasamy, S. (1997). *Sarvodaya Movement in Tamil Nadu—A Trend Analysis*, Unpublished synopsis of thesis submitted to Gandhigram Rural Institute, p. 2.
4. Augustine Thottakera (1992). *Gandhian Spirituality*, Centre for Indian and Inter-religious Studies, Italy, p. 11.
5. Paul Chowdhry, D. *op. cit.*, p. 14.
6. Parmeshwari Dayal (1986). *Gandhian Approach to Social Work*, Gujarat Vidyapith, Ahmedabad, p. 45.
7. Musumdar, Ammu M. (1964). *Social Welfare in India, Mahatma Gandhi's Contribution*, Asia Publishing House, Bombay, p. 158.
8. Khinduka, S.K. (1965). *Social Work in India*, Kitab Mahal Pvt. Ltd., Allahabad, p. IX.
9. Yasas, F.M. (1965). Gandhian Values and Professional Social Work Values, in *Khinduka, Ibid.*, pp. 75-76.
10. Gandhi, M.K. (1954). *The Story of My Experiments with Truth*, Navajivan, p. 4-5.
11. *Harijan*, 22-2-1942.

12. Devadoss, T.S. (1974). *Sarvodaya and the Problem of Political Sovereignty*, University of Madras, p. 521.
13. *Ibid.*, p. 523.
14. Gandhi, M.K. (1948). *Constructive Programme*, Navajivan, p. 7.
15. *Ibid.*, p. 11.
16. See details and the total picture of the Gandhian Constructive Programme in the Museum located at Gandhigram Rural Institute, Gandhigram, Tamil Nadu functioning since 1997.
17. *Gandhigram Calendar* (1999-2000), Gandhigram Rural Institute, pp. 10-11.
18. *Speech of Dr. M. Aram at the Golden Jubilee Celebrations of Gandhigram* at (Madras) Chennai in 1996.
19. The author has personal experiences in the field of Constructive Works in Gandhigram since 1980. It may be noted that he was a student of Gandhigram from 1971 to 1977.
20. For more details, see *GRI Newsletter* published by the Gandhigram Rural Institute-Deemed University, since 1976.
21. *Gandhigram Newsletter* published by the Gandhigram Trust, Tamil Nadu gives a full account of Constructive Programmes periodically.
22. Padmanabhan, V. (1996). *Grammar of Rural Development*, Sarvodaya Illakiya Pannai, Madurai. Sri. V. Padmanabhan was a Gandhian Worker, Constructive Worker and Social Worker. He was also known as ready reckoner of Village Industries.
23. Muniandi, K. (1985). *Gandhian Experiments on Education*, Gandhigram Rural Institute, Gandhigram, Tamil Nadu, p. 80.
24. Narayanasamy, S. (1993). Prohibition Movement: Action Programme, "*Sansthakul*", Vol. 22, No. 10, January, pp. 12-16.
25. Gandhigram Trust, Souvenir, *Gandhigram Golden Jubilee*, 1947-1997.
26. Involvement of GRI Shanti Sena Unit in the communal riot hit areas of Tamil Nadu.
27. M.L. Gujral (1986). *Thus speak Bapu or Dialogues between Gandhi's Spirit and the Scribe*, Gandhi Peace Foundation, New Delhi, p. 83.
28. *Ibid.*, p. 85.
29. Narayanasamy, S. (1997). Relevance of Constructive Programme, *Social Welfare* (Vol. 44, No. 4, July), pp. 12-14.
30. The author of the book has designed an undergraduate propramme is Gandhian Social Work during the academic year 2005-06 under the auspicial of Dept. of Gandhian thought and peace science, Gandhgram University, gandhgram. He has been guiding.

17

Mosaics on Constructive Work

Introduction

The constructive programme may otherwise and more fittingly be called construction of *Poorna Swaraj* or complete Independence by truthful and non-violent means.

Effort for attainment of Independence through so called violent and, therefore, necessarily untruthful means we know only too painfully. Look at the daily destruction of property, life and truth in the present war. (Gandhi, M.K., 1941, *Constructive Programme—its meaning and place*, Jitendra, T. Desai, Navajivan Mudranalaya, Ahmedabad, p. 5)

The primary aim of the Constructive Programme should be to secure for the worker his due share in production.—(Gujral, M.L., 1985, *Thus Spake Bapu, or Dialogues between Gandhi's Spirit and the Scribe*, GPF, New Delhi, p. 119)

The best preparation for, and even the expression of, non-violence lies, in the determined pursuit of the Constructive Programme. Anyone who believes that, without the backing of the constructive programme he will show non-violent strength when the testing time comes will fail miserably. It will be like the attempt of a starving, unarmed man to match his physical strength against a fully fed and panoplies soldier, foredoomed to failure—*Harijan*: April 12, 1942.

He who has no belief in the constructive programme has, in my opinion, no concrete feeling for the starved millions. He, who is devoid of the feeling, cannot fight non-violently—*Harijan*: April 12, 1942.

The execution of the constructive programme in its entirely means more than *Swaraj*: it means *Rama Raj*, Khudai Sultana or the Divine Kingdom. I am thirsting after such Raj. My God does not reside up above. He has to be realised on earth. He is here, within you, within me. He is omnipotent and omnipresent. You need not think of the world beyond. If we can do our duty here, the beyond will take care of itself—*Harijan*: January 4, 1946.

Nature of Constructive Work

'Constructive Work' signifies a programme that would lead to the reconstruction of both men and society by correcting the faults of private and public life. It differs from what is generally termed as 'Social Service' in that its object is not only to give relief to the afflicted, but also to eliminate the very need of that relief by removing the causes that give rise to it. Another of its ingredients, according to the Sarvodaya thinkers, is that it is performed of one's own accord. It is purely a moral action, which builds up morality in men. It is not actuated by any temptation or fear. Itself an expression of non-violence, it further aids in its growth. Gandhiji regarded constructive work to be 'the fulfillment of *Swaraj*' and the present Sarvodaya thinkers attach to it no less importance—rather more, because in the days of Gandhiji, its significance had been eclipsed by non-cooperation and civil disobedience. (*Source*: Vishwanath Tandon, 1965, *The Social and Political Philosophy of Sarvodaya after Gandhi*, Sarva Seva Sangh, Rajghat, Varanasi, India, pp. 163-164)

Constructive Programme as a Movement

Gandhi launched a movement of constructives progamme for economic betterment and for improving the tenor of social life for generation after generations. He also formed All India Village Industries Association, which was primarily an organization for the revival of cottage industries and betterment of rural life, in the centuries to come. The movement began with the emphasis of *Khadi* and it became the *Charkha* movement. Till this movement started, village reconstruction had not found its feet. For the first time the *Charkha* movement tied workers to village life and kept them there. The *Charkha* will continue to find its place in the centuries to come. India will not throw away the *charkha* till the last man improves his life and the *charkha* will have to be respected by the next generations.

The constructive programme is the long-term pre-requisite of a system of non-violent self-rule, without which political power or formal independence would prove to be a sham. The constructive programme includes individual and collective efforts on behalf of unity between diverse religious communities, the removal of social abuses such as untouchability, programmes of rural education and reconstruction, the decentralization of production and distributions, schemes for the improvement of health, sanitation and diet, the promotion of local handicrafts, and in general, concreted work by all to promote the common good (Sarvodaya). It may be underlined that where there is Sarvodaya, there is constructive programme, and the constructive programme is the heart of the Sarvodaya Movement. (*Source*: S. Narayanasamy, 1998, *Sarvodaya Movement in Tamil Nadu: A Trend Analysis*—Ph.D. Thesis, pp. 27-28.)

Communal Unity

Unity does not mean political unity alone. It means an unbreakable heart-unity. The first thing essential for achieving such unity is for every Congressman, whatever his religion may be, to represent in his own person Hindu, Muslim, Christian, Zoroastrian, Jew, etc. (*Source*: *Gandhi Diary*, 1998).

That unity is strength is not merely a copybook maxim, but a rule of life—*Young India*: May 11, 1921.

True unity comes of itself. No attempt has to be made for achieving it—*Young India*, October 21, 1926.

Unity is made of sterner stuff. It is not a showy nothing, to be merely named on a paper resolution. Unity to be achieved means solid action—*Young India*, January 15, 1925.

What does unity consist in and how can it be best promoted? The answer is simple. It consists on our having a common purpose, a common goal and common sorrows. It is best promoted by co-operating to reach the common goal, by sharing one another's sorrows and by mutual toleration—*My Picture of Free India*, p. 143.

Unity of Life

I believe in absolute oneness of God and, therefore, also of humanity. What though we may have many bodies? We have but one soul. The rays of the sun are many through refraction. But they have the same source—*Young India*, September 25, 1925.

I believe in the essential unity of man and, for that matter, of all that lives. Therefore, I believe that if one man gains spiritually, the whole world gains with him; and if one man falls, the whole world falls to that extent—*Young India*, December 4, 1924.

Seeking to realize oneness of life in practice, I cannot be happy if I see communities quarrelling with one another or men suppressing fellowmen —*Harijan*, March 2, 1934.

Mine is no narrow creed. It is one of realizing the essential brotherhood of man. To my mind, the message of the *Vedas* is unity of God and unity of all life in one God—*Harijan*, March 30, 1934.

I am a follower of Advaita or the theory of oneness of all. East and West, South and North are all one to me—*Harijan*, May 25, 1934.

I claim that human mind or human society is not divided into watertight compartments called social political and religious. All act and react upon one another—*Young India*, March 2, 1922.

Looking at society the entire world over, there is nothing but duality or plurality. Unity is conspicuous by its absence. This man is Hindu, that a Muslim, third a Christian, fourth a Parsi, fifth a Sikh, sixth a Jew. Even among these, there are sub-divisions. In the unity of my conception, there is a perfect unity in the plurality of designs—*Harijan*, July 13, 1947.

Behind the magnificent and kaleidoscopic variety, one discovers in Nature a unity of purpose, design and form, which is equally unmistakable—*Young India*, November 5, 1925.

In Nature, there is fundamental unity running through all the diversity we see about it. Religions are given to mankind so as to accelerate the process of realization of fundamental unity—*Young India*, August 20, 1934.

I think that we have to find unity in diversity.... We are all children of one and the same God and, therefore, absolutely equal—*Harijan*, February 2, 1934.

The forms are many, but the informing Spirit is one. How can there be room for distinctions of high and low when there is this all-embracing fundamental unity underlying the outward diversity? For, that is a fact meeting you at every step in daily life—*Harijan*, December 15, 1933.

Hindu-Muslim Unity

Hindu-Muslim unity consists in our having common purpose, a common goal and common sorrows. It is best promoted by co-operating to reach the common goal, by sharing one another's sorrows and by mutual toleration—*Young India*, February 25, 1920.

This unity cannot be a mere policy to be discarded it only when we are tired of *Swaraj*. Hindu-Muslim unity must be our creed to last for all time and under all circumstances—*Young India*, December 2, 1920.

Without unity between Hindus and Mussalmans, no certain progress can be made by the nation—*Young India*, July 28, 1921.

I am striving to become the best cement between the two communities. My longing is to be able to cement the two with my blood, if necessary. But before I can do so, I must prove to the Mussalmans that I love them as well as I love the Hindus. My religion teaches me to love all equally—*Young India*, September 25, 1924.

That 'unity is strength' is not merely a copybook maxim but a rule of life, is no case so clearly illustrated as in the problem of Hindu-Muslim unity. Divided, we must fall—*Young India*, May 11, 1921.

Hindu-Muslim unity means not unity only between Hindus and Mussalmans, but between all those who believe India to be their home, no matter to what faith they belong—*Young India*, May 11, 1921.

Hindu-Muslim unity is nothing, if it is not a partnership between brave men and women. We must trust each other always, but, in the last resort, we must trust ourselves and our God —*Young India*, September 29, 1921.

Hindu-Muslim unity will be very cheap and tawdry affair, if it has to depend upon mere reciprocation. Is a husband's loyalty dependent upon the wife's, or may a wife be faithless because the husband is a rake?—*Young India*, January 26, 1922.

What can be more natural than that Hindus and Mussalmans, born and bred in India, having the same adversities, the same hopes, should be permanent friends, brothers born of the same Mother India? The surprise is that we should fight, not that we should unite—*Young India*, August 21, 1924.

I believe with the late Poet Iqbal that the Hindus and the Muslims, who have lived together long under the Shadow of the mighty Himalayas and have drunk the waters of the Ganges and the Jamuna, have a unique message for the world—*Harijan*, March 16, 1947.

We Indians, of whatever religion, have to live together. We are of the same soil, we are nursed by the self-same Mother and we cannot go on killing each other if India is to live—*Harijan*, April 27, 1947.

We may think we are living, but disunited we are worse than dead. The Hindu thinks that in quarrelling with the Mussalmans, he is benefiting Hinduism; and Mussalman thinks that in fighting a Hindu, he is benefiting Islam. But each is ruining his faith—*Young India*, January 27, 1927.

For good or for ill, the two communities are wedded to India; they are neighbours, sons of the soil. They are destined to die here, as they are born here. Nature will force them to live in peace, if they do not come together voluntarily—*Harijan*, October 29, 1938.

Removal of Untouchability

So far as Harijans are concerned every Hindu should make a common cause with them and befriend them in their awful isolation. (*Source*: *Gandhi Diary*, 1998)

Untouchability means pollution by the touch of certain persons by reason of their birth in a particular state or family. It is an excrescence. In the guise of religion, it is always in the way, and erupts religion—Form Yeravda Mandir: p. 31.

There is an ineffaceable blot that Hinduism today carries with it. I have declined to believe that it has been handed to us from immemorial times. I think that this miserable, wretched, enslaving spirit of untouchability must have come to us when we were in the cycle of our lives at our lowest ebb… That any person should be considered untouchable in this sacred land passes one's comprehension—*Speeches and Writings of Mahatma Gandhi*, p. 387.

Untouchability is a sin against God and man. There is no warrant in the *Shastras* for untouchability as we practice it today—*Harijan*, March 2, 1934.

I consider untouchability to be a heinous crime against humanity. It is not a sign of self-restraint, but an arrogant assumption of superiority—*Young India*, December 8, 1920.

Untouchability is a snake with a thousand mouths, through each of which it shows its poisonous fangs. It defied definition. It needs no sanction from Manu or the other ancient lawgivers—*Young India*, July 11, 1927.

Untouchability is blot upon Hinduism and must be removed at any cost. Untouchability is a poison, which, if we do not get rid of it in time, will destroy Hinduism—*Harijan*, June 20, 1936.

And why do I say that untouchability is a curse, a blot and a powerful poison that will destroy Hinduism? It is repugnant to our sense of humanity to consider a single human being as untouchabile by birth. If you were to examine the scriptures of the world and the conduct of peoples other than Hindus, you do not find any parallel to the untouchability—*Harijan*, June 20, 1936.

I believe that if untouchability is really rooted out, it will not only purge Hinduism of a terrible blot, but its repercussion will be worldwide. My fight against untouchability is a fight against the impure in humanity—*Mahatma*, Vol. III. p. 203.

What I want, what I am living for and what I should delight in dying for is the eradication of untouchability, root and branch—*Mahatma*, Vol. III., p. 205.

Removal of untouchability means love for, and service of the whole world, and thus merges into Ahimsa. Removal of untouchability spells the breaking down of barriers between man and man, and between the various orders of Being—*From Yeravda Mandir*, p. 33.

Removal of untouchability means not merely touching the Harijans (untouchables), but also looking upon them as our own kith and kin; in other words, treating them in the same way as we would our own brothers and sisters. None is high, none low—*Bapu-ke-Ashirvad*, November 28, 1944.

They are not untouchables, we are untouchables. They eat and drink and think and feel even as we do. If a sum total of their virtues and vices and the privileges they are denied were to be made and compared with our virtues and vices and the privileges we enjoy and deny to them, I am sure in God's books we should find our debit side far heavier than theirs—*Young India*, May 13, 1926.

Untouchability is repugnant to reason and to the instinct of mercy, pity, and love. No man can consider another man inferior to himself. He must consider every man as his blood brother. It is the cardinal principle of every religion—*Speeches and Writings of Mahatma Gandhi*, p. 930.

It is a sin to believe that anyone else is inferior or superior to ourselves. We are all equal. It is the touch of sin that pollutes us, and never that of a human being. None are high and none are low for who would devote his life to service. The distinction between high and low is a blot on Hinduism, which we must obliterate—*The Diary of Mahadev Desai*, p. 286.

The distinction of high and low is at the bottom of untouchability. So long as the idea of high and low is not abolished, untouchability cannot be said to have been abolished—*Conversations of Gandhiji*, p. 60.

In battling against untouchability and in dedicating myself to that battle, I have no less an ambition than to see a complete regeneration of humanity. It may be mere dream, as unreal as the silver in the seashell. It is not so to me while the dream lasts, and, in the words of Romain Rolland: "Victory lies not in realization of the goal, but in a relentless pursuit after it—*Harijan*, March 25, 1933.

In dealing with the monster of untouchability, my own innermost desire is not that the brotherhood of Hindus only may be achieved, but it essentially is that the brotherhood of man—be he Hindu, Mussalman, Christian, Parsi or Jew—may be realized—*Harijan*, February 16, 1934.

I do want *Moksha*. I do not want to be reborn. But if I have to be reborn, I should be born as an untouchable, so that I may share their sorrows, sufferings, and the affronts levelled at them, in order that I may endeavour to free myself and them from that miserable condition.... If I should die with any of my desires unfulfilled, with my service of the untouchables unfinished, with my Hinduism unfulfilled, I may be born again amongst the untouchables to bring my Hinduism to fulfillment—*Harijan*, September 12, 1936.

Prohibition

We may not leave to the future government the fate of lakhs of men and women, who are labouring under the course of intoxicants and narcotics. We have to discuss ways of weaning the drunkard and the opium addict from this course. (*Source*: *Gandhi Diary*, 1998)

India has the capacity and the opportunity to lead the world in the matter of prohibition. Can she forego the revenue derived from this degrading traffic? She must, if she is to live—*Harijan*, September 15, 1946.

The positive side of prohibition must run side by side with the negative. The positive consists in providing the drinker with counter-attractions, giving him health and innocent amusement—*Harijan*, September 15, 1946.

We shall not be able to combat drink evil successfully till prohibition comes... without prohibition it is impossible to bring about sober habits among the labouring population in India—*Harijan*, January 19, 1934.

India is a country in which total prohibition can succeed. People are not habitually given to drink. It is not a fashionable vice. The climate does not demand its use—*Harijan*, January 19, 1934.

In no part of the world is prohibition as easy to carry out as in India, for, with us it is only a minority that drinks. Drinking is generally considered disrespectable. And there are millions, I believe, who have never known what drink is—*Harijan*, July 31, 1937.

Total prohibition is prohibition against sales of intoxicating drinks and drugs, except under medical prescription by a practioner licensed for the purpose and to be purchasable only at Government depots maintained therefore, *Harijan*, July 31, 1937.

Khadi

Khadi connotes the beginning of economic freedom and equality for all in the country. It must be taken with all its implications. It means a wholesale swadeshi mentality, a determination to find all the necessities of life in India, and that too, through the labour and intellect of villages. (*Source*: *Gandhi Diary*, 1998)

Khadi, to me, is the symbol of unity of Indian humanity, of its economic freedom and equality and, therefore, ultimately, in the poetic expression of Jawaharlal Nehru, 'the livery of India's freedom', *Mahatma*, Vol. VI, p. 20.

Habitual use of *Khadi* is a sign that the wearer identifies himself with the poorest in the land, and has patriotism and self-sacrifice enough in him to wear *Khadi*, even though it may not be so soft or elegant in appearance as foreign fineries, nor so cheap—*Harijan*, January 27, 1940.

Khadi is the breath of national life like *Swaraj*. It cannot be given up. To give up *Khadi* would be to sell the masses—the soul of India—*Harijan*, January 20, 1927.

We must be prepared to be satisfied with such cloth as India can produce, even as we are thankfully content with such children as God gives us. I have not known a mother throwing away her baby, even though it may appear ugly to an outsider. So should it be with the patriotic women of India about Indian manufactures—*Young India*, July 6, 1927.

I deny that any *Khaddar* is ugly. What of the dead sameness of machine-made article is not a sign of ugliness, but it is a sign of life, even as absence of sameness in the millions of leaves of a tree is no sign of its ugliness. As a matter of fact, it is the variety about the leaves, which gives a tree its life-like beauty.... And why should the cost of *Khaddar*, good or bad, worry us if every penny we pay for it goes directly into the pockets of the starving millions?—*Young India*, June 17, 1926.

The art that is in the machine-made article, appeals only to the eye; the art in *Khadi* appeals first to the heart and then to the eye—*Mahatma*, Vol. III, P. 292.

Khaddar delivers the poor from the bonds of the rich and creates a moral and spiritual bond between the classes and the masses. It restores to the poor somewhat of what the rich have taken from them—*Young India*, March 17, 1927.

Khaddar is the concrete and central fact of *Swadeshi*. *Swadeshi* without *Khaddar* is like the body without life, fit only to receive a decent burial or cremation—*Young India*, June 17, 1926.

Khadi is the central sun, round which the other village industries resolve like so many planets—*Harijan*, January 20, 1940.

Khadi Economics

Khaddar economics is wholly different from the ordinary. The latter takes no note of the human factor. The former wholly concerns itself with the human. The latte is frankly selfish, the former necessary scarily unselfish. Competition and, therefore, prices are eliminated from the conception of *Khaddar*—*Young India*, July 16, 1931.

Village Industries

Village economy cannot be complete without the essential

industries such as hand grinding, hand pounding, soap making, paper making, match making, tanning, oil pressing, etc. (*Source*: *Gandhi Diary*, 1998)

All should make it a point of honour to use only village articles, whenever and wherever available. Given the demand, there is no doubt that most of our wants can be supplied from our villages. When we have become village-minded, we will not want limitations of the West or machine-made products, but we will develop a true national taste in keeping with the vision of a New India, in which pauperism, starvation and idleness will be unknown—*The Constructive Programme*, p. 11.

The idea behind the village industries scheme is that we should look to the villages for the supply of our daily needs, and that when we find that some needs are not so supplied, we should see whether, with a little trouble and organization, they couldn't be profitably supplied by the villagers. In estimating the profit, we should think of the villager, not of ourselves—*Harijan*, November 23, 1934.

In a nutshell, of the things we use, we should restrict our purchases to the articles, which villages manufacture. There, we should think of the villager, not of ourselves—*Harijan*, November 23, 1934.

In a nutshell, of the things we use, we should restrict our purchases to the articles, which villages manufacture. Their manufactures may be crude, we should think of the villager, not of ourselves—*Harijan*, November 23, 1934.

In a nutshell, of the things we use, we should restrict our purchases to the articles, which villages manufacture. Their manufactures may be crude. We must try to induce them to improve their workmanship, and not dismiss them because foreign articles or even articles or even articles produced in cities, that is, big factories, are superior—*Harijan*, November 30, 1934.

Village Sanitation

Instead of having graceful hamlets dotting the land, we have villages, looking like dung-heaps. It is the duty of everyone to make our village models of cleanliness in every sense of the word. (*Source*: *Gandhi Diary*, 1998)

Some foreign observers have testified that, of all the nations of the earth, India comes, perhaps, to the top in the observance of personal cleanliness. But I fear that it is not possible to say the same of corporate, in other words, village, cleanliness. In yet other words, we have not made much advance beyond the family interest. We would sacrifice everything for the family as distinguished from the village i.e., in a sense, the nation—*Harijan*, February 8, 1935.

Members of a family will keep their own home clean, but they will not be interested in the neighbour's. They will keep their courtyard clean of dirt, insects and reptiles, but will not hesitate to shove all into the neighbour's yard. As a result of this want of corporate responsibility, our villages are dung heaps—*Harijan*, February 8, 1935.

Nai Talim/New Education

Basic Education links the children, whether of the cities or the villages, to all that is best and lasting in India. It develops both, the body and mind of the child. (*Source*: *Gandhi Diary*, 1998)

Basic education links the children, whether of the cities or villages, to all that is best and lasting in India—*Epigrams from Gandhiji*, p. 168.

This education is meant to transform village children into model villagers. It is principally designed for them. The inspiration for it has to come from the villages—*My Views on Education*, p. 113.

The object of basic education is the physical, intellectual and moral development of the children through the medium of a handicraft... The emphasis laid on the principle of spending every minute of one's life usefully is the best education for citizenship, and incidentally makes basic education self-sufficient—*Harijan*, April 6, 1940.

Basic Education

Basic education must become literally education for life. All educational activity of the Government should be on basic education lines. If I had my way, I would conduct adult education drives also through a basic craft. In my opinion, cotton spinning and the allied processes are crafts par excellence for this purpose—*Harijan*, August 25, 1946.

Literary education is of no value, if it is not able to build up a sound character—*Speeches and Writings of Mahatma Gandhi*, p. 214.

Real education is impossible through a foreign medium—*Young India*, September 1, 1921.

Real education consists in drawing the best out of yourself. What better book can there be than the book of humanity?—*Harijan*, March 30, 1934.

By education I mean an all-round drawing out of the best in child and man-body, mind and spirit—*Harijan*, July 31, 1937.

Man is neither mere intellect, not the gross animal body, nor the heart or soul alone. A proper and harmonious combination of all the three is required for the making of the whole man and constitutes the true economics of education—*Harijan*, December 19, 1938.

In India, where more than eighty per cent of the population is agricultural and another ten per cent industrial, it is a crime to make education merely literary and to unfit boys and girls for manual work in after-life. Our children must, from their infancy, be taught the dignity of such labour—*Young India*, Sept. 1, 1921.

Both Basic Education and Adult Education constitute a big field of work meant to transform village children and adults into model villagers.

Basic Education links the children, whether of the cities or villages, to all that is best and lasting in India. It develops both the body and the mind, and keeps the child rooted to the soil with a glorious vision of the future in the realization of which he or she begins to take his or her share from the very commencement of his or her career in school.

...If I had the charge of Adult Education, I would begin with the general and political education of the villager by word of mouth.

By Education, I mean drawing out the best from the body, mind and soul of the children.

Basic Education is meant to transform village children into

model villagers. It is principally designed for them. The inspiration for it has come from the villages.

The object of Basic Education is the physical, intellectual and moral development of children through the medium of a handicraft.

EWE-24
—*Evil Wrought by the English Medium*
R.K. Prabhu (1958)

According to Gandhi, "The New Education Scheme is not a little of literary education and a little of craft. It is full education through the medium of a craft".

Gandhi abundantly made it clear that the aim of his *Nai Talim* was to teach a craft not merely mechanically as is generally done today but scientifically, in order to develop the physical as well as the intellectual potentialities of the child. His objective was to impart an all-round and integrated education to children.

Gandhi enunciated the principle of Basic Education in which academic subjects were to be taught through the medium of productive activity like agriculture, gardening, animal husbandry, cottage industries and the like. He was very particular that the students should learn the principles of self-help, self-reliance and dignity of manual labour along with their academic pursuits.

The aim of New Education was not to make schools self-supporting for saving financial expenditure of the state. The main objective was to impart good education to children through production work.

The emphasis of Basic Education laid on the principles of spending every minute of one's life usefully is the best education for citizenship, and incidentally makes education self-sufficient.

What is the meaning of Education?

It simply means knowledge of letters. It is merely an Instrument, and an Instrument may be well used or abused. The same instrument that may be used to cure a patient may be used to take his life, and so may knowledge of letters. We daily observe that many men abuse it and very few make good use of it; and if this is a correct statement, we have proved that more harm has been done by it than good.

The ordinary meaning of education is knowledge of letters. To teach boys reading, writing and arithmetic is called primary education. "A peasant earns his bread honestly. He has ordinary knowledge of the world. He knows fairly well how he should behave towards his parents, his wife, his children and his fellow villagers. He understands and observes the rules of morality. But he cannot write his own name, what do you propose to do by giving him knowledge of letters? Will you add an inch to his happiness? Do you wish to make him discontented with his cottage or his lot? And even if you want to do that, he will not need such an education, carried away by the flood of western thought we came to the conclusion, without weighing pros and cons, that we should give this kind of education to the people." (*Hind Swaraj*, pp. 87-88)

To Gandhi students were "the hope of the future".

Gandhi was dissatisfied with the use of a foreign language as the medium of instruction in educational Institutions.

Gandhi desired radical changes in the existing curricula which were too 'bookish' and out of time with the realities of life.

Gandhi said, "Students must not take part in party politics. Because they are students searches, not politicians".

Adult Education

Adult education means, first, true political education of the adult by word of mouth. (*Source*: *Gandhi Diary*, 1998)

If I had charge of adult education, I should begin with opening the minds of the adult pupils to the greatness and vastness of their country. The villager's India is contained in his village. If he goes to another village, he talks of his own village as his home. Hinduism is for him a geographical term. We have no notion of the ignorance prevailing in the villages—*My Views on Education*, p. 115.

My Adult Education means, first, true political education of the adult by word of mouth. Side by side with the education by the mouth will be the literary education. This is itself a specialty—*My Views on Education*, p. 115.

"My Adult Education means, therefore, first, true political Education of the adult by word of mouth".

If I had charge of Adult Education, I should begin with opening the greatness and vastness of their country. The villager's Indian is contained in his village.

Adult Education center run by any Gandhian Institution may be exhibited.

Goal of Education

The goal is character building—an all round drawing out of the best in the child and the man—*Construction Programme by Mahatma Gandhi.*

Some work for Adult Education is being done in many places. It is mostly concentrated among the mill-hands and the like in big cities. No one has really touched the village. Mere three R's and lectures on politics will not satisfy me. (Adult Education of my conception must make man and women better citizens all round). To work out the syllabus and to organize the work of Adult Education is a more difficult task than preparation of the seven years' course for children.

The common central feature of both will be the imparting of Education through the village crafts. Agriculture will play a very important part in Adult Education under the basic scheme. Literary instruction must be there. Much information will be given orally. There will be books, more for the teachers than the taught. We must teach the majority has to behave towards the minority and *vice-versa*. (The right type of adult Education should teach neighbourliness and cut at the very root of untouchability and the communal problem).

—*D.G. Tendulkar*, p. 290, Vol. 6.

As to Adult Education, Gandhi observed that it had become clear to him that the scope of basic education had to be extended.

It should include the education of everybody at every stage of lifr —*D.G. Tendulkar*, p. 289

Women's Uplift

Woman is nothing if she is not self-sacrifice and purity personified—*Young India*, November 19, 1925.

For the courage of self-sacrifice woman is any day superior to man, as I believe man is to woman for the courage of the brute—*Harijan*, November 5, 1938.

Woman is the incarnation of *Ahimsa. Ahimsa* means infinite love, which again means infinite capacity for suffering. Who but woman, the mother of man, shows this capacity in the largest measure? Let he forget that she ever was or can be the object of man's lust. And she will occupy her proud position by the side of man as his mother, maker and silent leader—*Young India*, October 17, 1929.

A woman, I hold, is the personification of self-sacrifice, but unfortunately, to day, she does not realize what a tremendous advantage she has over man. As Tolstoy used to say, they are labouring under the hypnotic influence of man. If they would realize the strength of non-violence, they would not consent to be called the weaker sex—*India's Case for Swaraj*, p. 401.

To call the women the weaker sex is a libel; it is man's injustice to woman. If by strength is meant brute strength, then indeed is woman less brute than man. If by strength is meant moral power, than woman is immeasurably man's superior. Has she not greater intuition, is she not more self-sacrificing, has she greater courage? Without her, man could not be. If non-violence is the law of our being, the future is with woman—*Young India*, April 10, 1930.

Woman is not helpless. She must never regard herself as weaker than man. She should not, therefore, beg for any man's mercy nor depend upon him—*Bapu-ke-Ashirvad*, Septober 10, 1945.

Woman will not regard herself as dependent, weak or helpless. She is not really pure. Her purity makes her conscious of her strength. I have always held that it is physically impossible to violate a woman against her will. The outrage takes place only when she gives way to fear or does not realize her moral strength—*The Role of Women*, p. 111.

Women may not look for protection to men. They must rely on their own strength and purity of character and on God, as did Draupadi of old—*The Role of Women*, p. 118.

Why should Indian women feel so helpless? Is bravery the monopoly of men only? Women, of course, do not generally carry swords, though the Rani of Jhansi did and outdid all her contemporaries in the valour of the sword. Still, all cannot become Ranis of Jhansi. But all women can emulate the example of Sita, who even the mighty Ravana dared not touch. Ranis of Jhansi could be subdued—*Harijan*, October 27, 1946.

Woman in our country is brought up to think that she is well only with her husband or on the funeral pyre. I would far rather see India's women trained to wield arms than that they should feel helpless—*Harijan*, October 27, 1946.

There is no occasion for women to consider themselves subordinate or inferior to men. Languages proclaim that woman is half of man and, by parity of reasoning, man is half of woman. They are not two separate entities, but halves of one. The English language goes further and calls woman the better half of man. Therefore, women should resort to civil rebellion against all undesirable and unworthy restraints—*Harijan*, March 23, 1947.

Woman is described as man's better half. As long as she has not the same rights in law as man, as long as the birth of a girl does not receive the same welcome as that of a boy, so long we should know that India is suffering from partial paralysis. Suppression of woman is a denial of *Ahimsa*—*Harijan*, August 18, 1940.

Woman is the companion of man, gifted with equal mental capacities. She has the right to participate in very minutes detail in the activities of man, and she has an equal right of freedom and liberty with him—*Speeches and Writings of Mahatma Gandhi*, p. 423.

I will far rather see the race of man extinct than that we should become less than beasts by making the noblest of God's creation the object of lust—*Young India*, July 21, 1921.

Woman must cease to consider herself the object of man's lust. The remedy is more in her hands than men. She must refuse to adorn herself for men, including her husband, if she will be an equal partner with man. I cannot imagine Sita ever wasting a single moment on pleasing Rama by physical charms—*Young India*, July 21, 1921.

Would that woman will realize the power that she has latent in her for good, if she has also for mischief. It is in her power to make the world more lovable both for her and her partner, whether as father, son, or husband, if she would cease to think of herself as weak, and fit only to serve as a doll for man to play with—*Harijan*, November 14, 1936.

Women: Advice To

If you women would only realize your dignity and privilege, and make full use of it for mankind, you will make it much better than it is. But man has delighted in enslaving you and you have proved willing slaves till the slaves and the slaveholders have become one in the crime of degrading humanity. My special function from childhood has been to make woman realise her dignity. I was once slaveholder myself, but Ba proved an unwilling slave and thus opened my eyes to my mission. Her task was finished. Now I am in search of a woman who would realize her mission—*Letters to Rajkumari Amrit Kaur*: p. 100.

If you (women) want to play your part in the world's affairs, you must refuse to deck yourselves for pleasing man. If I was born a woman, I would rise in rebellion against any prevention on the part of man that woman is born to be his plaything—*Young India*, February 20, 1920.

Refuse to decorate yourselves, don't go in for scents and lavender waters; it must come out of your heart, and then you will captivate not man, but humanity. It is your birth right. Man is born of woman, he is flesh of her flesh and bone of her bone. Come to your own and deliver your message again—*Young India*, February 20, 1920.

It is my firm conviction that a fearless woman, who knows that her purity is her best shield, can never be dishonoured. However beastly the man, he will bow in shame before the flame of her dazzling purity—*Harijan*, March 1, 1942.

When a pure woman adds bravery and motherliness to her purity, she becomes at once a magnet in a way no man can... For woman is sacrifice personified. When she does a thing in the right spirit, she moves mountains—*Young India*, December 22, 1921.

Woman has circumvented man in a variety of ways in her unconsciously subtle ways, as man has vainly and equally unconsciously struggled to thwart woman in gaining ascendancy over him. The result is a stalemate—*Young India*, October 17, 1928.

It is not wrong to say that woman is the root of all evil for a sensual man, just as a gold mine is veritable hell for the covetous. But, for the world at large, gold may be beneficially used in a variety of ways—*The Diary of Mahadev Desai*, p. 167.

Man has converted woman into a domestic drudge and an instrument of his pleasure, instead of regarding her as his helpmate and better half. The result is a semi-paralysis of our society—*Harijan*, February 12, 1939.

To me, this domestic slavery of woman is a symbol of our barbarism. In my opinion the slavery of the kitchen is a remnant of barbarism mainly. It is high time that our womankind was freed from this incubus. Domestic work ought not to take the whole of a woman's time—*Harijan*, June 8, 1940.

> *"...It is physically impossible to violate a woman against her will. The outrage takes place only when she gives way to fear or does not realize her moral strength".*
>
> —*Young India II*, p. 862

"In a plan of life based on Non-violence, woman has as much right to shape her own destiny as man has to shape his".

Gandhi—*Constructive Programme*, p. 14

"Independence would be incomplete without the cooperation of women".

The Kasturba Gandhi Memorial Trust which collected more than a crore and a quarter of rupees in 1946 aims at the welfare and education of women and children in rural areas only through the agency of woman workers.

Man is born of woman; he is flesh of her flesh and bone of her bone. T-2-300

Woman is the incarnation of *chinga*. *Ahimsa* means infinite love, which again means infinite capacity for suffering. T-5-227

Woman is, by habit or nature, queen of the household. She is not designed to organize on a large scale. XXV-153

Woman is the embodiment of sacrifice and suffering and her advent to public life should, therefore, result in purifying it in restraining unbridled ambition and accumulation of property. T-2-367

Woman is more fitted than man to make exploration and take bolder action in *ahimsa*. MM-294

Women are special custodians of all that is pure and religious in life. MM-293

A women's intuition has often proved truer than man's arrogant assumption of superior knowledge. T-2-51

According to Gandhi, "Woman who knows and fulfils her duty realizes her dignified status. She is the queen, not the slave, of the household, over which she presides".

Every woman will tell the curious that with the disappearance of the spinning wheel vanished India's happiness and prosperity. T-2-38

The woman who knows and fulfills her duty realized her dignified status. MM-294

The woman has circumvented man in a variety of ways in

her unconsciously sub-ways, as the man has vainly and equally consciously struggled to thwart the woman in gaining ascendancy over him. T-2-367

The duty of motherhood, which the vast majority of women will always undertake, requires the qualities, which men need not possess. T-5-227

A fearless woman who knows that her purity is her best shield can never dishonoured. MM-301

There is no occasion for woman to consider themselves subordinate or inferior to men. MM-297

Woman is the companion of man, gifted with equal mental capacities.

If by strength is meant moral power, then woman is immeasurably man's superior. T-3-33

If non-violence is the law of our being, the future is with woman. T-3-33

To call woman the weaker sex is a libel; it is man's injustice to woman. T-3-33

Who can make a more effective appeal to the heart then woman?

Man is born of woman; he is flesh of her flesh and bone of her bone. T-2-300

Man, the law-giver, will have to pay a dreadful penalty for the degradation he has imposed upon the so-called weaker sex.

Men to be men must be able to trust their women-folk, even as the latter are compelled to trust them. T-2-349

Marriage is not an act or service. It is a comfort man or woman seeks for himself or herself. XXVI-285

Contraceptives are an insult to womanhood. MM-288

If you want to play your part in the world's affairs, you must refuse to deck yourselves for pleasing men. T-2-300

It is degrading both for man and woman that woman should be called upon or induced to forsake the hearth and shoulder the rifle for the protection of the hearth. T-5-227

If we would be pure, if we would save Hinduism, we must rid ourselves of this poison of enforced widowhood.
MM-299

If what passed as non-violence did not enable people to protect the honour of woman, or if it did not enable woman to protect their own honour, it was not non-violence. T-7-30

Why should men arrogate to themselves the right to regulate female purity? MM-29

Widowhood imposed by religion or custom is an unbearable yoke and defiles the home by secret vice and degrades religion.
MM-229

The restoration of spinning to its central place in India's peaceful campaign for deliverance from the imperial yoke gives her woman a special status. T-5-206

If we all could give our own definitions of God, there would be as many definitions as there are men and woman.
XXVI-224

Marriage must cease to be a matter of arrangement made by parents for money. MM-289

Languages proclaim that woman's is half of man, and by parity of reasoning, man is half of woman. MM-297

I am the only one whom you may find it hard to get rid of, for I have always counted myself as a woman. T-7-87

I have mentally become a woman in order to steal into her heart. MM-291

My own opinion is that, just as fundamentally man and woman are one, their problem must be one in essence.
MM-294

My quarrel with the advocates of contraceptives lies in their taking for granted that ordinary mortals can not exercise self-control. MM-289

What is but *ahimsa* that draws thousands of women to me in fearless confidence? T-5-291

For the courage of self-sacrifice, woman is anytime superior to man, as I believe man is to woman for the courage of the brute. MM-294

Woman, I hold, is the personification of self-sacrifice but unfortunately today she does not realize what a tremendous advantage she has over man. MM-291

Any young man who makes dowry a condition to marriage, discredits his education and his country and dishonours womanhood. MM-298

A smattering of English is worse than unless; it is an unnecessary tax on our woman.

Man has regarded woman as his tool. She has learnt to be his tool and in the end found it easy and pleasurable to be such, because when one drags another is his fall, the descent is easy.
T-4-45

Wives should not be dolls and objects of indulgence, but should be treated as honoured comrades in common service.
Constructive Programme—p. 18

Education in Health and Hygiene

The very high death rate among us is, no doubt, due largely to our growing poverty, but it could be mitigated if the people were properly educated about health and hygiene.

Observance of the fundamental laws of health and hygiene is necessary to cure illness. Resort to nature-cure according to your resources. (*Source: Gandhi Diary*, 1998)

It is health, which is real wealth, not pieces of silver and gold—*Harijan*, June 29, 1935.

Perfect health can be attained only by living in obedience to the laws of God, and defying the power of Satan—*The Health Guide*, p. 19.

He who takes indigestion and constipation lightly does not know the A-B-C of the rules of health. These two are the root-cause of innumerable ailments—*The Health Guide*, p. 23.

No one need in the search of health, leave a country where the Himalaya, the King of Mountains, exercise undisturbed sway, and which is watered by such mighty rivers as the Ganges, the Indus, and the Brahmaputra. A country, where millions of men enjoy prefect health, should be enough to supply the princes' needs on that score—*Young India*, January 8, 1925.

The real key to health lies in the conservation of vital energy—*Key to Health*, p. 46.

The joy of possessing perfect health is not to be compared with any other, and perfect health is unattainable by slaves. Slavery of one's animality is perhaps the worst of all—*Key to Health*, p. 49.

Only that man can be said to be really healthy, who has sound mind in a sound body. The relation between the body and the mind is so intimate that, if either of them got out of order, the whole system would suffer—*The Health Guide*, p. 16.

We have to acquire the faculty of keeping well under all weathers—a difficult task. I know. But it is not beyond human reach. The mind plays a great part in it. If we can completely detach ourselves from the externals, we can attain that state—*The Health Guide*, p. 230.

The remedy of the mind lies in the mind itself. In other words, it means that by meditating upon God alone, all our sorrows come to an end—*From a Letter to Vidya Hingorani*, March 3, 1932.

No man whose character is not pure can be said to be really healthy. The body, which contains a diseased mind, can never be anything but diseased—*The Health Guide*, p. 16.

A pure character is the foundation of health in the real sense of the term, and we say that all evil thoughts and evil passions are but different forms of disease—*The Health Guide*, p. 16.

Men's sana in corpore sano is perhaps the first Law of Humanity. A healthy mind in a healthy body is a self-evident truth. There is an inevitable connection between mind and body. If we were in possession of healthy minds, we would shed all violence and, naturally obeying the laws of health, we would have healthy bodies without an effort—*Constructive Programme*, p. 18.

The practice of Naturopathy became an Integral element of his constructive programme, and in 1994 he established in the village of Uruli, near Poona, a nature cure clinic

> *"If all the Medicines in the world were thrown into the bottom of the sea the health of mankind would improve; it would, of course, harm the fish".*
>
> —*Oliver Wendal Holmes*

In his youth Gandhi always wanted to be a Doctor. His brother objected; their father was opposed to the dissection of dead bodies and wanted Mohandas to prepare for the bar.

As early as 1906, while in South Africa, he wrote articles on health in the *Indian Opinion* and later published them under the title 'Guide to Health'.

The book '*Key to Health*' was written by Gandhi during 1943-44.

While Gandhi was in South Africa, a Doctor friend of his—Dr. Pranjivan Mehta—used to treat Gandhi with drugs for general lassitude.

At the outbreak of the Boer War I 1899 Gandhi organized

and led an ambulance corps of 1,100 Indians that served on many battle fronts.

Gandhi read a manual on obstetrics and assisted in the delivery of his fourth son, Ramdas born in Durban in 1897. In 1909, when their fifth and last son was born, Gandhi delivered the child entirely by himself.

Gandhi designed simple, easy-to-use latrines that did not require a scavenger to clean them, since the excreta was covered with earth and allowed to become manure.

In 1917, Gandhi was laid down with severe dysentery and was, as a result, reduced to a skeleton.

Once, in Africa, he (Gandhi) asked his wife to clean the commode used by a clerk who had been born an untouchable; she began to cry. Gandhi was not satisfied when she carried the pot, he wanted her to do it cheerfully. Shouting, "I will not stand this nonsense in my house", he threw her out of the house, and relented only when she pleaded with him.

Inspite of the popular prejudice against tamarind, it has been found that it is a good aperient and blood purifier. I gave copious doses of tamarind to one of the inmates suffering from Malaria with very good effect and have tried it in several cases of constipation.

Gandhi recommended a 40 day course of pure, sweet, thin mango juice as the finest "kaya-kalpa ousshada" (rejuvenating tonic) to those who were weak and emaciated.

Gandhi was married at the age of 13. The sense of guilt he experienced at the time of his father's death because of his failure to control his sexual desire occurred when he was 16. He renounced sex in 1906 at the age of 37, though the more or less successful practice of self-control had been going on since 1901.

Gandhi's many-sided public life did not permit him to read extensively on the subject of sex. As late as 1947 in his letter to Bose he said, "What is Freudian philosophy? I have not read any writing of his.

Gandhi: *My Experiments with Truth*, p. 256.

In 1924, Gandhi underwent an operation for appendicitis.

As a devout practitioner, he believed that he would live to be 215 years old—"the traditional life span of a Hindu Sage".

Gandhi laid great stress on spiritual purity as a requirement of good health, maintaining that the "body which contains a diseased mind can never be anything but diseased".

Some of the long fasts Gandhi undertook seriously undermined his health.

In February 1943, Gandhi, at the age of 73, undertook a 21 day fast as an appeal to God to clear this 'misunderstanding'. Although Gandhi survived the fast, his health suffered, and in subsequent months, he came down with a succession of ailments—malaria, amoebic, dysentery, hookworm, and acute anaemia.

Gandhi advocated sleeping in the open. He often recommended that cloths need not be worn at night when sleeping with a sheet.

> *"If our eyes were not blinded by foolish habit, we should see that the body looks most handsome only in that condition".*
>
> Gandhi: *Guide to Health*, p. 59

Physical well-being is useless if it does not lead to spiritual uplift is central to Gandhi's philosophy of health.

Mother Tongue: Provincial Languages

The neglect of our mother tongue had led to disastrous results. The disservice caused to India by this neglect of its great languages cannot be measures. How can the masses make their contribution to the Independence movement, unless they are explained every step in all its implications in their own languages? (*Source*: *Gandhi Diary*, 1998)

Our love of the English language in preference to our own mother tongue has caused a deep chasm between the educated and the politically-minded classes and the masses. The languages of India have suffered impoverishment. We flounder when we make the vain attempt to express abstruse thought in the mother tongue. There are no equipments for scientific terms. The result has been disastrous. The masses remain cut off from the modern mind. We are too near our own times correctly to measure the disservice caused to India by this neglect of its great languages. It is easy enough to understand that, unless we undo the mischief, the mass mind must remain imprisoned. The masses can make no solid contribution to the construction of *Swaraj*. It is inherent in *Swaraj* based on Non-violence that every individual makes his own direct contribution to the Independence movement. The masses cannot do this fully, unless they understand every step with all its implications. This is impossible, unless every step is explained in their own languages.

—*D.G. Tendulkar*, pp. 25-36.
Constructive Programme by M.K. Gandhi, p. 20.

College Education provides a career. It is a passport for entrance to the charmed circle. Pardonable hunger for knowledge cannot be satisfied otherwise than by going through the usual rut.

They do not mind the waste of precious years in acquiring knowledge of an utterly foreign language, which takes the place of the mother tongue. The sin of it is never felt. They and the teachers have made up their minds that the indigenous languages are useless for gaining access to modern thought and the modern sciences. I wonder how the Japanese are faring. For their Education, I understand, is all given in Japanese? The Chinese Generalissimo knows very little, if anything, of English.

—*D.G. Tendulkar*, p. 29

The question of language as such does not fall within the scope of *Nai Talim*, but the question of the medium of instruction does and that must always be the mother tongue. This point cannot be over-emphasised.

—*D.G. Tendulkar*, p. 300.

Common/National Language

For all-India intercourse we need from the Indian stock, a language which the largest number of people already know and which the others can easily pick up. That language is indisputably Hindi (Hindustani). (*Source: Gandhi Diary*, 1998)

Equally important is the question of the national or all-India language. (It can never be English, which is undoubtedly the language of foreigners and international commerce, but Hindustani alone can be the national language.) At present, it has two forms. In order to understand both the forms of the national language, Hindi and Urdu, and for their natural synthesis, we must learn the Devanagari and the Persian scripts. I find it lacking even in my immediate surroundings. All our signboards must be written in both the scripts and there should be none amongst us who cannot easily read and write either. —*D.G. Tendulkar*, p. 300.

We are slaves and have hugged the language of those who have kept us enslaved. It has become a fashion to blame the Englishman for all our ills. I have not hesitated to blame them for many things they have done. I have never charges them with compelling us to adopt precious years of our lives to learning the English language, our ambition being to be able to speak English as Englishman, and our breast swells with pride when an Englishman pats us on our back for speaking flawless English. Think of the time and energy of our youth expended on learning English language, as if it was our mother tongue, and calculate by simple multiplication the energy that are lost to the nation. —*D.G. Tendulkar*, p. 50.

Language is but a poor vehicle of one's thought. What I have said is bound to suffer from the limitations of that vehicle. —*D.G. Tendulkar*, p. 92.

It gave me joy to find that it held our prospect of success. I see no reason why what was at one time the common language of both the Hindus and the Mussleman are descended from ancestors that spoke and wrote a common language. It should require far less labour than to create two different languages, Urdu and Hindi. —*D.G. Tendulkar*, p. 305.

National languages should enable one to understand and speak both forms of speech and write in both the scripts.

Constructive Programme by M.K. Gandhi, p. 21.

In 1920, a deliberate attempt was begun to recognize the importance of Indian languages for the political education of the masses, as also of an all-India common speech which politically minded.

Constructive Programme by M.K. Gandhi, p. 21.

Economic Equality

Working for economic equality means abolishing the eternal conflict between capital and labour. A violent and bloody revolution is a certainty one day unless there is a voluntary abdication by the rich of riches, and the power that riches give, and sharing them for the common good. (*Source: Gandhi Diary*, 1998)

Economic equality of my conception does not mean that everyone would literally have the same amount. It simply means that everybody should have enough for his or her needs—*Harijan*, October 6, 1946.

I do not believe in dead uniformity. 'All men are born equal and free'—is not Nature's law in the literal sense. All men are not born equal in intellect, for instance; but the doctrine of equality will be vindicated if those who have superior intellect will use it not for self-advancement at the expense of others, but for the service of those who are less favoured in that respect than they—*Harijan*, October 6, 1946.

The real meaning of economic equality is: "To each according to his need". That is the definition of Marx. If a single man demands as much as a man with wife and four children, that would be violation of economic equality—*To Ashram Sisters*, p. 105.

We are all absolutely equal. But equality is of souls and not bodies. Hence, it is a mental state. We need to think of and to assert equality because we see great inequalities in the physical world. We have to realize equality in the midst of this apparent external by any person over any other, is a sin against God and man—*Young India*, June 4, 1931.

While we are born equal, meaning that we have a right to equal opportunity, all have not the same capacity. It is in the nature of things impossible. For instance, all cannot have the same height, or colour or degree of intelligence, etc.; therefore, in the nature of things, some will have ability to earn more and others less—*Young India*, November 26, 1931.

If we wish to develop in us the capacity to look on all as equals, we should aim at—getting only what the rest of the world gets. Thus, if the whole world gets milk, we may also have it. We may pray to God and say: 'O God, if you wish me to have milk, give it first to the rest of the world'—*To Ashram Sisters*, p. 105.

Welfare of *Kisans*: Peasant

Swaraj is a mighty structure. Eighty crores of hands have to work at building it. Of these *kisans*, i.e. the peasantries are the largest part. In fact, being the bulk of them (probably over 80%) the *kisans* should be the Congress. (*Source: Gandhi Diary*, 1998)

The *Kisan* or the peasant whether as a landless labourer or a labouring proprietor comes first, He is the salt of the earth, which rightly belongs or should belong to him, not to the absentee landlord or *Zamindar*. But in the non-violent way, the labourer cannot forcibly eject the absentee landlord. He has so to work as to make it impossible for the landlord to exploit him—*Press Report*: October 26, 1944.

In my opinion, the *Kisan* must not be used for power politics. I consider it contrary to the non-violent method. *Kisans* must be properly organised. To this end, special organizing bodies or committees should be formed where there are none, and those already in existence should be reformed and strengthened. Those who would know my method of organizing *Kisans* may profitably study the movement in Champaran where *Satyagraha* was tried for the first time in India with the result everyone knows. It became a mass movement, which remained wholly non-violent from start to finish. If affected over twenty lakhs of

Kisans. The struggle centred round one specific grievance, which were century-old. There had been several violent revolts to get rid of the grievance. The *Kisans* were suppressed. The non-violent remedy made them politically conscious, and they succeeded in achieving their end in barely six months. The workers may profitably study the *Kisan* movements in Kheda, Bardoli and Borsad. The secret of the success lies in a refusal to exploit the *Kisans* for political ends outside their own personal and felt grievances. Poor wages for landless labourers, wages that cannot provide sufficient food, clothing or shelter, lack of cheap credit for the marginal farmer, lack of power and other inputs, remission of land revenue during periods of droughts, etc., and absentee landlordism—all these are the wrongs suffered which they understand. (Gujral, M.L., 1985, *Thus Spoke Bapu or Dialogues between Gandhi's Spirit and the Scribe*, GPF, New Delhi, p. 118)

Welfare of Labourers

Ahmedabad Labour Union is a model for all India to copy. Its basis is non-violence, pure and simple. If I had my way, I would regulate all the labour organizations of India after the Ahmedabad model. (*Source*: *Gandhi Diary*, 1998)

Labour is more than money—*Harijan*, October 16, 1945.

When labour is intelligence enough to organize itself and learns to act as one man, it will have the same weight as money, if not much greater—*The Wit and Wisdom of Gandhi*, p. 102.

Labour is far superior to capital. Without labour, gold, silver and copper are a useless burden. It is labour, which extracts precious ore from the bowels of the earth—*Harijan*, September 7, 1947.

Capital controls labour because it knows the art of combination. Drops in separation can only fade away. Drops up co-operation make the ocean, which carries on its broad bosdom grey-hounds—*Harijan*, September 7, 1947.

A true and non-violent combination of labour would act like a magnet, attracting to it all the needed capital—*Harijan*, September 7, 1947.

Labour should be made conscious of its duty, from whose performance rights follow as a matter of course—*Press Report*, October 27, 1944.

Like a ship without direction or destination, labour without an ideal is fruitless—*Bapu-ke-Ashirvad*, May 22, 1945.

Labour, in my opinion, must not become a power in the hands of the politicians on the political chessboard. It must, by its sheer strength, dominate the chessboard—*Selections from Gandhi*, p. 134.

A nation may do without its millionaires and without its capitalists, but nation can never do without its labour—*Speeches and Writings of Mahatma Gandhi*, p. 1045.

Welfare of Tribals: Adivasis

Service of *adivasis* is also a part of the Constructive Programme. The *adivasis* are several crores in whole of India. There are several workers involved in this much-needed service, and yet their number is too few. (*Source*: *Gandhi Diary*, 1998)

The *adivasis* or the tribals are not an inconsiderable group as you say. There are over two crores or 23 million of them spread all over India—from Assam in the North-East, through Bihar, Madhya Pradesh, Rajasthan, Gujarat and Maharashtra in the West, and from North to South. Little work was done among them during the period of the British rule except by Christian missionaries who, with few exceptions like Verrier Elwyn, actually alienated them from the stream of Indian nationalism, and were mainly interested in their conversion to Christianity. Of the Congressman, Thakkar Bapa did some work among Bhils in Gujarat and Balasahib Kher threw himself with his usual zeal into this much needed service in Thana in the 1940's of this century. But, by and large, this difficult work was completely ignored.

It should have received a fillip after political independence was gained, but his did not happen. Congressmen, as the other parties, never took to constructive work, and the Constructive Programme was given a complete go-by. Congressmen, and the Congress Governments became wholly engrossed in the exercise of power and the fruits power brings. They failed to realize that it was difficult to make good their claim to be one nation, unless every group acquired a living consciousness of being one with all others. They forgot that service of the tribals was not only humanitarian but solidly national and designed to bring them close to true independence.

If a sizable section of our people has to be brought into the national stream, both the ruling and the other parties should stop using the *Adivasis* for their own ulterior ends, as they have been recently doing in Assam and elsewhere, and begin in all earnestness constructive work among them. (Gujral, M.L., 1985, *Thus Spoke Bapu, or Dialogues between Gandhi's Spirit and the Scribe*, GPF, New Delhi, p. 120)

Eradication of Leprosy

Leper is a word of bad odour. Yet they are as much a part of our society as the tallest among us. Lepers are much in need of attention, but their lot is neglected. (*Source: Gandhi Diary*, 1998).

'Leper' is a word of bad odour. India is perhaps a home of lepers, next only to Central Africa. Yet, they are as much a part of society as the tallest among us. But the tall absorb our attention, though they are least in need of it. The lot of the lepers, who are much in need of attention, is studied neglect. I am tempted to call it heartless, which it certainly is, in terms of non-violence—*Harijan*, November 2, 1947.

Why should there be a stigma about leprosy any more than about other infectious diseases? Real leprosy is attached to an unclean mind. To look down upon fellow human beings, to condemn any community or class of men, is a sign of diseased mind far worse than physical leprosy. Such men are real lepers of society—*Harijan*, November 2, 1947.

Students

Students are the hope of the future. It is from these young men and women that the future leaders of the nation are to rise.

Students must not take part in party politics. They may not resort to political strikes. They must do all sacrificial spinning in a scientific manner. They should be *khadi* users all through and use village products. (*Source: Gandhi Diary*, 1998)

A student's life has been rightly likened to the life of a *Sanyasi*. He must be the embodiment of simple living and high thinking. He must be discipline-incarnate. His pleasure is derived from his studies. They do provide real pleasure when study ceases to be a tax the student has to pay. What can be a greater pleasure than that a student marches from knowledge?—*Harijan*, August 17, 1947.

The life of a student is to correspond to the life of a *Sanyasi* up to the time his studies end. He is to be under the strictest discipline. He cannot marry nor indulge in dissipation. He cannot indulge in drinks and the like. His behaviour is to be a pattern of exemplary self-restraint—*Harijan*, August 17, 1947.

How can we understand the duty of students today? We have fallen so much from the ideal. The parents take the lead in giving the wrong direction. They feel that their children should be educated only in order that they may earn wealth and position. Education and knowledge are thus being prostituted and we look in vain for the peace, innocence and bliss that the life of a student ought to be—*Young India*, January 29, 1925.

Our students are weighed down with cares and worries when they should really be 'careful for nothing'. They have simply to receive and to assimilate. They should know only to discriminate between what should be received and what rejected—*Young India*, January 29, 1925.

I owe all I am to my parents. I felt towards them as Shravana is said to have done towards his parents. But, now-a-days, it has become the fashion with some young men to adopt the superior attitude and pose as paragons of perfection. In my opinion, the maintenance of one's aged and infirm parents is a first charge upon grown-up sons. They may not marry if they are not in a position to support their parents. They may not take up public work till this primary condition is fulfilled. They must starve so that their parents may be fed and clothed—*Young India*, June 25, 1925.

Students have to become nation-builders. The base imitation of the West, the ability to speak and write correct and polished English will not add one brick to the temple of Freedom—*Young India*, June 9, 1927.

Students must become pioneers in conservation reform, conserving all that is good in the nation and fearlessly ridding society of the innumerable abuses that have crept into it—*Young India*, June 9, 1927.

Students have to react upon the dumb millions. They have to learn to think, not in terms of a province, or a town, or a class, or a caste, but in terms of a continent and of the millions who include untouchables, drunkards, hooligans and even prostitutes, for whose existence in our midst every one of us is responsible—*Young India*, June 9, 1927.

Students and Character

Students have to search within and look after their personal character. Purity of personal life is the one indispensable condition for building a sound education. No man or women with an impure heart can possibly appear before the Great White Throne. All our learning or recitation of the *Vedas*, correct knowledge of Sanskrit, Latin, Greek and what not, will avail us nothing, if they do not enable us to cultivate absolute purity of heart. The end of all knowledge must be building up of character—*Young India*, September 8, 1927.

The student life is meant for the cultivation of self-restraint in everything—*Harijan*, April 1, 1933.

All your scholarship, all your study of Shakespeare and Wordsworth would be in vain, if at the same time you do not build your character, and attain mastery over your thoughts and actions—*To The Students*, p. 189.

Your education is absolutely worthless, if it is not built on a solid foundation of truth and purity. If you, boys, are careful about the personal purity of your lives, and if you are not careful about being pure in thought, speech and deed, then I tell you that you are lost, although you may become perfect, finished scholars—*With Gandhiji in Ceylon*, p. 75.

I do not care what you learn or what you do not learn in your school, if you will observe two conditions. One condition is that you must be fearlessly truthful against heaviest odds, under every circumstance imaginable. A truthful boy, a brave boy, will never a think of hurting even a fly. He will defend all the weak boys in his own school and help, whether inside school or outside the school, all those who need his help. A boy who does not observe personal purity of mind and body and action, is a boy who should be driven out of any school—*With Gandhiji in Ceylon*, p. 105.

Do not lie under any circumstances whatsoever. Keep nothing secret, take your teachers and your elders into your confidence and make a clean breast of everything to them. Bear ill-will to none: do not say an evil thing of any one behind his back; above all, 'to thine ownself be true' so that you are false to no one else. Truthful dealing, even in the least little things of life, is the only secret of a pure life—*Young India*, December 10, 1925.

Never lose faith in God and, therefore, in yourselves; and remember that if you allow refuge to a single evil thought, a single sinful thought, remember that you lack that faith. Untruthfulness, uncharitableness, violence, sensuality—all these things are strangers to that faith. Remember that we have in this world no enemy greater than ourselves. No one can harm us so much as we can ourselves—*Young India*, October 27, 1927.

Students and Politics

Students should have the greatest freedom of expression and of opinion. But, in my opinion, they may not have freedom of action whilst they are studying—*To The Students*, p. 111.

Students cannot afford to have party politics. They may hear all parties, as they read to all sorts of books, but their business is to assimilate the truth of all and reject the balance. That is the only worthy attitude that they can take—*Harijan*, January 26, 1941.

I hold it to be quite wrong on the part of students and pupils to take part in political demonstrations and party politics. Such ferment interferes with serious study and unfits students for solid work as future citizens—*Wit and Wisdom of Mahatma Gandhi*, p. 219.

Power politics should be unknown to the student world. Immediately they dabble in that class of work, they cease to be students and will, therefore, fail to serve the country in its crisis—*Harijan*, January 26, 1941.

The students should know that the cultivation of nationalism is not a crime but a virtue—*Harijan*, September 18, 1937.

Before I close this topic, may I say a few more words on what the students should do and what they should not do?

1. Students must not take part in party politics. They are students and researchers, not politicians.
2. They should not resort to political strikes. All differences with teaching staff and management should be settled peacefully and amicably.
3. They must all do either sacrificial spinning in a scientific manner or perform other bread or body labour in addition to their studies.
4. They will be *Khadi* wearers all through and use village products to the exclusion of all analogues things, foreign or machine-made.
5. They should honour the National Flag and harbour neither communalism nor untouchability in their hearts.
6. They will make it a point to give first-aid to their injured neighbours and do scavenging and cleaning in the neighbouring villages and instruct village children and adults.
7. They will learn and teach the National Language, in one or both scripts—Davanagari or Persian.
8. They will translate into Hindustani or the mother tongue everything new they may learn, and transmit it to the villagers.

9. They will do nothing in secret, will be above board in all their dealings, will lead a life of self-restraint, shed all fear, be always ready to protect all their weak fellow students, and be ready to quell riots by non-violent conduct at the risk of their lives.
10. They will be scrupulously correct and chivalrous in their behaviour towards their girl fellow students.

For working our programme I have sketched for them, the students must find time. I know that they waste a great deal of time in idleness. By strict economy of time, they can save many hours. I would, therefore, advise patriotic students to lose some period, not at a stretch but spread over their period of study. They will find that a year or more, so given, will not be a waste of time. The effort will add to their equipment—mental, moral, and physical—and they will have made, even during their studies, a substantial contribution to the social and economic freedom movement. (Gujral, M.L., 1985, *Thus Spoke Bapu, or Dialogues between Gandhi's Spirit and the Scribe*, GPF, New Delhi, pp. 133-134)

Constructive Programmes of Vinobaji

Cow Protection

Cow service may be included as one more item in the Constructive Programme. I would phrase it as improvement of cattle.

Cow protection, is one of the most wonderful phenomena in human evolution. It takes the human being beyond his species. The cow to me means the entire subhuman world. Man, through the cow, is enjoys his identity with all that lives. Why the cow was selected for apotheosis is obvious to me. The cow was in India the best companion. She was the giver of plenty. Not only did she give milk but she also made agriculture possible. The cow is a poem of pity. One reads pity in the gentle animal. She is the mother to millions of Indians. Protection of the cow means protection of the whole dumb creation of God.

The ancient seer, whoever he was, began with the cow. The appeal of the lower orders of creation is all the more forcible because it is speechless.

A Hindu who protects the cow should protect every animal. But taking all things into consideration, we may not cavil at his protecting the cow because he fails to protect the other animals. The only question, therefore, to consider is whether he is right in protecting the cow. And he cannot be wrong in so doing if non-killing of animals generally may be regarded as a duty for one who believes in *ahimsa*. And every Hindu and, for that matter, every man of religion, does so. The duty of non-killing animals generally and therefore of protecting them must be accepted as an indisputable fact. It is then so much to the credit of Hinduism that it has taken up cow protection as a duty. And he is a poor specimen of Hinduism who stops merely at cow protection, when he can extend the arm of protection to other animals. The cow merely stands as a symbol, and the protection of the cow is the least he is expected to undertake.—(Gujral, M.L., 1985, *Thus Spoke Bapu, or Dialogues Between Gandhi's Spirit and the Scribe*, GPF, New Delhi, pp. 121-122)

Cow Protection Movement

Gram Swaraj Conference was held at Paunar from Dec. 25-27, 1978 and it turned into the conference of cow protection movement. Vinobaji declared that he would go on fast unto death if the Government of Kerala and West Bengal fail to enact legislation on cow protection. The representatives of both State governments requested an extension of time for bringing legislation on cow protection. However, Vinoba was gracious and granted 113 days but, these two States did not take action and became silent. Subsequently, Vinoba declared his fast and he would happy to die during fasting.

In Tamil Nadu Cow Protection Committee was constituted With Shri S. Jaganathan as the President and Shri R. Varadhan as the Secretary. *Satyagrahis* in Tamil Nadu stopped taking cows to Kerala plunging in to action at the important places like Cumbum, T. Kallupatti, Batlagundu, Arokiapuram, Koothiar

Gundu Medu, Alagapuri and Oddanchatram. In Nellai District, cow protection movement was gaining momentum under the leadership of Shri R.T.P. Subramaniam. In Trichy District, three hundred people were arrested in this connection. A Farmer's rally was organized on 22-4-1979 and all the farmers presented a petition to the then Chief Minister of Kerala requesting to pass legislation seeking cow protection. Madurai district cow protection conference was organized at Cumbum on 1-4-1979 and a similar conference was held at Trichy on 16-9-1979 in which Shri R.K. Patel and Shri Radhakrishna Bajaj participated and addressed the gathering. A State level conference of cow protection took place at Madurai on 29-9-1980. The Governor of Tamil Nadu Shri Prabhudas Patwari inaugurated it and Shri S. Jaganathan presided over the conference. In the meanwhile a legislation was passed in Tamil Nadu ensuring cow protection. Tamil Nadu Sarvodaya Mandal sought the blessings of Kanchi Kamakodi Peedam for the growth of cow protection movement. However, Sarvodaya Movement prepared the people in support of the cow protection movement. (*Source:* S. Narayanasamy, 1998, *Sarvodaya Movement in Tamil Nadu—A Trend Analysis*—Ph.D. Thesis, p. 107)

Nature Cure

The working of Nature's processes in the human breast is mysterious and baffles interpretation—*Young India*, May 9, 1929.

Nature abhors a vacuum. Therefore, construction must keep pace with destruction—*Young India*, May 19, 1929.

Nature abhors weakness—*Young India*, May 13, 1927.

The laws of Nature are changeless, unchangeable, and there are no miracles in the sense of infringement or interruption of nature's laws—*Harijan*, April 17, 1937.

Marvellous as the progress of physical sciences undoubtedly is, it only humbles us and enables us to know that we know hardly anything of the mysteries of Nature—*Harijan*, January 9, 1937.

The essence of Nature Cure is that we learn the principles of hygiene and sanitation, and abide by those laws as well as the laws relating proper nutrition. Thus does every one become his own doctor—*Harijan*, September 1, 1946.

Nature cure connects a way of life which has to be learnt, it is not drug cure as we understand it—*Key to Health*, p. 63.

Nature curė is not like a doctor giving medicine in a bottle. It is really the natural way of keeping health and happiness—*Press Report*, March 15, 1946.

The man who eats to live, who is friends with the five powers—earth, water, ether, sun, and air—and who is servant of God, the Greater of all these, ought not to fall ill. If he does, he will remain calm relying on God and die in peace, if need be—*Harijan*, September 1, 1946.

Nature cure implies an ideal mode of life and that, in its turn, presupposes ideal living conditions in towns and villages. The name of God is, of course, the hub round which the Nature cure system revolves—*Harijan*, May 26, 1946.

Whether you get or not, what does it matter? The more reliance we place on God, the more peace of mind we shall have. *Vaidyas* and doctors are there, of course, but they take us farther away from God. Nature cure treatment takes us nearer to God. I will have no objection whatever if we could do even without it. But why be afraid of fast or avoid pure air? The meaning of Nature cure is to go nearer Nature, that is God—*From a Letter to Anand, T. Hingorani*, January 9, 1945.

"Human Body, The living temple of God, and a living Miraculous machine, is self-relevant in maintaining Health, as well as curing ill health (Diseases) through the Natural Medicines produced in its own factory"—Mahatma Gandhi.

Naturopathy

There is a growing awareness today about health and fitness among the masses. Large sections of health conscious people have started reviewing and questioning the modern life style. Most healthcare specialists today believe that most of the diseases from which the mankind is afflicted today are the outcome of the wrong living habits, wrong eating habits and wrong thinking habits i.e. Faulty living style, unnatural food habits and of the increasing pollution of the environment. That is why a system like Naturopathy is gaining more and more acceptance across the globe.

Nature cure is an art as well as a science of healthy living and a drugless system of healing based on well-founded philosophy. It has its own concept of health and disease and the principles of treatment.

Nature cure is defined as a system of man building in harmony with the constructive principles of nature on physical, mental, moral and spiritual planes of living. It has a great primitive, curative and rehabilitative health potential.

In fact, Nature cure is a very old method of living and curing diseases. The main concepts of Nature cure are morbid matter theory and the concept of vital force. The fundamental difference between Nature cure and other systems is that its theory and practice are purely based on a *'Holistic View Point'* unlike the latter's approach, which is specific. Nature cure does not believe in the specific cause of disease and its specific treatment but takes into account the totality of factors responsible for the disease such as one's unnatural habits, thinking, working, sleeping, relaxation, sexual indulgence, etc. It also considers the environmental factors involved that disturb the normal functioning of the body and lead it to a morbid, weak and toxic state. For treatment purpose, Nature cure primarily tries to correct all the factors responsible for the diseases and allows the body to recover itself. A Nature cure physician simply helps in nature's effort to overcome disease by applying correct natural modalities and controlling the natural forces to work under safe limits. The five main modalities of treatment in nature are Air, Water, Heat, Mud and Space.

Naturopaths believe that the human body is composed of five great elements (or *Pancha Maha Bhootas*). Imbalances of these create diseases. These five elements include Air, Water, Earth, Heat and Space. Treatment by these is what is called Nature Cure. Mahatma Gandhi, the father of our nation was an ardent advocate of Nature cure. He added Rama Naam

(Prayer) as a modality to it. Apart from above stated Pancha Maha Bhoot therapies. i.e. Air therapy, Fire therapy, Hydro therapy, Mud therapy, Fasting, Nutrition and Dietetics, some other therapies such as Exercise, Massage, Electrotherapy, Yoga, Chromo-therapy, etc. are also practices by naturopaths. [(*Source*: K.D. Sharma, (2002), "Yoga and Naturopathy: The true science of healing," *Indian Journal of Traditional Knowledge*, National Institute of Science Communication, New Delhi, Vol. 1 (I), p. 24)]

Bhoodan

Pochampalli is the village where the first *Bhoodan* (Land Gift) was offered to Acharya Vinoba Bhave on April 18, 1951. During the 2002, a special function was organized at Pochampalli on April 18 to celebrate India's first *Bhoodan*. To celebrate the occasion, admirers of *Bhoodan* Movement had come to this village from several parts of India. Shri Amarnath Bhai, Chairperson of Sarva Seva Sangh; Shri Yashpal Mittal, Coordinator of Golden Jubilee functions; Shri Lavanam, well-known social worker and Jt. Secretary of Gandhi Smarak Nidhi; Shri Vendat Rama Rau, Chairperson, Andhra Pradesh Sarvodaya Mandal; Shri G.V. Subba Rao, Secretary of Andhra Pradesh Sarvodaya Mandal were among them.

Pochampalli is the place where Shri Vinoba Bhave received the gift of 100 acres of land for the first time in India from the hands of Shri Ram Chandra Reddy. After this land gift, Vinobaji started his marathon *Bhoodan Yatra* of 80 thousand kilometers, which took him 13 years to complete.—(*Source: Sansthakul*, June 2002, p. 12)

Bhoodan Movement

In 1951, Vinoba started a *Bhoodan* Movement (Land Gift). It began with a voluntary gift of 100 acres of land by a landlord Shri Ramachandra Reddy at Pochampalli in Andhra Pradesh, in an area affected by Marxist violence. Vinoba calculated; India had 10 million landless families and they required 50 million acres of land, which was one sixth of the country's cultivable, land, namely 300 million acres. The assumption was that each landless family would need about 5 acres of land for its support.

Vinoba Bhave walked on foot from state to state and asked every landlord for one sixth of his land. Thousands of acres poured in as free gifts. The *Bhoodan* Movement attracted national and international attention. Socialist leaders like Jayaprakash Narayan joined the movement. The *Bhoodan* led to *Gramdan*. Now the village community could redistribute the land and start a new programme of cooperative farming or group and individual farming. Also allied programmes like animal husbandry, rural industry, village health and the village as a whole in a new social climate could plan sanitation, village education, etc.

Thus *Gramdan* became the basis of Integrated Rural Development at Yelwal in South India in 1957, a national meet took place in which the top political leaders participated including the President of India and the Prime Minister and the Chairmen of leading political parties. A joint declaration was issued supporting the *Gramdan* approach to rural development. It was suggested that the government should co-ordinate its development programme with the *Gramdan* movement leading to Sarvodaya socio-economic order.

Over the last five decades, we have, no doubt, made a significant change in the process of planning our rural development programmes. Earlier it was chalked out by the Planning Commission and then at the State headquarters. But now we have accepted the need for district level planning. However, district is also a very large area for making any specific development plan by taking into consideration the available resources and local needs. We need to go further down. Considering the variation in the quality of our natural resources and opportunities at the village level and the need for taking up block level or taluk level planning. J.C. Kumarappa, born in 1892, an economist trained in London and New York, joined Gandhi in 1929. He also emphasized the need for micro-level planning and productive schemes under the Community Development Programme. His criticism of the Community Development Programme was unforgiving. Most of its funds, he said, were taken up for unproductive schemes like road building. Moreover, the "persons who have co-operated (with the Government) belong to a small section of the public, though moneyed and influential." But the *Harijans* "are notoriously neglected, the poor are still standing apart suspiciously." "Generally speaking," he summed up "the atmosphere around officials and gram sevaks is not one of love for rural people and their life but one of their own employment and advancement." The insensitivity of public officials was compounded by their brief, handed down from above, which was completely at odds with the physical realities of Indian agriculture. The variety of *swadeshi*, which Kumarappa himself promoted emphasized local rather than national self-reliance, working towards what he called the "economy of performance" (roughly synonymous with what we, in the late 20th century, less elegantly term "sustainable development"). As he once remarked: "If we produce everything we want from within a limited area, we are in a position to supervise the methods of production, while, if we draw our requirements from the ends of the earth it becomes impossible for us to guarantee the conditions of production in such places." Proof of his far-sightedness in matters ecological is provided by the following remarks in his Madurai report:

On water conservation: "The irrigation tanks are as a rule silted up and eroded.... If these tanks are desilted four or five feet, much of the cry for water will cease and the farmers can get two or three crops a year where even getting one is a gamble today. Attention to these tanks will give us control over floods and reduce erosion. If properly advised and guided the villagers will gladly extend their co-operation in such schemes.... This is a programme that will quickly raise the production of food several fold and thereby better village conditions in a very short time."

On fertilizer over-use: "There are no facilities (in the agricultural demonstration centres) for soil and water analysis. In the absence of these, no artificial or chemical manures should be used. Now such fertilizers are being supplied at favourable rates. They may prove ruinous in the end. At present the Government seems more anxious to dispose of their fertilizers than to observe the ill effects of their use indiscriminately on all kinds of fields in the course of years."

On forest protection: "Water supply depends on an efficient forest policy. The Government is overanxious on the revenue production of forests rather than their being a conserving ground for water. Every village should have its common lands properly taken care of."

On the protection of artisans: "Welfare of villagers rests on the occupations open to those who are not fully employed on the land. (Village) industries provide the necessary complement to work on land. A few stray attempts are being made to help with the *ghani*—oil grinder, *khadi* work, bee-keeping, etc. But these are not considered an essential feature of the development (work) and suffer from a lack of emphasis—All village industries will have to be resuscitated to put life into rural parts."

For while the environmentalists of today are unaware of his name and work, they are only taking up where he left off. High on their green agenda figure the things Kumarappa talked of in his "Report on Rural Development Work in Madurai District" of 1956 and in numerous other writings of the forties and fifties: soil fertility, water conservation, forest protection, resource recycling, handicraft production—all this not by government patronage but through the renewal and revitalization of decentralized "community" systems for the management of water, pasture and forests.

Bhoodan in Tamil Nadu

Madurai district Constructive Workers Association was established in collaboration with Gandhigram in Tamil Nadu. The association started functioning under the leadership of N.M.R. Subburaman who was known as Madurai Gandhi. Some of the volunteers joined workers home at Gandhigram and carried out village service. The summer camp was organized to train college students and farmers. Besides, Farmers Association was founded with an object to work for the rights to the farmers through non-violent method. Shri S. Jaganathan evinced much interest in this field. He was encouraged, motivated and guided by Shri J.C. Kumarappa, a noted Gandhian economist. The struggles and *Satyagrahas* like 'Kallanthiri Farmers Struggle', 'Sholavandan *Satyagraha*' and 'Natchikulam Sugarcane *Satyagraha*' was organized by S. Jaganathan and ultimately he developed a deep interest in solving the land problem. While Vinoba Bhave was working for *Bhoodan Movement*, Shri S. Jaganathan from Tamil Nadu joined him in Uttar Pradesh and gained direct grassroots experience under the leadership of Vinoba Bhave.

With the blessings of Vinoba Bhave, S. Jaganathan came back to Tamil Nadu and started *Bhoodan* activities. In the year 1952, he organized a conference at Madurai. O.P. Ramasamy Reddiar, Sardar Vedaratnam, N.M.R. Subburaman and *Khadi* workers joined together and decided to work for *Bhoodan* Movement in Tamil Nadu. As a result *Bhoodan* Committee was formed. The Secretariat for the *Bhoodan* in Tamil Nadu started functioning in the premises of "Students Seva Centre" located at Shenoy Nagar, Madurai. In the year 1952, on October 2, *Padayatra* under the leadership of Shankar Rao Dev was conducted from Rameswaram to Palakadu. During the second leg of his *Padayatra*, he covered the distance from Kanyakumari to Vedaranyam. Shri Shankar Rao Dev, Shri Dada Darmadhi Kari and Vimala Thakkar conducted *Padayatras* from time-to-time in Tamil Nadu. Shri Jayaprakash Narayan, who added a feather in the cap, i.e., "*Jeevan Dan*" in the *Bhoodan* Movement and Shri K. Kamaraj, the then Tamil Nadu Congress Committee leader joined together and toured extensively different areas like Chengalpet, Madurai, Ramanathapuram, Tirunelveli, Tanjore, Coimbatore and North Arcot. They took about fifteen days to cover all the said districts in Tamil Nadu. Totally 5200 acres of land for bhoodan, Rs. 26,368 being sampattidan, ploughs and bullocks were received as a token of *bhoodan*.

It was not until April 18, 1951, however, that a spark ignited the tinder of non-violent revolution. This was the gift by a landlord of 100 acres of land to Vinoba for distribution among the landless *Harijans* in the village of Pochampalli in the Telegram district of Andhra Pradesh. Thus was born *Bhoodan*—

the first and most spectacular of a series of "dan" programmes promoted by the movement. There is no doubt that Vinoba saw the gift as a sign from God, indicating the way in which non-violent social change could and should be pursued. To those who joined him in promoting the new programme, it was also a visible manifestation that "the gift of grace"—the mark of the genuine charismatic leader—had been bestowed on Vinoba. Gandhi's true successor in India had at last clearly emerged from the shadows.

It is significant that the first land gift was made in a village in an area raven by violent social conflict. Since 1948, the Communists in Telengana had been actively promoting a violent peasant revolution along the lines favoured by Maoists in China. Vinoba's visit to the area was in the nature of a "peace mission". But he was concerned not merely to preach but also, and more importantly, to find a viable alternative to violent revolution. Although sympathetic to many of the declared aims of the Communists, he believed that their philosophy was antithetical to that of Sarvodaya and, indeed, that Sarvodaya was destined to be the ideology that would finally overcome the advancing ideology of Communism. This implied that Sarvodaya was a positive ideology in its own right and not simply a negative to Communist revolutionism—a view that was encouraged when land gifts were made in areas not dominated by the Communists. However, the forcible seizure convinced him of how serious was their plight and that land was the key to the social revolution in India. A land revolution, to be achieved peacefully by appealing for voluntary donations of land from the landlords, was thus defined by Vinoba as the critical element in India's non-violent revolution. The appeal to landlords might be couched in the language of charity, and Vinoba was certainly concerned to elicit from landlords a sense of compassion—a virtue that he was to place alongside those of truth and non-violence—but justice was the name of the exercise. As Vinoba explained: 'In a just and equitable order of society, land must belong to all. That is why we do not beg for gifts but demand a share to which the poor are rightly entitled'.

In spreading the message of *Bhoodan*, Vinoba adopted the traditional way of an Indian *rishi*: a *padayatra*, or pilgrimage on foot, marching from village to village. Vinoba was not averse to employing modern means of communication. (His general attitude was to welcome science and its application, while insisting that science must be married to non-violence if mankind is to survive in the modern world.) But he was aware that the non-violent revolution was a revolution from below to be made by ordinary people and that direct communication with them in the manner and language they understood was the best procedure or tactic. His initial success in obtaining land gifts in Telengana, followed by even greater success in Uttar Pradesh, in any case rapidly won widespread publicity of the conventional kind both in India and throughout the world outside. Nehru, impressed by the power of non-violence in Telengana where military force was being used to crush the Communists and anxious to encourage a climate conducive to the acceptance of the Government's own land reforms, was among the first to praise Vinoba's work. In December 1951, the Sarva Seva Sangh then adopted *Bhoodan* as part of its own programme, a decision which facilitated the organization of *Padayatras* by others as well as by Vinoba. The targets for *Bhoodan* were set and exceeded until, amid enthusiasm acres was set to be reached by 1957, which was heralded, in the movement, as "the Year of the Land Revolution".

However, the interest of the public in the movement centred not on its strategy for non-violent revolution but on its *Bhoodan* programme. The movement was commonly referred to as "the *Bhoodan* movement" and represented as a uniquely Indian approach to land reform: its deeper significance was scarcely appreciated. In an effort to underline the real meaning of *Bhoodan* as a step towards a new caring and sharing society, Vinoba devised other *dan* programmes. These included: *Shramdan* (gift of labour); *Sadhandan* (gift of subsidiary means of production, such as bullocks, to enable *Bhoodan* recipients to till their new lands); *Buddhidan* (gift of money, income, or wealth); and *Jeevandan* (gift of dedication of one's life to the cause). Taken together, these signified that everybody had something he or she could share with others; some might have more than others but there were no 'have-nots'. Of these *dans*,

Sampattidan was potentially the most significant. Although it was put forward as a proposal that each donor should devote a proportion of his income to social welfare work, behind it lay Gandhi's theory of trusteeship, interpreted in a socialist way. In the words of a resolution of the Sarva Seva Sangh: "The basic principle behind *Sampattidan Yojna* is that such means of production as are not directly in the hands of the producers, should vest in the society or village community.... The one-sixth share now claimed leads to the recognition of the principle that any individual possessing property and wealth is not its owner but only a trustee holding them for the whole community."[24] Two other programmes are also worth noting. One was the establish of a *Shanti Sena* or Peace Force—an idea originally mooted by Gandhi but which he had not been able to realize. In 1958, following Vinoba's call for 70,000 volunteers to act as a non-violent police force (particularly in the context of communal conflicts), the *Shanti Sena* was finally set up. The other programme, also dating from 1958, was Sarvodaya Patra, which called for a pot in each home into which the children were asked to keep a handful of grain daily. The practical purpose of the programme was to provide the means of subsistence for the movement's workers, but it also embodied a large purpose: it was intended to symbolize that the activities of the workers enjoyed the support and sanction of the people. In addition to the above-mentioned programmes, the movement continued to emphasis what had been the best-known item in Gandhi's Constructive Programme: the production of *khadi* as a village industry.

Promotion of the *Bhoodan* Silver Jubilee by speeding up land distribution inevitably led the Sarvodaya workers involved, such as Nirmala Deshpande, to develop close contacts with various Government authorities. As we have seen, Mrs. Gandhi had already promised Vinoba that the Government would celebrate the inauguration of the *Bhoodan* Silver Jubilee year. In fulfillment of this promise, the President of India, Fakhruddin Ali Ahmed, addressed a meeting at Hyderabad on 18 April 1975, in which he described the *Bhoodan* Movement as a "new and essentially Indian approach" to the land problem:

"It is land reform not by threat or coercion but by change of heart... It gains a new relevance now with the incidence of sporadic violence." In a message to the nation, the Prime Minister made a similar point: "It (*Bhoodan*) shuns violence and confrontation. We cannot afford to slacken our defences against violence which seems to lurk below the surface in human beings and in social groups, waiting to demolish values and undermine institutions and conventions." (*Source: Non-violent Revolution in India*, Geoffrey Ostegaard, 1985, GPF, New Delhi, pp. 5-6, 16-17, 181)

Gramdan

Gramdan grew naturally out of *Bhoodan* as a consequence of all, or almost all, the landowners in a village donating all their land in the village. This occurred first, as early as May 1952, at Mangroth in Uttar Pradesh where the donated land was vested in the village community and subsequently distributed among the villagers in pieces, which varied according to each family's capacity and needs. Some of the families then formed a cooperative farm, the others continuing to farm as family units. The radical implications of *Gramdan* when compared with *Bhoodan* soon became apparent. Whereas *Bhoodan* involved donations from individuals, *Gramdan* involved also community action; under *Bhoodan* individual ownership of land was retained but under *Gramdan* it was abolished and the land "villagized"; and, thirdly, whereas the beneficiary of *Bhoodan* was an individual or group of individuals, the beneficiary of *Gramdan* was the whole village community. In short, the move from *Bhoodan* to *Gramdan* represented a move from a basically individualist programme (and one which could be criticized for increasing the fragmentation of landholdings) to a basically socialist programme. Despite the more radical character of *Gramdan*, the number of villages opting for it increased until nearly 2,000 had done so by the end of 1956. In 1957, therefore, instead of the movement ruefully lamenting the failure to meet its *Bhoodan* target, it announced that its sights were now set on ending private ownership of land altogether. The original target was absorbed in this new resolve; the target, henceforth, was *Gramdan* as the basis for establishing *Gramswarajya*.

After 1959, the emphasis was placed increasingly on spreading the *Gramdan* idea and the objective of arousing "the latent capacity of the people and to harness it for village development". In so far as the villagers required help from outside in their task of reconstruction, the main responsibility for supplying it, suggested Vinoba, rested on the Government. This attitude was encouraged by expectations aroused at the Yelwal conference, although some workers remained uneasy about the implied dependence of a movement for non-violent revolution on the cooperation of the Government.

Jayaprakash Narayan's decision to devote himself full time to *Gramdan* work in Musahari gave a much-needed boost to the miracle of other Sarvodaya workers in Bihar, when in October 1970, having taken the advice of Vinoba, they decided to launch consolidation work in the smallest district in the State and the one deemed most favourably disposed towards *Gramdan*. The work was to be done through a *Gramswarajya* Samiti and supervised by veteran workers, such as Krishnaraja Metha and Nirmala Deshpande. (*Source: Non-violent Revolution in India*, Geoffrey Ostegaard, 1985, GPF, New Delhi, pp. 18, 21, 35.)

Gramdan Development Activities

During Vinoba's *Padayatra*—walking tour, a huge gift of village *Gramdan* was received in Madurai district. The entire Thirumangalam taluk was in the process of covering under *Gramdan*. A similar situation also prevailed in Batlagundu area. In order to assess the extent of area covered under *Gramdan* and its legal aspects, a survey committee was constituted on 16-1-1957 under the chairmanship of the Madurai District Collector. Deputy Development Commissioner, Shri S. Jaganathan and Shri R. Gurusamy as members of the said committee. On the recommendation of this committee, State level *Bhoodan* Board was formed on 25-1-1959. The State Bhoodan Board was initially headed by Shri K. Arunachalam with members, namely Shri

K. Kamaraj, Shri P.S. Chinnadurai, Shri S. Jaganathan, Shri P. Jeevanantham, Shri Ma.Po. Sivagnanam, Shri S.R. Subramaniam, Shri K. Venkatachalapathy and Shri A. Avaiyan as the Secretary. Since 1970 *Bhoodan* Board functioned under the presidentship of Swamy Vidyananda Saraswathi in Madurai District. Subsequently, a ten *Gramdan* Sarvodaya Cooperative Society was registered. Gandhi Smarak Nidhi in Tamil Nadu took necessary efforts to carry out constructive programmes in all the ten *Gramdan* villages. Tamil Nadu Sarvodaya Sangh Vannangulam, Koniyampatty, Palapatty and old Batlagundu provided necessary assistance to the *Gramdan* development activities. A well-wisher of Sarvodaya from Quakers group based in England, Mr. Donald Groom provided financial assistance to dig wells in Batlagundu area. At that time, Shri R.R. Keithan's 60th birthday was celebrated at Batlagundu in a grand manner. During this period, Sarvodaya Ashram at Batlagundu (now at Kanavaipatty) was founded and Shri A. Avaiyan was made the Secretary. Shri Meyer from Germany during the year 1967 and Shri Javani from Italy during the year 1969 started associating with *Gramdan* development programmes by providing financial assistance. Ultimately, they became instrumental in organizing Meyer Trust with effect from 18-4-1974 and Sarva Seva Sangh with effect from 30-12-1978 and they were registered as an independent organization. (*Source*: S. Narayanasamy, 1998, *Sarvodaya Movement in Tamil Nadu—A Trend Analysis*—Ph.D. Thesis, pp. 103-104)

Shanti Sena

Gandhi thought of "Peace Brigades" or "*Shanti Senai*" as early as 1938 in the context of communal riots in India. He wrote in the *Harijan* on 18.06.1938.

"Some time ago I suggested formation of a Peace Brigade whose members would risk their lives in dealing with riots especially communal? The idea was that this brigade should substitute the police and even the military. This reads ambition. The achievement may prove impossible. Yet, if the Congress is to succeed in its non violent struggle, it must develop the power to deal peacefully with such situations".

In that article Gandhiji listed the qualifications and attributes of a member of the peace brigade:

1. He or She must have a living faith in non-violence. This is impossible without a living faith in God.
2. The messenger of peace must have equal regard for all the principal religions of the earth.
3. Peace work can be done singly or in groups.
4. The messenger of peace will cultivate through personal service, contacts with the people in his locality.
5. A peace bringer must have a character beyond reproach and must be known for his strict impartiality.
6. A peace brigade will not wait till the conflagration breaks out, but will try to handle the situation in anticipation.
7. There should be a distinctive dress worn by the members of the peace brigade so that they would be recognized without difficulty.

This list of qualifications and attributes gives an idea of the way Gandhiji's mind was working at that time regarding Shanti Sena.

Gandhiji's life and death gave a brilliant demonstration of what a Shanti Sainik (Peace Soldier) should be like. In his last years he functioned as a shining embodiment of the ideal of Shanti Sena. His own wonderful performance at Calcutta is part of history.

One-Man-Boundary-Force

Gandhiji's lonely trek in the village of riot-torn Noakali is also part of history. Lord Mountbatten called Gandhiji "the One-Man-Boundary-Force".

Let me quote Mountbatten "In the Punjab we have 55 thousand soldiers and large-scale rioting on our hands. In Bengal our forces consist of one man and there is no rioting. As a serving officer, as well as an administrator, may I be allowed to pay my tribute to the One-Man-Boundary-Force".

It was in his magnificent death that Gandhiji demonstrated to the world the brilliance of *Shanti Sena* in action. He showed to the world what a peace soldier par excellence could be like. He will ever remain an unending source of inspiration for generations to come

After Mahatma Gandhi

After Gandhiji passed away it was given to Acharya Vinoba Bhave to pick up the thread and give a creative impetus to the Gandhian movement. He discovered *Bhoodan* (land gift) developed it into *Gramdan* (Village Gift) and the movement began to manifest new dimensions.

When Vinobaji was in Kerala State in 1957, he realized the urgent need of developing *Shanti Sena*. He started an eight-member group of *Shanti Sena*, which included the late Shri Kelappan and Shri Janardhanan Pillai. These friends took five vows:

1. To practice truth and non-violence.
2. To serve the people without consideration of reward.
3. To keep aloof from political parties and power politics.
4. To be above caste and community differences and treat all religions as equal.
5. To devote maximum time to *Bhoodan* work.

The *Shanti Sena* programme progressed from strength to strength. The All India Shanti Sena Mandal was established under the auspices of Sarva Seva Sangh. For many years Shri Jayaprakash Narayan was the Chairman of All India Shanti Sena Mandal. [(*Source*: M. Aram and N. Radhakrishnan (1984), *Training Youth in Non-Violence—The Shanti Sena* (Peace-Brigade) of Gandhigram Rural University, pp. i-iv)]

The Need for a Shanti Sena

The basic problem of the whole world today is the establishment of peace. Perhaps in no other age has there ever been such a world-hunger for peace. There are countries whose whole way of thought, up to yesterday, was deeply dyed with violence; today even those countries long to find release from violence. True, they go on increasing their arrangements, but nevertheless they are wondering how to get rid of them. The sheer inertia of habit makes for the stock-piling of arms. But intellectually people have come to understand that arms will achieve nothing—nothing, that is, except losses for the poor and the blocking of all progress in real welfare consequent on the immense expenditure of resources on the army. Even those countries where revolutions have taken place through bloodshed today desire peace. Why? Because whereas in former days the weapons were in the hands of men, it is no longer: men are now in the hands of their weapons. If the spark of war should now set the world on fire, no man will be able to control it. Mankind has, therefore, lost faith in the possibility of solving its problems through war or violence. That in itself is a great thing to have happened and the way forward is now open. If arms can no longer settle our disputes, then some other way of settling them must be found. That is what the *Shanti Sena* is designed to do.

The *Shanti Sena* is not a new proposal. We owe both the word and the idea behind it to Bapu, who himself endeavoured to give it a practical shape. He was both its first commander and its first soldier. As commander he issued the order: 'Do or die', and as a soldier he obeyed it. That is, his life and actions give us a complete picture of what the *Shanti Sena* is. No doubt, he also expounded his ideas freely in words, but it was through action, through life, that his thought was most fully expressed.

When I set out alone for the Shivarampalli Conference, I made up my mind to return by way of Telengana. I used to say, in explaining my purpose, that I was the *Bhoodan-Yajna* movement which came out of that journey; but my intention was to go as a *Shanti Sainik* to see the conditions and to help in whatever way might prove possible. The thought of *Shanti Sena*, in fact, has thus been constantly in my mind.

But although, these ideas were in the back of my mind, it was only when I was touring in Kerala that it became clear to me that I should undertake the organization of a *Shanti Sena*. People used to ask me, in those days, what were the conditions, which caused me to come to this decision. I replied that the idea itself did not originate from the actual conditions before me; the concept of *Shanti Sena* had already been present in my mind, and in Kerala the outline had taken on a new clarity. This new clarity of vision might have come to me anywhere (for India is in such an explosive condition that the explosion may happen at any place) but in fact it came in Kerala.

Another thought had already been much in my mind: *Gramdan*, the ending of individual ownership in land etc., will not be able to bring about a revolution by peaceful methods, unless the people also feel at the same time that our ideas offer them a powerful means of self-defence even in the present state of affairs (that is, even while unjust differences remain). These distinctions, this cleavage between high and low, are a cause of un-peace and if they are got rid of, there is no doubt that un-peace will also disappear. But having said that, are we to be content to go on like this?—"If conflict breaks out, what can we do? We have blazed a trial, and pointed it out to the people—the way of ending individual ownership and working constructively together. If they follow the trial, well and good. If they don't, the seeds of conflict are bound to grow in the evil conditions of today. We have shown them a way, but if they will not walk in it they must taste the bitter fruits of their refusal. What can we do?"—If we are content to take that line, our talk of a peaceful revolution is nothing but a 'talk'. It will not cut any ice with the people. Their hearts will not be touched by it, and neither will our own hearts find any inward peace in it. It is, therefore, necessary, even for the healthy growth of those processes of peaceful revolution in which we are already engaged, that we should make ourselves responsible for peace. This does not mean that we dare to think that we can save the world. That power does not lie in us, but in the nature of non-violence. It is our faith that non-violence can claim to save the world, which it does possess strength to do and that is the goal towards which we must strive. With this in mind I put forward in Kerala the plan for a *Shanti Sena*, and in accordance with that plan I set up the tiny nucleus of a *Shanti Sena* and made a public announcement of it. (*Source*: Vinoba, 1963, *Shanti Sena*, Sarva Seva Sangh, Rajghat, Varanasi, India, pp. 9-12)

Training of Shanti Sainiks

Gandhiji converted the masses into *Satyagrahis* and forced the British to leave India. But it was not an easy task. A *Satyagrahi* must be a highly disciplined person. And a disciplined person is one who lives in such a way as to cause least discomfort, to others. Spinning on the *Charkha* was not only a productive work that the Mahatma gave to those who had nothing to depend on but also a source of discipline. That is why he made *Charkha* compulsory for all, poor or rich.

Once Gandhiji was in South India. Over 5,000 poor women came to receive him. They sat in rows on their *Charkha* singing patriotic songs in harmony. A British author accompanying Gandhiji was awe stricken on seeing this scene and said, "I see Gandhiji's discipline is more effective than British Army discipline and so, I feel that Gandhiji's army will win in India's struggle for freedom through non-violence."

Gandhiji created a huge army of dedicated men and women who were prepared to sacrifice themselves. It is these people who gave strength to Gandhiji and made India free. They all worked in one or more of the constructive programmes of Gandhi—*khadi*, prohibition, communal harmony, and removal of untouchability. Their training was imparted in *Ashrams* as well as jails and in the *Satyagraha* movements he launched from time-to-time. It was only to discipline people, that he stopped some of these movements, when people became violent.

World Needs Shanti Sena

India needed such bands of disciplined non-violent soldiers after independence too. But the man who inspired hundreds and thousands of people to join his army of peace was no more there to lead the people. The mind-set of India changed rather fast after Independence, particularly after Gandhiji's assassination in 1948. Non-violence was no longer the weapon for conflict resolution. We returned to the primitive principle of eye for eye; the result—we are one of the most-violent nations of the world today.

The violence in which India is in stepped today is not limited to human relations alone. Rape of nature; cruelty to animals and increasing distance between haves and have-nots are only some of the reflections of the worldview India has cultivated during the last 50 years. India, nay the world as a whole, must return to the Gandhian ways to ensure peace. The United Nations, instead of sending armed forces to quell violence as in Timor (in Indonesia), should send *Shanti Sena*. True, it cannot happen today or may be even in the next couple of decades but if the concept of Army of Peace as it is understood today is gradually changed to the Gandhian concept of *Shanti Sena*, the world will move further towards peace. May be, to begin with, *Shanti Sena* with weapons and *Shanti Sena* of *Satyagrahis* consisting of Nobel Laureates and other persons of repute are sent together; and a *Shanti Sena* without weapons, but with terrific moral force, acts first to restore peace.

Potential of Shanti Sena

The Potential of *Shanti Sena* is not limited to fire fighting alone. It has to be productive so that peace is not disturbed. For this to happen need for agencies which can train people to prevent the breach of peace cannot be over emphasized. We have to build a society in which there is ample scope for even the criminals to become good citizens.

Let it be clear that *Shanti Sena* is not a professional outfit for a chosen few. It is a concept that covers all the people, the people who are engaged in self-fulfilling tasks and activities. The frustrated unemployed cannot be *Shanti Sainiks*. Quite often we reduce this concept to youth brigades formed at colleges and universities. *Shanti Sena* is for more than this. Training in peace making is a must. As such, they can be treated as adhoc *Shanti Sainiks* not yet fully trained to perform the functions of *Satyagrahis*.

Weapons of Shanti Sena

The weapons that the *Shanti Sena* uses are dialogue, negotiations, service, love, faith and prayers, community service of the needy, the poor, the marginalized, sick and helpless, is equivalent to parade. What we need today urgently is the establishment of centers of *Shanti Sena* all over the world to bring about reconciliation in conflict situations and to prevent any breach of peace. Such centers would be autonomous receiving cooperation and help from people as well as governmental agencies. (*Source*: Anil Dutta Mishra, 2002, *Rediscovering Gandhi*, Mittal Publications, New Delhi-110 059, pp. 149-151)

Key to Sources

MM	—	Mind of Mahatma Gandhi (Ed. Prabhu and Rao), 3rd Edition, 1968.
T	—	(Followed by Vol. Nos.) Mahatma (D.G. Tendulkar), Vols. 1-8: 2nd Edition, 1960, Publications Division.
I to XXVI	—	The collected works of Mahatma Gandhi—Publications Division.
TIG	—	Truth is God (Ed, R.K. Prabhu), 1955.
MOG	—	The Message of the Gita, R.K. Prabhu (1959)
MGCG	—	Mahatma Gandhi—Correspondence with the government 1959.
CP	—	Constructive Programme by M.K. Gandhi.

REFERANCES

Arunachalam, K., *Gandhi: The Peace Maker.*
Bhave, Vinoba, *Shanti Sena.*

Bose, N.K., *Studies in Gandhism.*

Chandrand Devanesan, *The Making of Mahatma.*

Desai, Narayan, *Handbook for Satayagrahis*, Gandhi Peace Foundation, New Delhi, 1980.

Devadoss, T.S., *Sarvodaya and The Problem of Political Sovereignty*, University of Madras.

Dhare, O.G. Dhavan, *The Political Philosophy of Mahatma Gandhi.*

Divakar, N.D., *Social Reform Movements in India*, Popular Prakashan, Bombay.

Diwakar, R.R., *Saga of Satyagraha*, Bharthiya Vidya Bhavan, Bombay, 1969

Doctor, Adi H., *Sarvodaya: A Political and Economic Study.*

Gandhi, M.K., *Constructive Programme—Its Meaning and Place*, Navajivan Publishing House, Ahmedabad, 1945.

——., *An Autobiography or The Story of My Experiments with Truth*, Navajivan Publishing House, Ahmedabad.

——., *Satyagraha in South Africa*, Navajivan Publishing House, Ahmedabad.

——., *Satyagraha*, Navajivan Publishing House, Ahmedabad.

——., *An Autobiography or The Story of My Experiments with Truth.*

——., *Ashram Observances in Action.*

——., *Basic Education.*

——., *Constructive Programme: Its Meaning and Place.*

——., *Ethical Religion.*

——., *From Yeravada Mandir.*

——., *Hind Swaraj.*

——., *Key to Health.*

——., *Sarvodaya.*

——., *Satyagraha in South Africa.*

——., *Truth is God.*

——., *Sarvodaya*, Navajivan Publishing House, Ahmedabad.

Gangal, S.C., *The Gandhian Way to World Peace*, Vora & Co., Publishers Pvt., Ltd., Bombay, 1960.

Gregg Richard, B., *The Power of Non-violence*, Navajivan Publishing House, Ahmedabad, 1960.

Hriman, S. Narayan, *Relevance of Gandhian Economics.*

Kantowsky, Detlef, *Sarvodaya—The Other Development*, Vikas Publishing House, New Delhi.

Kantowsky, Detlef, *The Political Philosophy of Mahatma Gandhi and Sarvodaya*, Lakshmi Narayan, Agarwal, Agra, 1972.

Louis Fisher, *Gandhi: His Life and Message.*

Malhotra, S.C., *From Civil Disobedience to Quit India*, Punjab University, Chandigarh, 1979.

Mashruwala, K.G., *Towards Sarvodaya Order*, Navajivan Publishing House, Ahmedabad.

Pyarelal, *Towards New Horizons*, Navajivan Publishing House, Ahmedabad, 1959.

Ramanamurthy, V.V., *Essential Writings of Gandhi*. Gandhi Peace Foundation, New Delhi

Sethi, J.D., *Trusteeship*, The Gandhian Alternative Gandhi Peace Foundation, New Delhi.

Sharma, K.D., Yoga and Naturopathy: The True Science of Healing, *Indian Journal of Traditional Knowledge*, National Institute of Science Communication, New Delhi, Vol. 1 (I), p. 24, 2002.

Sharp, Gene, *The Politics of Non-violent Action*, Porter Sargent Publishers, Boston, 1975.

——., *Gandhi Wields the Weapon of Moral Power*, Navajivan Publishing House, Ahmedabad, 1960.

Shridharani, *War without Violence*.

Soman, R.J., *Peaceful Industrial Relations—Their Science and Technique*, Navajivan Publishing House, Ahmedabad, 1959.

Tandon, Vishwanath, *Sarvodaya After Gandhi*, Navajivan Publishing House, Ahmedabad.

Tandon, Vishwanath, *The Social and Political Philosophy of Sarvodaya after Gandhi*, Sarva Seva Sangh Prakashan, Varanasi, Rajghat, 1965.

Unnithan, T.K.N., *Gandhi and Social Change*, Rawat Publications, Jaipur, 1956.

18

Constructive Work: Futuristic Trends

We are racing towards the twenty-first century. The closer we get to the next century the greater becomes the need to understand what awaits us in the future and to foresee it in order to be better prepared for the twenty first century. There are many institutions in the world that conduct forecasts of the future. Gandhian Institutions, in particular must be faced with the addressing the issues relating to the Constructive Programmes as designed by Gandhiji in the fourth decade of the twentieth century. It will be almost sixty years by 2000 A.D., since the Constructive Programmes of Gandhiji came into practice. The core of the programme is the synthesis between the material and moral advancement of human society.

Present Scenario

Serious and sustained threads to the survival of the environment and the well being of the human kind pose the greatest challenge to the 21st century. There is perhaps no other hope for the strife-torn world, not only in the 21st century but for all centuries to come, but to accept the Gandhian paradigm for establishing a qualitatively better, sustainable social order nationally and globally. Let us enter the dawn of the 21st century realizing the need of constructive programmes and resolving to do what we can to improve the quality of human life. What a different 21st century it would be, if constructive programmes are in full swing.

Nelson Mandela's prophetic words that the twenty-first century belongs to Gandhi appear to be more than a mere ripple among to-day's intelligentsia. The International Community is increasingly turning to Gandhi who was a phenomenon of this century. There is greater awareness of the Gandhian model of development and almost everywhere, political pundits, economic experts and even religious leaders are analyzing the Gandhian model and Constructive Programmes with considerable interest. No doubt, Constructive Programme would be the heart of Gandhian Revolution in the centuries to come. According to Gandhi, the Constructive Programme is the truthful and non-violent way of winning *Purna Swaraj*. If the Constructive Programme could be successfully worked out, the end of it would be the wholesome independence we want. Gandhi launched a movement of Constructive Programme for economic betterment and for improving the tenor of social life for generation after generations. The Gandhian Constructive Programme was a movement of the people, by the people, for the people. Sarvodaya movement headed by the Gandhi Peace award winner Dr. A.T. Ariaratne in Sri Lanka is a living example for Constructive Programme. There are some outstanding Gandhian Institutions in India to show the way for constructive work.

Creative Programme

The Constructive Programme was the instrument of creative revolution. Gandhi's Creative Revolution was a political, economic, educational, social and moral revolution the grandest creative revolution the world has ever seen culminating in one of the greatest political triumphs of history—without blood-shed and without rancour. For half of a century and more the Gandhian Constructive Programme was the only testament of hope for our village masses and they have never once gone back to their earlier past of despair. Gandhi himself drew immense strength from the awakened masses of the villages as he stroke blow after blow at the mighty edifice of British rule in India and ultimately shattered it. The memory and experience of the Constructive Programmes never died out from the memory of the people. The Constructive Programme is central to the understanding of Gandhi's concept of *Swaraj*, which was for him a step towards the ultimate goal of "*Ramraj*", the kingdom of God, where an equal share was given "even Unto This Last". In short, Constructive Programme was a revolutionary programme, which changed the landscape of life.

Principles of Constructive Programme

1. It is performed on its own accord. It is purely a moral action which strengthens morality in man.
2. Co-operation and mutual aid are the importance of constructive work. Voluntariness and sharing are the core of constructive activities.
3. Self-reliance and self-help is another important principle of Constructive Programme.
4. The fourth principle of Constructive Programme is building from below.
5. Constructive Programme is the concrete expression of the spirit of non-violence.
6. Decentralisation is another important principle of Constructive Programme.

The Content

Constructive Programme is an integral part of non-violence and it is essentially village work. The eighteen items, which Gandhiji included in the programme were indispensable for the emancipation of the nation through non-violence, Gandhi wrote a small booklet, titled "Constructive Programme—Its meaning and place" on the train from Sevagram to Bardoli. He had listed the following original thirteen items in the year 1941. (1) Communal Unity, (2) Removal of Untouchability; (3) Prohibition; (4) *Khadi*; (5) Village Industries; (6) Village sanitation; (7) *Nai Talim* or Basic Education, (8) Adult Education, (9) Uplift of Women, (10) Education in Health and Hygiene, (11) Provincial Languages, (12) National Language, (13) Promotion of Economic Enqality. In 1945, Gandhi added five more items: (1) *Kisans*, (2) Labour, (3) *Adivasis*, (4) Lepers, (5) Students.

After Gandhiji's death, the following items were added by his followers to strengthen the movement:

(1) Cow protection (2) Nature cure, (3) *Bhoodan*, (4) *Gramdan*, (5) *Shanti Sena*. Gandhi's abstract ideas immediately took concrete forms in his 19-point Constructive Programme which was the blue-print for social resurgence, the espousal of *Sarvadharma Samabhava* (equal respect for all religions), the craft based, skill oriented, value creating *Nai Talim* (new education), the trusteeship concept, decentralized planning, local self-government, village self-sufficiency all of which were all-embracing frame of the non-violent revolution aimed at a new social order.

New Items in the Future

Moreover, the list is not complete and new items can be added as and when necessary. The items may be named which required equal attention towards the twenty, first century; (1) Population Control, (2) Resource Exhaustion, (3) Pollution, (4) Afforestation, (5) Restoration of Ecology, (6) Prevention of profiteering, (7) Prevention of hoarding, (8) Prevention of black markets, (9) Prevention of Smuggling, (10) Prevention of Corruption, (11) Electoral Reform, (12) Prevention of Aids, (13) Moral or Spiritual Education, (14) Home for the homeless, (15) Prevention of Disability and Welfare of the Disabled, (16) Removal of hunger, (17) Service to Refugees, (18) Rehabilitation of the Prisoners, (19) Child and bonded labour, (20) Family Welfare, (21) Prevention of Beggary, (24) Protection for the victims of inter-caste marriage, (25) Prevention of suicides, (26) Uplift of slum dwellers, (27) Rain Water Harvesting, (28) HIV/AIDS prevention.

Significance of the Programme

Of these Gandhiji attached the greatest importance to the economic items and particularly to *Khadi*. Gandhiji considers economic problems in terms of the moral well-being of man. His economic outlook is determined by the ideals of non-possession, non-stealing, bread-labour and *swadeshi*. India's future lies in the practice of *swadeshi*. The future of India is intrinsically connected with the future of its villages. There are ever increasing problems. With courage, conviction and abiding faith in the teaching of Gandhi, we have to tackle the problems of poverty, ignorance, malnutrition, unsanitary conditions, population explosion and the caste system. In every village, there should be a body of servants of the nation engaged in constructive work to achieve social, moral, and economic freedom. It should be organised democratically from the bottom upwards. Five adult constructive workers should form a unit. Two contiguous Panchayats should elect a leader. Fifty first-grade leaders should elect a second-grade leader and so on till they covered the entire country. In this way, Panchayati Raj bodies can play a vital role in the Constructive work and service. In the centuries to come, we may encourage 'Service-worship" instead of "Leader-worship" so as to make the upcoming centuries as "Constructive Service". In order to imbibe the spirit of service among youths, "Indian Constructive Service" (ICS) cadre may be created in the schools, colleges and villages. The existing (NSS) "National Service Scheme" in the colleges and schools may be renamed as the (NCS) "National Constructive Service" or (ICS) "Indian Constructive Service" in the future. Further, we may observe 21st century as a century of Constructive Programmes as an integral part of Non-violence.

In conclusion, it may be emphasized that the lamp of life will burn high in the huts of the world community only when the Constructive Programmes are in full swing.

19

Creative Programmes for Peace

The following are the peace programmes suggested in the New Millennium so as to maintain Peace and harmony:

Programmes for Peace

- Praying with 2000 youth for peace by 2000 A.D.
- Organizing an inter-religious prayer with 2000 youth.
- Organizing world youth conference with 2000 youth representing 200 from each of the ten major religions.
- Organizing 2000 kms. "Drive for Peace" from south to north with two hundred dedicated youth.
- A massive peace march involving 2000 youth from all religions.
- Conducting *Poojas/Bhajans* in 2000 temples/churches/ mosques with 2000 spiritual youth.
- *Weekly School of Non-violence*: Non-violence is the focal point of teachings of great masters. Such a weekly school may provide a capsule of peace and non-violence for the youth. The ultimate aim of the school is to help the participants in solving the present day problems in a non-violent way.
- *"Each One, Meet One for Peace"*: for example: A member of a caste 'A' can meet a member of another caste 'B' and they can mobilize a group for peace and harmony.
- *Village Get-together*: Every month, on a full moon day, a community gathering may be encouraged. Leaders of all caste groups in a village will come to the common platform/village assembly and they may sort out any problems cropping from time-to-time.

- *Community Prayer*: Congregational prayer may be conducted and all the children, youth, women and elders could participate in it. Each caste group will take care of each week and there could be recitation from spiritual texts, like *Gita, Bible* and *Quran*.
- *Cycle Rally/Bullock Cart Rally for Peace*: May be encouraged by involving youth in the village.
- *Peace March*: Within the village a march covering 3 to 5 villages could be organized involving all caste groups and community leaders.
- *Peace Club*: Existing youth club in the village may act as peace club and *rasikar narpani mandrams* (means Cine Actors Association in villages) may be encouraged to promote peace.
- *Peace Slogans and Quotations*: It may be displayed in the public walls of a village.
- *Zone of Peace*: Every village/panchayat must be recognised as a primary zone of peace and any area affected by violence may be declared as an anti-zone of peace. Anti-zone of peace must be given priority and it must be diagnosed with utmost care.
- *Weapon-free Village*: Door to door searches within the village must be carried out so as to create weapon-free village. Any person/family found possessing dangerous weapon must be taken into task. Government should clearly specify item of weapons that each family/village may posses. So that life killing weapons will not be used for the communal violence.
- Traditional Peace Workers in the villages may be identified and their techniques for peace and harmony may be made known to others.
- *Village Peace Brigade*: It is necessary to have a village peace brigade (*Shanti Sena* Unit) in every village. A village where youth club exists may form peace brigade from the existing unit. Village peace brigade will undertake both preventive and curative aspects of the village conflicts. It will not allow any problem reaching

the police and the court. Besides, it will involve in the development programmes of the village.

- *Bala Shanti Sena*: It means children's peace brigade. Such a unit could be established in the elementary school and with the non-school children attending the non-formal education centers.
- *Joint Caste Council Meeting*: Although we believe in casteless society, the villagers may be advised including the urban areas to have joint caste council meetings with a view to exchange views among themselves and to discuss the minutes details relating to their community.
- *Sports and Games*: At the village level, sports and games may be promoted through the district youth centers (Nehru Yuva Kendra) with a view to involve all the caste groups.
- *Zero Conflict Village*: On an average 10-12 quarrels/skirmishes/conflicts within a village take place in a month. Such a petty quarrels may lead to bigger conflicts. In order to encourage zero conflict at the grassroots level, a suitable award may be given to the village where no conflict is observed.
- *A Register (Calendar) of Conflicts*: Every village should be encouraged to maintain a Diary of conflicts both minor and major. So that one can trace out the origin of any type of violence.
- *Communal Harmony Wing*: Like a police wing for prohibition, there could be a wing for communal harmony within the police force and such a wing should not use any weapons and they will act like a *Shanti Sainiks*. The only weapon is love.
- A training school for peace and harmony may be conducted in every District.
- *Inter-religious Festival (IRF)*: Like any other village festival, inter-religious festival may be organized once in six months or once a year. All religions can take part in it.
- *Training for Youth in Peace and Non-violence*: Like a

military training, every youth in a village may be trained in peace an non-violence.

- *Inter-dining*: Peace tea party may be encouraged.
- *District Peace Academy* (*DPA*) may be created specially or a wing in the District Collectorate may be created with a team of trained peace workers to look after communal clashes in the district and maintain a documentation cell relating to the communal harmony and peace.
- *Makkal Nala Paniyalar as Samuthaya Amaithi Paniyalar*: As on today, there are about 13,000 people's welfare workers in Tamil Nadu and they were appointed in the year 1990. All these workers may be oriented towards peace and harmony.
- *Peace Education through Adult Education*: Adult Education Centre (AEC) may function as Peace Education Centre (PEC). Curriculum on peace and harmony may be included in the syllabus on adult education.
- *Peace Prayer Club*: There are prayer clubs praying for the welfare of individuals falling sick as observed in the weekly Tamil magazines like *Kumudam* and *Ananda Vikatan*. The same prayer club may also conduct prayer for communal harmony.
- *Defender of Peace Award*: Such of those who dedicated their life for peace and harmony may be recognized with an award and citation on the occasions like Sarvodaya Day or International Peace Day.
- *Padayatra or Peace Pilgrim*: There was a lady who walked 5,000 miles for peace and harmony under the banner of "peace pilgrimage". Similarly, individual *padayatras* or group *padayatras* may be undertaken in the riot-hit villages.
- *Vigilance Committee*: A strict vigilance committee may be constituted to monitor village conflicts.
- *Shanti Sena Training Camp*: A periodical *Shanti Sena* training programmes could be conducted. Such training will provide a methodology for conflict resolution.

- *Slogans for Peace*: "Say 'yes' to Non-violence" and "Say 'no' to Violence" campaigns may be organized.
- *Peace News*: Newspapers keep on highlighting only news relating to violence. The same paper could highlight peace work being carried out.
- *Cinemas*: Movies highlighting violence should be curbed, cine actors and actresses will appeal to the people to work for harmony.
- *Cinema Slides*: Local cinema theatres will prepare slides on peace and screen it. So that the message will reach the heart of the village.
- *Peace Songs*: It will be played throughout to heal the heart of the affected.
- *Vahana Yatra*: A team of peace workers will go in a vehicle from one village to another village with a peace message. The team will look after relief measures.
- Mobile school of peace in villages through youth.
- *Peace Bus*: The peace bus technique will create peace in the riot-hit areas. The bus will carry effective speakers and the prayer group to organize street plays. Peace bus will literally reach the doorsteps of the village.
- *Peace and Academic Curriculum*: No regular school is giving peace education. Peace values are not taught for the benefit of younger generation. One of the subjects or some lessons on peace will be prescribed in the school curriculum.
- *Highlights of Violence*: Evil-effects and side effects of violence may be highlighted through media or through the distribution of leaflets. The consequences of violence abroad may also be brought to the notice of younger generation.
- *Counselling Services*: Personal counselling may be provided and individuals may be given an opportunity to release their tension.
- *Peace Begins with Neighbours*: All the neighbours come together and plan for peace. Periodical family gathering/get-together may be encouraged.
- *Sponsors of Violence*: A deliberate sponsors of violence

or donors of violent groups may be identified and to prevent to violence by way of arresting the flow of money for violence.

- *Everybody is a Peace Worker*: We should float the idea among the public that everybody can play the role of peace worker. From servant maid to scavenger and bus conductor to office goer can be a peacemaker. Manchester College in USA advocates that bank worker/manager could be a peace worker.
- *Human Chain for Peace and Harmony*: Human chain at the village level must be tried instead in the big cities/towns. Human chain should emanate from the heart.
- *T-Shirt or Banian for Peace*: Now-a-days plenty of T-Shirts and *banians* with colourful pictures are available in the market. Those T-Shirts may be used to carry the peace message.
- *Peace Flag*: Every village is used as the heart of party flags. In order to bring an understanding between the parties and caste groups, a peace flag may be hoisted in the village involving all for harmonious living.
- *Mobile Peace Centre*: A mobile team in each block/district may go round and identify sensitive areas (red spots). It generates ideas and supply materials on peace.
- Peace Ring may be exchanged between the community leaders.
- *Peace Posters*: A suitable peace posters may be displayed in the important places to the attention of the public.
- Peace Pillar or Peace Park may be created wherever possible.
- Peace Arches may be erected to serve as a reminder of the public.
- *Pledge for Peace*: A peace pledge in vernacular may be administered to the public in the village.
- *Weekly Medical Camp for Peace*: A medical camp, as a novel experiment may be conducted every week in one village affected by the caste and communal flare-up, to install confidence in the minds of the poor and

downtrodden and maintain unity among the villagers. The medical camp would enable the villagers to share all information on the activities of the anti-social elements with police and help put an end to illegal activities. Such camps would help us in establishing a friendly relationship with the public and know their problems, besides, the members of the rival communities, who have not seen eye-to-eye since trouble broke out could stand in the same queue to get treatment. (*The Hindu*, September 22, 1997, p. (4)

Involvement of Children for Peace

- Leadership school for peace and development.
- Introducing Gandhi to school children.
- Imparting inter-religious knowledge.
- A booklet highlighting importance of all religions with background pictures may be made available.
- Encouraging children to collect pictures of inter-religious leader.
- Highlighting significant contributions of inter-religious leaders: Each week, each leader.
- To conduct yoga/meditation classes.
- Preparing of *Shanti Sena* caps and present to children.
- Display board for "Thought for the day on Gandhi and Peace".
- Role play "Training how to solve children's conflict by themselves".
- Preparation of a statement showing all details regarding minor conflicts among school children during school hours.
- Convening monthly/quarterly meeting of *Shanti Sena* Programme for coordinators from different schools.
- Conducting inter-religious tours.
- Taking children to all temples/church/mosque on rotation basis.
- *Shanti Sena* subscription fees Rs. 5 per quarter.

- Organizing school *Shanti Sena* rally.
- Cultivating the habit of wearing *khadi* among children—maintaining any day as '*Khadi* day' in a week.
- Celebration of peace festival—all religious parents will gather in the school.
- Teaching "Swimming for Children" and "Traffic Regulation".
- Cultivating savings habit—How Gandhi was economical?
- Imparting poverty education to affluent children.
- Organizing peace exhibition.
- Elocution/Essay competitions on peace science.
- Encouraging children to open "Sarvodaya patra" for peace at home.
- Children's *Shramdan* programme.
- Teaching inter-religious songs.
- Regulating marching and drilling.
- Training in first aid.
- Arranging films and documentaries on Gandhi/ communal harmony and evils of conflicts.
- Creating an informal dialogue with leaders involved in the process of conflict resolution.
- Preparing skits/drama on various problems and conflicts.
- Organizing group peace games.
- Children's rally for peace.

Summer Courses

- Gandhi Summer School for Children (GSSC).
- Young Peace Workers Scheme or Young Peace Scientist Scheme (YPSS).
- Summer Course for Young Constructive Workers (SCYCW).
- Summer Mobile School of Peace (SMSP).
- Summer Spiritual Camp for Youth (SSCY).

- Summer Inter-religious Dialogue (SIRD).
- Summer Youth Festival (SYF).
- Summer Trekking for Youth (STY).
- Summer Discourses on *Gita/Bible*/ and *Quran* for youth.
- Summer Institute of Youth Development and Peace (SIYDP).
- Summer Course on Handicrafts, Photography and Paintings.

Have a fun in the summer and bite philosophy in the middle.

20

Gandhi's Thought for Ending World Crisis

- A born democrat is a born disciplinarian
- Act locally and think globally
- A calculating mind cannot attain self-realisation
- A devotee is ever absorbed in God
- A good man's thought never goes in vain
- A good thought is like fragrance
- A keen sense of honour turns every privation into a joy
- A life of service must be one of humility
- A man cannot borrow faith or courage from others
- A man without an ideal is like a ship without a rudder
- A mind consciously unclean becomes clean by fasting
- A nation's culture resides in the hearts and soul of the people
- A needless word is also a violation of truth
- A policy may be changed, a creed can not
- A pure fast, like duty, is its own reward
- A religion worth the name does not admit of any coercion
- A *Satyagraha* bids good-bye to fear
- A servant of the people never needs to offer defence
- A slave has no freedom even to do the right thing
- A thoughtless life is like that of a beast
- A troubled mind causes more suffering than an ulcer
- A true pacifist is a true *Satyagrahi*

- A true source of rights is duty
- A wise man attains peace only through renunciation
- A word uttered from a pure heart is never in vain
- A word uttered never hurts ultimately
- A worthy heir always adds to the legacy that he receives
- A wrong ceases to be wrong only when it is righted
- Adversity is the crucible in which friendship is tested
- *Ahimsa* abhors sects. It discovers unity in diversity
- *Ahimsa* and truth are as my two lungs
- *Ahimsa* is an attribute of the brave
- *Ahimsa* is not a policy with me, but a creed, a religion
- *Ahimsa* is the farthest limit of humility
- Alone can be a leader, who never loses hope
- All true art is an expression of the soul
- All true art must help the soul to realize it
- An egotistical utterance should always be regarded as false
- As we approach our ideal, we become more truthful
- Be your own judge and you will be truly happy
- Beauty lies not in complexion, but in truth alone
- Belief in God is the corner-stone of all religions
- Belittling one's mother-tongue is like disparaging one's mother
- Better to die once than to die daily
- Blindness in a leader is unpardonable
- Character is more eloquent than speech
- Chastity needs no purdah, it needs only God's protection
- Confession of error works like a broom, sweeps away filth. Confession does no less
- Confession of one's guilt purifies and uplifts
- Cowards have no sense of justice
- Death is a friend, which brings deliverance from sufferings

- Debts are redeemed by deeds, not by words
- Deeds like seeds take their own time to fructify
- Demands of equity supersede the letter to law
- Despair corrodes man
- Dirt is misplaced matter
- Disbelief is a treacherous mate
- Discipline is learnt in the school of adversity
- Disciplined agitation is the condition of national growth
- Divine guidance often comes when the horizon is the blackest
- Do not crave to know the views of others, nor base your intent thereon; to think independently for oneself is a sign of fearlessness
- Do not listen to rumour; but, if you do, do not believe it
- Do what you think is your duty
- Each one prays according to his own light
- Education, which does not mould character, is absolutely worthless
- Envy devours him who harbours it
- Even a minute wasted is irrecoverable
- Even if he is your relation, do not try to hide his faults
- Every individual is a mobile temple
- Every one has a divine spark of truth
- Everything is right and proper in its place
- Evil by itself has no legs to stand upon
- Evil thoughts are also a sign of illness; let us therefore avoid evil thought
- Faith alone is the sun of life
- Faith demands no proof
- Faith is tested when situation is most difficult
- Faith steers the ship
- Faith transcends reason, but it is not opposed to it
- Fear vanishes only with the annihilation of the ego
- Fearlessness is the first requisite of spirituality

- For a fighter the fight itself is victory
- Freedom is not for the faint-hearted
- Gift of life is the greatest of all gifts
- Give all, gain all
- Keep all, lose all
- Give up mental laziness and do some basic thinking
- God alone can take life, because he alone gives it
- God alone knows what tomorrow will bring
- God is omnipresent, hence it is that he speaks to us through stones, trees, insects, birds, beasts etc
- God is our helm as well as our helmsman
- God needs no reminder
- God never answers the prayers of arrogant
- God never forsakes him, whose surrender to him is complete
- God sometimes does try to help utmost those, whom he wishes to bless
- God turns his back on those who quarrel among themselves
- God watches us all not with a view to punish but to chasten
- Good is self-existent, evil is not
- Government that exists by terror does not deserve to exist at all
- Great caution is necessary when a man represses his nature
- Guidance is not dictatorship
- Hate is supplest form of violence
- He alone can offer sacrifice, who is pure, fearless and worthy
- He alone knows the charm of solitude, who has deliberately taken to it
- He alone who truly serves is a good house holder. He goes on giving without expectation of return
- He, who concentrates on any one thing with singleness

of purpose, will ultimately acquire the capacity to do everything

- He, who denies the existence of God denies his own
- He, who does not know the art of living, cannot know the art of dying
- He, who does not labour and yet eats, eats stolen food
- He, who doubts the existence of God, perishes
- He, who finds faults in others, cannot see his own
- He, who does not know himself is lost
- He, who forgets God forgets himself
- He, who harps on his woes, multiplies them manifold
- He, who has all but God on his side, has nothing
- He, who has God on his side, has all
- He, who has not in him the quality of infinite patience, cannot observe non-violence
- He who in his distress turns to God is not troubled by any fear
- He, who is face to face with God, does not speak, indeed, he cannot
- He who is face to face with the God does not speak
- He, who is not upset by bad news will not be elated over good news
- He, who is the dirt of everybody's feet is near to God
- He, who lacks peace and firmness, cannot realize God
- He, who loses his individually, loses all
- He, who remembers everything else, but forgets life
- He, who remembers God, can afford to forget everything
- He, who serves the poor, is great in the eyes of God
- He, who treads the path of truth, never stumbles
- He, who walks in tune with the rhythm of life is never weary
- He, who wants to please all, will please none
- How shall we please God, how praise him? By serving his creature: man

- How wrong it is to ask others to be clean, when we ourselves remain unclean
- Humility is the key to quick success
- I am not consistent with the past, I am consistent with the truth
- I do not believe that the end justifies the means
- I have no weapon but love to wield authority over anyone
- I know where I stand and have a strong belief in myself
- If a man is in distress, the key to his happiness lies in labour
- If capital is power, so is work
- In faith there is no room for despair
- If God loves you, what does it matter if you are rejected by men?
- If God resides in every heart, then who dares hate whom?
- If I am to die by the bullet of a madman, I must do so smiling
- If the inside is clean, the outside is bound to be so
- If we do not give up our ideal, the ideal will never forsake us
- If we obey the law of God, we need no man-made laws
- If we will take care of to day, God will take care of tomorrow
- If you have the will, there is sure to be the way
- If you say inner beauty, the outer will pale into insignificance
- Illness should not beset one whose body and mind are wholly sound
- Imitation is sincerest flattery
- In complete non-violence, there is complete absence of hatred
- In egoism lies all trouble

- In faith there is no room for despair
- In the dictionary of *Satyagraha* there is no enemy
- Industrialism is going to be a curse for mankind
- Inner strength grows by prayer
- Intuition is lame if it is not supported by reason
- Irregularity never goes well with non-attachment
- It is irreligion to give the religious sanction to a brutal custom
- It is man's habit to forget his own faults and see those of others
- It is not possible to see God face to face unless you crucify the flesh
- It is possible to endure a diseased body, but not a diseased mind
- It is sin to reject anyone as helpless, who has God for his support
- It is sinful to multiply one's wants unnecessarily
- It is unmanly for any person to claim superiority on a fellow being
- Just as drop-by-drop the lake fills up, so also every minute of sincere prayer nourishes the soul
- Just as I have the right to eat and drink, so also have I the right to do my work in my own way—this is *swaraj*
- Just time spent in service is the only fruitful life
- Justice without generosity may easily become shylock justice
- Keep all, lose all
- Let us fear God and we shall cease to fear man
- Let us not think of big things, but of good ones
- Life and death are like the two sides of a coin
- Life is an endless service of experiments
- Life is not for making money
- Life is not for merry-making
- Life is unreal, death is real

- Life persists in the midst of destruction
- Life spent in service is the only fruitful life
- Living with God, there are no difficulties
- Loyalty to the country is always subordinate to loyalty to God
- Lying is the mother of violence
- Man can move mountains by faith
- Man finds himself by losing his self
- Man himself is the cause of his happiness as well as his misery
- Man is not all body but he is something definitely higher
- Man is the embodiment of his thoughts
- Man is truly known by the humility of his heart
- Man is where his mind is, not where his body is
- Man must never suppress his inner voice even if he stands alone
- Man often becomes what he believes himself to be
- Man or any living being is a part of the divine
- Man spoils matters much more by speech than by silence
- Man's capacity for self-deception is strange
- Mere confession of wrong doesn't erase it
- Mind is at the root of all sensuality
- Millionaires, who earn without work, are parasites
- Misunderstanding lies in distrust
- More people die of worry than of natural causes
- More potent than the spoken word is a pure thought
- My definition of true *shastra* is the chosen word that gives us life
- My patriotism is subservient to my religion
- Nature cure implies an ideal mode of life
- Neither do nor read anything without understanding it
- Never be stirred by passion
- No joy can compare with the joy of doing one's duty quietly

- No sacrifice is worth the name unless it is a joy
- Nobody progresses without opposition
- Noise does not cancel noise, silence does
- Non-cooperation is not a hymn of hate
- Non-cooperation with evil is a sacred duty
- Non-cooperation with evil is as much a duty as is co-operation with good
- Non-violence like charity must begin at home
- Not to do evil is the only truth of life
- Nothing can work without rules
- Nothing is ever achieved without toil
- Nothing is impossible for a true devotee
- Nothing is impossible for pure love
- Nothing the heart gives away is gone; it is kept in the hearts of others
- Nothing turns out right so long as there is no harmony between body, mind, and soul
- One does not become dull by remaining quiet in meditation
- We must never try to impose one's views on others
- One ounce of practice is worth tones of learning
- One perfect man can dispel untruth even though the untruthful be legion
- Only he can be a leader who never loses hope
- Only he who is prepared to suffer can pray to God
- Opposition makes the man
- Our existence is purely momentary
- Our greatest enemy is not the foreigner, nor anyone else our enemies are we ourselves; that is, our desires
- Our salvation can only come through the farmer
- Outward peace is useless without inner peace
- Pain is often the precision of pleasure
- Patience and perseverance overcome mountains
- Performance of one's duty should be independent of public opinion

- Physical weakness is not the real weakness; weakness of the mind alone is the real weakness
- Politics, divorced of religion, has absolutely no meaning
- Power comes from sincere service
- Practice makes perfect
- Prayer changes things
- Prayer is like a spiritual bath
- Prayer needs a heart, not a voice without the heart, words have no meaning
- Prayer needs no speech
- Pride swallows up a man completely
- Public opinion alone can keep a society pure and healthy
- Pure love removes all weariness
- Pure thought is far more potent than speech
- Purity asks for no external protection
- Purity is tested only when pitted against impurity
- Real weakness is internal, not outward
- Reflection shows that heaven is here on our earth, not in the sky above
- Religion is no religion if it becomes mechanical
- Religion is not a garment to be cast off at will
- Religion is outraged when an outrage is perpetrated in its name
- Religion is that which comprehends all
- Religions are meant to tame our savage nature, not to let them loose
- Renunciation is true enjoyment
- Revolution is exclusive property of no nation, no tribe
- Sacrifice is fruitful only to the extent that it is pure
- Sacrifice with regret is no sacrifice
- Satisfaction lies in the effort, not in the attainment
- *Satyagraha* is essentially a weapon of the truthful
- *Satyagraha* is nothing but '*tapasya*' for truth

- Self-indulgence leads to destruction
- Self-respect knows no consideration
- Self-suffering is the truest test of sincerity
- Selfishness and fear must go if one is to realize God
- Selfishness keeps us worrying forever
- Selfless action is a source of strength
- Service without humility is selfishness and egotism
- Silence inspired by fear is no silence
- Silence is a part of spiritual discipline of a votary of truth
- Silence is above all
- Silence is essential for one, whose life is an incessant search for truth
- Slavery to the environment dulls a man's mind
- Suffering willingly undergone never harms the sufferer
- Suicide is a sin
- Superstition and truth cannot go together
- Suppression of women is a denial of *ahimsa*
- *Swadeshi* in the purest form is the acme of universal service
- *Swaraj* for the masses is impossible without the charkha
- *Swaraj* is the abandonment of the fear of death
- *Swaraj* won without sacrifice cannot last long
- Sweets are the fruits of patience
- Tear down the purdah with one mighty effort
- That government is best which governs the least
- That which does not serve in practice, how can it be religion?
- That which looks for mercy from an opponent is not non-violence
- The advantages of solitude can be realized only by experience
- The alter of literature claims special incense
- The blind one is he, who hides his shortcomings

- The breach of one rule inevitably leads to the breach of other rule
- The essence of religion is morality
- The first service is latrine cleaning
- The force of arms is powerless when matched against the force of love
- The greatness of a person lies in his heart, not in his head; that is intellect
- The greatest men of the world have always stood alone
- The golden rule is to dare to do the right at any cost
- The heart has no language. It speaks to the heart
- The heart's earnest and pure desire is always fulfilled
- The human body is like a musical instrument
- The ideal that marriage aims at is of spiritual union
- The joy of life lies in divesting oneself of life's cares
- The light of knowledge can never dawn on the proud
- The non-attached person cannot own anything
- The policy of tit for tat is not conducive to friendship
- The real ornament of woman is her character, her purity
- The religion knows no territorial limits
- The right that accrues from the performance of duty endures
- The scale of religion is in the heart
- The sole aim of journalism should be service
- The soul dries up without the company of the God
- The spirit becomes unclean if the heart is not washed with prayer
- The victories of truth have never been won without risks
- The way of non-violence and truth is as sharp as razor's edge
- There are occasions when silence is wisdom
- There can be no perception without steadfastness of mind
- There can be no safety for us save in the lap of God

- There is a divine purpose behind every physical calamity
- There is a lot of difference between living faith and a mere desire for faith
- There is goodness and greatness in simplicity, not in wealth
- There is limit to violent action
- There is no room for patronage among equals
- There is no sin like cowardice
- There is not a single moment in life when man cannot serve
- There is nothing more glorious than to die whilst you are striving
- There is nothing that can't be attained by patience
- There is victory in death
- Thought pierces even a wall of steel
- To a starving person, bread alone will be God
- To be guilty of a lapse small or big is certainly bad, but to hide it is even worse
- To be in a minority is often a blessing
- To conceal ignorance is to increase it
- To confess an error or sin as soon as it is discovered is to purge it out
- To enjoy life one should give up the lure of life
- To entertain good thoughts is one thing, to act upon them is another
- To make an allegation is one thing, to prove it is another
- To remember God and forget others is to see God even in them
- To serve is my religion
- To speak truth, you have to weigh your words
- To try to suppress another is always suicidal
- To utter a *mantra* without knowing its value is unmanly
- True beauty after all consists in purity of heart
- True happiness does not come from obtaining what one

likes. It comes from cultivating a liking for what one dislikes

- Truth and love are faces of same coin
- Truth is God and the way to him is non-violence
- Truth is superior to man's wisdom
- Truth is the exclusive property of no single scripture
- Truth is the law of our being
- Truth is the right destination of God
- Truth should be accompanied by firmness of purpose
- Untouchability poisons Hinduism as a drop of arsenic poisons milk
- Untruth and violence are twin sisters
- Verily, the land belongs to one, who labours on it
- Vice flourishes in darkness it vanishes in the light
- Violence dies when it ceases to evoke response from its object
- Virtue is in fighting alone, be the opponent one or many
- Violence is preferable to importance
- Violence is the weapon of the weak, non-violence is that of the strong
- We become what we yearn after
- We have made ourselves what we are
- We must be true to ourselves
- We seek the company of the good, for that is food for our soul
- What barrier is there that love cannot break
- What does it matter if people look upon us as dreamers!
- What is gained by violence must be lost before superior violence
- What is in the mind must come out, sooner or later
- What one does must be well done
- What seems impossible is not always really so
- When a man lays bare his heart, God enters it
- When a man sleeps under the sky, who can rob him

- When a man works for an ideal, he becomes irresistible
- When all forsake you, God shall be with you against the whole world
- When God cares, why should we be full of cares?
- When man indulge in pleasures, the indulgence consumes the man
- When man realizes himself, he is saved
- When reason and faith are in conflict, it is better to prefer faith
- When *'seva'* (service) wags its tongue it looses all its value
- When the ego dies, the soul awakes
- When the self dies, god fills the void
- When the soul awakes, all sorrow vanishes
- When the world rejects man, God befriends him
- When we give anything, we must give the truest part of ourselves
- Whenever men begin to see beauty in truth, true art emerges
- Where there is fear, there can be no true love
- Where there is fear, there is no religion
- Where there is light there is also shadow
- Wherever the crisis is, the fire of love will melt it
- Why fear death, when its threat is never present
- Why seek outside that which is within you
- With others? Why need there be any reason for that?
- With whom will you be angry?
- With yourself? Do that everyday
- Without selfishness how can there be fearlessness
- You can't lead a true life without suffering
- You may throw dust at the sun, it will not dim its lustre

Bibliography

Ahmad Razi, *Indian Peasant Movement and Mahatma Gandhi*, Shabd Prakashan, Delhi, 1987.

Alexander, Horace, *Gandhi Through Western Eyes*, Asia Publishing House, New Delhi, 1969.

Anjaria, J.J., *An Essay on Gandhian Economics*, Vora and Co., Bombay, 1944.

Appadorai, A., *Documents on Political Thought in Modern India*, Vol. 1, Oxford University Press, New Delhi, 1981.

Arunachalam, K., *Gandhian Approach to Rural Development*, Sarvodaya Ilakkiya Pannai, Madurai, 1981.

Arunachalam, K. and Jiyapragasam S., *Gandhian Techniques for the Liberation of Weaker Sections*, Sarvodaya Ilakkiya Pannai, Madurai, 1987.

Bandyopadhyaya, J., *Social and Political Thought of Gandhi*, Allied Publishers, Calcutta, 1969.

Bakshi, S.R., *Gandhi and His Social Thought*, Criterion Publications, New Delhi, 1986.

Bakshi, S.R., *Gandhi and Dandi March*, Criterion Publications, New Delhi, 1988.

Bakshi, S.R., *Gandhi and Indians in South Africa*, Antique Publishers, New Delhi, 1988.

Bakshi, S.R., *Gandhi and Khilafat*, Gitanjali Publishing House, New Delhi, 1985.

Bakshi, S.R., *Gandhi and Concept of Swaraj*, Criterion Publications, New Delhi, 1988.

Bakshi, S.R., *Gandhi and the Mass Movements*, Atlantic Publishers and Distributors, New Delhi, 1988.

Bakshi, S.R., *Gandhi and Ideology of Non-violence*, Criterion Publications, New Delhi, 1986.

Bharati, K.S., *Socio-Religious Thoughts of Mahatma Gandhi*, Dattsons, Nagpur, 1989.

Bharati, K.S., *The Social Philosophy of Mahatma Gandhi*, Concept Publishing Company, New Delhi, 1991.

Biswas, S.C. (Ed.), *Gandhi: Theory and Practice Social Impact and Contemporary Relevance*, Indian Institute of Advanced Study, Shimla, 1969.

Bose, Anima, *Peace and Conflict Resolution in the World Community*, Vikas Publishing House Pvt. Ltd., 1991.

Bose, Anima, *Dimensions of Peace and Non-violence: The Gandhian Perspective*, Gian Publishing House, New Delhi, 1987.

Bose, N.K., *Gandhiji the Man and His Mission*, Bharatiya Vidya Bhawan, Bombay, 1966.

Bose, N.K., *Selections from Gandhi*, Navajivan Publishing House, Ahmedabad, 1972.

Bose, R.N., *Gandhian Technique and Tradition*, Research Division All India Institute of Social Welfare and Business Management, Calcutta, 1956.

Bose, R.N., *Our Gandhian Heritage*, Bookland Private Limited, Calcutta, 1970.

Brown, M. Judith, *Gandhi Prisoner of Hope*, Oxford University Press, Delhi, 1992.

Chakrabarti, Mohit, *Gandhian Mysticism*, Atlantic Publishers and Distributors, New Delhi, 1989.

Chakrabarti, Mohit, *Gandhian Humanism*, Concept Publishing Company, New Delhi, 1992.

Chatterjee, Partha, *Nationalist Thought and the Colonial World*, Oxford University Press, New Delhi, 1986.

Chatterjee, D.K., *Gandhi and Constitution Making in India*, Associated Publishing House, New Delhi, 1984.

Chaudhury, P.C. Roy, *Gandhiji and International Politics*, Navajivan Publishing House, Ahmedabad, 1970.

Chaudhury, P.C. Roy, *Gandhi and his Contemporaries*, Sterling Publishers Pvt. Ltd., New Delhi, 1986.

Chaudhary, Ramnarayan, *Bapu as I saw him*, Navajivan Publishing House, Ahmedabad, 1959.

Chetty, K.M. Rathnam, *Sarvodaya and Freedom: A Gandhian Appraisal*, Discovery Publishing House, New Delhi, 1991.

Chopra, Pran, *The Sage in Revolt: A Remembrance*, Gandhi Peace Foundation, New Delhi, 1972.

Choudhuri, Manmohan, *Exploring Gandhi*, The Gandhi Peace Foundation, New Delhi, 1987.

Dadhich, Naresh, *Gandhi and Existentialism*, Rawat Publications, Jaipur, 1993.

Dantwala, M.L., *Gandhian Reconsidered*, Padma Publications Ltd., Bombay, 1945.

Datt, D.K., *Social, Moral and Religious Philosophy of Mahatma Gandhi*, Intellectual Book Corner, New Delhi, 1980.

Desai, Mahadev H., *Day-to-Day with Gandhi*, (Secretary's Diary) Sarva Seva Sangh Prakashan, Varanasi, 1973.

Desai, V.A., *Ashram Observers in Action*, Navajivan Publishing House, Ahmedabad, 1955.

Dharmadhikari, Dada, *Philosophy of Total Revolution*, Sarva Seva Sangh Prakashan, Varanasi, 1982.

Diwakar, R.R., *Saga of Satyagraha*, Gandhi Peace Foundation, New Delhi, 1969.

Dutt, Vishnu, *Gandhi, Nehru and the Challenge*, Abhinav Publications, New Delhi, 1979.

Erikson, Erik H., *Gandhi's Truth: On the Origins of Militant Non-violence*, Faber and Faber Limited, London, 1970.

Fischer, Herbert, *Mahatma Gandhi Personality and Leader (of his Time)*, K.P. Bagchi and Company, Calcutta.

Fischer, Louis, *The Essential Gandhi*, George Allen and Unwin Limited, London, 1962.

Fischer, Louis, *The Life of Mahatma Gandhi*, Jonathan Cape, London, 1962.

Galtung, John, *The Struggle for Peace*, Peace Research Centre, Gujarat Vidyapith, Ahmedabad, 1984.

Gandhi, M.K., *Hind Swaraj or Indian Home Rule*, Navajivan Publishing House, Ahmedabad, 1938.

Gandhi, M.K., *An Autobiography or The Story of My Experiments with Truth*, Navajivan Publishing House, Ahmedabad, 1927.

Gandhi, M.K., *Satyagraha in South Africa*, Navajivan Publishing House, Ahmedabad, 1928.

Gandhi, M.K., *Basic Education*, Navajivan Publishing House, Ahmedabad, 1952.

Gandhi, M.K., *To the Perplexed*, Bharatiya Vidya Bhavan, Bombay, 1966.

Gandhi, M.K., *Non-violence in Peace and War*, Vol. I & II, Navajivan Publishing House, Ahmedabad, 1960.

Gandhi, M.K., *Satyagraha (Non-violent Resistance)*, Navajivan Publishing House, Ahmedabad, 1958.

Gangal, S.C., *Gandhian Thought and Techniques in the Modern World*, Criterion Publications, New Delhi, 1988.

Gangarde, K.D. and Misra, R.P., *Conflict Resolution through Non-violence Role of the Universities*, Concept Publishing Company, New Delhi, 1990.

Gangarde, K.D. *Gandhian Ideal Development and Social Change*, Northern Book Centre, New Delhi, 1991.

George, S.K. and Ramachandran G., *The Economics of Peace: The Cause and the Man*, Peace Publishers, New Delhi, 1992.

Ghosh, Sudhir, *Gandhi's Emissary*, Rupa and Co., Calcutta, 1967.

Gujral, M.L., *Thus Spoke Bapu or Dialogues between Gandhi's Spirit and the Scribe*, Gandhi Peace Foundation, New Delhi, 1985.

Hasan, Z., *Gandhi and Ruskin*, Shree Publishing House, New Delhi, 1980.

Hasan, Z., *Gandhi and the Harijans*, Shree Publishing House, New Delhi, 1986.

Holmes, J.H. and Harrington, D.S., *The Enduring Greatness of Gandhi: An American Estimate*, Navajivan Publishing House, Ahmedabad, 1982.

Holmes, J.H., *Gandhi and Non-violence*, Akashdeep Publishing House, New Delhi, 1988.

Horsburgh, H.J.N., *Non-violence and Aggression: A Study of Gandhi's Moral Equivalent of War*, Oxford University Press, London, 1968.

Hunt, James D., *Gandhi and the Non-conformists, Encounters in South Africa*, Promilla & Co. Publishers, New Delhi, 1986.

Hunter, Doris A., and Mallick Krishna, *Non-violence: A Reader in the Ethics of Action*, Gandhi Peace Foundation, New Delhi, 1990.

Huttenback, Robert A., *Gandhi in South Africa: British Imperialism and the Indian Question, 1860-1914*, Cornell University Press, London, 1971.

Iyer, Raghavan, *The Moral and Political Thought of Mahatma Gandhi*, Oxford University Press, Chicago, 1973.

Jack, A. Homer (Ed.), *The Gandhi Reader*, Samata Books, Madras, 1984.

Jain, Pratibha, *Gandhian Ideals Social Movements and Creativity*, Rawat Publications, Jaipur, 1985.

Jesusdasan, Ignative S.J., *A Gandhian Theology of Liberation*, Gujrat Sahitya Prakashan, Anand, 1987.

Joshi, Pushpa, *Gandhi on Women*, Navajivan Publishing House, Ahmedabad, 1988.

Karunakaran, K.P., *Gandhi-Interpretations*, Gitanjali Publishing House, New Delhi, 1985.

Kataria, Sunita, *Gandhi's Reactions to World Affairs*, Kanishka Publishing House, Delhi, 1990.

Keer, Dhananjay, *Mahatma Gandhi: Political Saint and Unarmed Prophet*, Popular Prakashan, Bombay, 1973.

Khanna, Suman, *Gandhi and the Good Life*, Gandhi Peace Foundation, New Delhi, 1985.

Khan, Afaque, *Gandhian Approach to Communalism: A Critical Study*, Ajanta Publications, Delhi, 1986.

Kripalani, K. (Ed.), *All Men are Brothers*, Navajivan Publishing House, Ahmedabad, 1960.

Kripalani, J.B., *Gandhian Thought*, Gandhi Smarak Nidhi, New Delhi, 1961.

Kumarappa, J.C., *Economy of Permanence*, Akhil Bharat Sarva Seva Sangh Publication, Rajghat, Kashi.

Lewis, Martin Deming, *Gandhi Maker of Modern India*, D.C. Health and Company, Boston, 1966.

Lohia, Rammanohar, Marx, *Gandhi and Socialism*, Rammanohar Lohia Samata Vidyalaya Nyasa, Hyderabad, 1978.

Mallick, B.K., *Gandhi—A Prophecy*, Hall The Publisher Ltd., Oxford, 1948.

Mathur, J.S., *Non-violence and Social Change*, Navajivan Publishing House, Ahmedabad, 1977.

Mathur, J.S., *Peace, Non-violence and World Order (Gandhian Perspective)*, Vohra Publishers and Distributors, Allahabad, 1990.

Malhotra, S.L., *Gandhi, Punjab and the Partition*, Publication Bureau, Punjab University, Chandigarh, 1983.

Millser, William Robert, *Non-violence—A Chrestian Interpretations*, George Allen and Unwin Ltd., London, 1964.

Mishra, Anil Dutta, *Fundamentals of Gandhism*, Mittal Publications, New Delhi, 1995.

Mishra, Anil Dutta (Ed.), *Gandhian Approach to Contemporary Problems*, Mittal Publications, New Delhi, 1996.

Misra, K.P. and Gangal, S.C., *Gandhi and the Contemporary World: Studies in Peace and War*, Chanakya Publications, Delhi, 1981.

Mishra, R.P., *Gandhian Model of Development and World Peace*, Concept Publishing Company, New Delhi, 1988.

Mishra, Sweta, *Democratic Decentralisation in India*, Mittal Publications, New Delhi, 1994.

Mishra, S.N., *Rural Development and Panchayati Raj*, Concept Publishing Company, New Delhi, 1980.

Moon, Penderel, *Gandhi and Modern India*, The English Universities Press Ltd., London, 1968.

Mukherjee, Hiren, *Gandhiji: A Study*, People's Publishing House, New Delhi, 1991.

Mukherjee, Subrata and Ramaswamy, Sushila, *Facts of Mahatma Gandhi*, Deep and Deep Publications, New Delhi, 1994.

Nambodiripad, E.M.S., *The Mahatma and the Ism*, People's Publishing House, New Delhi, 1959.

Nanda, B.R., *Gandhi Pan-Islamism Imperialism and Nationalism*, Oxford University Press, Bombay, 1989.

Nanda, B.R., Joshi, P.C., and Krishna Raj, *Gandhi and Nehru*, Oxford University Press, Delhi, 1979.

Narain, Jai, *Economic Thought of Mahatma Gandhi*, Sehgal, New Delhi, 1991.

Narayan, Shriman, *Selected Works of Mahatma Gandhi*, Navajivan Publishing House, Ahmedabad, 1956.

Narayan, Shriman, *Vinoba—His Life and Work*, Popular Prakashan, Bombay, 1970.

Narasimhaiah, C.D. (Ed.), *Gandhi and the West*, University of Mysore, Mysore.

Ostergaard Geoffrey, *Non-violent Revolution in India*, Gandhi Peace Foundation, New Delhi, 1985.

Patel, Jehangir P. and Sykes Marjoril, *Gandhi: His Gift of the Fight*, Friends Rural Centre, Rasulia, 1987.

Patel, C.N., *Mahatma Gandhi in his Gujarati Writings*, Sahitya Academy, New Delhi, 1981.

Patel, V.T. (Ed.), *Studies on Gandhi*, Sterling Publishers Pvt. Ltd., New Delhi, 1983.

Pandey, B.P., *Gandhi Sarvodaya and Organisations*, Chugh Publications, Allahabad, 1988.

Parekh, Bhikku, *Colonialism, Tradition and Reforms: An Analysis of Gandhi's Political Discourse*, Sage Publications, New Delhi, 1989.

Polak, H.S.L., Brailsford, H.N., and Lawrence Lord Pethick, *Mahatma Gandhi the Father of Modern India*, Anmol Publications, New Delhi, 1986.

Prabhu, R.K., and Kelekar, Ravindra, *Truth called Them Differently (Tagore-Gandhi Controversy)*, Navajivan Publishing House, Ahmedabad, 1961.

Prabhu, R.K., and Rao, V.R., *The Mind of Mahatma Gandhi*, Navajivan Publishing House, Ahmedabad, 1967.

Prasad, L.G., *Religion, Morality and Politics according to Mahatma Gandhi*, Classical Publishing Company, New Delhi, 1991.

Prasad, Nageshwar (Ed.), *Gandhi and the Contemporary World*, Radiant Publishers, New Delhi, 1993.

Prasad, K.M., *Sarvodaya of Gandhi*, Raj Hans Publications, New Delhi, 1984.

Prasad, Nageshwar, *Hind Swaraj: A Fresh Look*, Gandhi Peace Foundation, New Delhi, 1985.

Puri, Rashmi Sudha, *Gandhi on War and Peace*, Praeger, New York, 1987.

Pyarelal and Nayar Sushila, *In Gandhiji's Mirror*, Oxford University Press, Delhi, 1991.

Radhakrishnan, S., *Mahatma Gandhi: Reflections on his Life and Work*, Jaico Publishing House, Bombay, 1956.

Radhakrishnan, S. (Ed.), *Mahatma Gandhi 100 Years*, Gandhi Peace Foundation, New Delhi, 1968.

Ram Suresh, *Vinoba and his Mission*, Akhil Bharat Sarva Seva Sangh Prakashan, New Delhi, 1956.

Ramchandran, G. and Mahadevan, T.K., *Quest for Gandhi*, Gandhi Peace Foundation, New Delhi, 1970.

Rani Asha, *Gandhian Non-violence and India's Freedom Struggle*, Shree Publishing House, New Delhi, 1981.

Rao, U.S. Mohan (Ed.), *The Message of Mahatma Gandhi*, Publication Division, Ministry of Information and Broadcasting, Government of India, New Delhi, 1968.

Rao, P. Nagaraja, *Mahatma Gandhi*, Guru Gobind Singh Department of Religious Studies, Panjabi University, Patiala, 1972.

Rao, K.L. Seshagiri, *Mahatma Gandhi and Comparative Religion*, Motilal Banarsidass Publishers, Delhi, 1990.

Rattan, Ram, *Gandhi's Thought and Action*, Kalinga Publications, Delhi, 1991.

Reddy, B.S., and Gandhi Gopalkrishna, *Gandhi and South Africa 1914-1948*, Navajivan Publishing House, Ahmedabad, 1993.

Roy, Ramashray, *Gandhi: Soundings in Political Philosophy*, Chanakya Publications, Delhi, 1984.

Roy, Ramashray, *Contemporary Crisis and Gandhi*, Discovery Publishing House, Delhi, 1986.

Sethi, J.D., *Gandhian Critique of Western Peace Movements*, Chanakya Publications, Delhi, 1989.

Shah, Kantilal, *Vinoba on Gandhi*, Sarva Seva Sangh Prakashan, Varanasi, 1985.

Sharma, Shri Ram, *Gandhi: The Man and the Mahatma*, Rajan, Chandigarh, 1985.

Sharma, Sudarshan, *The Influence of Gandhian Ideology on Indo-Anglian Fiction*, Soni Book Agency, New Delhi, 1982.

Sheean Vincent, *Mahatma Gandhi: A Great Life in Brief*, Publications Division, New Delhi, 1990.

Singh, Ramjee, *Gandhi and the Modern World*, Classical Publishing Company, New Delhi, 1993.

Singh, Ramjee, *Gandhi and the Twenty-first Century*, Peace Publishers, New Delhi, 1993.

Singh, Ramjee, *The Relevance of Gandhian Thought*, Classical Publishing Company, New Delhi, 1988.

Singh, T.P., *Bhoodan and Gramdan in Orissa: An Analytical Study*, Sarva Seva Sangh Prakashan, Varanasi, 1973.

Smith, Adam, *An Inquiry into the Nature and Causes of Wealth of Nations*, The Modern Library, New York, 1937.

Solanki, A.B., *The Technique of Correlation in Basic Education*, Navajivan, Bombay, 1958.

Sonnleitner, Michael W., *Gandhian Non-violence Levels of Satyagraha*, Abhinav Publications, New Delhi, 1985.

Swaminathan, K. and Patel, C.N., *A Gandhi Reader*, Orient Longmen, Madras, 1988.

Tahtinen, Unto, *The Core of Gandhi's Philosophy*, Abhinav Publications, New Delhi, 1979.

Tendulkar, D.G., *Mahatma (Life of Mohandas Karamchand Gandhi)*, The Publications Division, Ministry of Information and Broadcasting, Govenment of India, New Delhi, 1962.

Thakur, Gourikant, *Mahatma Gandhi's Philosophy of Satyagraha*, Kishor Vidya Niketan, Varanasi, 1988.

The Collected Works of Mahatma Gandhi, The Publications Division, Ministry of Information and Broad casting, Government of India, New Delhi, 1969.

Thomson, Mark, *Gandhi and his Ashrams*, Popular Prakashan, Bombay, 1993.

Tikekar, Indu B., *Integral Revolution: An Analytical Study of Gandhian Thought*, Sarva Seva Sangh Prakashan, Varanasi, 1965.

Tondon, Vishwanath, *The Social and Political Philosophy of Sarvodaya after Gandhi*, Sarva Seva Sangh Prakashan, Varanasi, 1970.

Topa, Ishwara, *Ethos of Non-violence*, Navajivan Publishing House, Ahmedabad, 1964.

Unnithan, T.K.N., *Gandhi and Social Change*, Rawat Publications, Jaipur, 1979.

Venkatramani, M.S. and Shrivastava, B.K., *Roosevelt—Gandhi, Churchil*, Radiant Publishers, New Delhi, 1983.

Vir, Dharma, *Gandhi Bibliography*, Gandhi Smarak Nidhi, New Delhi, 1967.

Vinoba, Bhave, *Swaraj Sastra*, Sarva Seva Sangh Prakashan, Varanasi, 1963.

Wadhwan Madhuri, *Gandhi Between Tradition and Modernity*, Deep and Deep Publications, New Delhi, 1991.

Watson, Blanche, *Gandhi and Non-violent Resistance (The Non-Cooperation Movement of India)*, Anmol Publications, New Delhi, 1989.

Watson, Francis and Tennyson Hallam, *Talking of Gandhi*, Sangam Books, Bombay, 1957.
Weber, David R. (Ed.), *Civil Disobedience in America—A Documentary History*, Cornell University Press, Ithaca, 1978.
Weber, Thomas, *Conflict Resolution and Gandhian Ethics*, The Gandhi Peace Foundation, New Delhi, 1991.
Woodcock George, *Gandhi*, Fontana, London, 1972.
Yarker, P.M. (Ed.), *John Ruskin—Unto This Last*, Collins Publishers, London & Glasgow, 1970.

Index

20-point programme target, 177
Academic programmes, 192
Adivasis, 107, 191, 198, 236-237, 269
Adult Education Centres, 196, 275
Adult Education, 42, 107, 190, 215, 217-218, 269, 275
Advisors for Sustainable Development, 162
Agraha, 90-91
Agricultural demonstration centres, 249
Agriculture-based village, 171
Ahimsa, 6-7, 39, 49, 97, 99, 185-186, 209, 219-220, 223, 226, 243, 282, 291
AIDS prevention, 199, 270
Ambedkar, 121
American Museum of Natural History in New York, 164
Andhra Pradesh Sarvodaya Mandal, 247
Anti-Gandhian, 89
Anti-zone of peace, 273
Apex courts, 78
Architect of modern India, 122, 149
Army of Peace, 263
Artificial Limb Centre, 128
Ashram Sisters, 233-234
Autonomy, 119, 121

Bala Shanti Sena, 274
Balwadi centres, 197
Barbarism, 222
Basic education, 14, 105, 107, 146, 186, 190, 196, 214-216, 218, 269
Batlagundu, 243, 257
Bhagvad Gita, 4, 8, 93, 176
Bhoodan, 107, 247-248, 250-255, 260, 270
Biodiversity, 55, 164
Block development schemes, 162
Boycott, 105, 111-113
Bravery, 50, 220, 222
Bread-labour, 14, 88, 101, 271
Brotherhood, 8, 10, 21, 95, 98, 176, 190, 205, 210
  international, 41
  universal, 8, 10
Buddhism, 4, 9-10, 92
Bullock Cart Rally for Peace, 273

Capitalist world, 136
Casteless society, 40, 193, 197, 274
Celibacy, 99-100
Ceylon, 240
Character building, 84, 86-87, 218
Cheema, Shabbir, 160
Christianity, 6, 10, 236
Civil disobedience, 4, 7, 105, 111, 113-115, 203
Civil power, 166
Classless society-liberty, 21

Coalmine workers, 111
College Education, 231
Committee on Administrative Arrangements for Rural Development, 122
Communalism, 80, 121, 183, 241
Communism, 18-21, 252
Community Development Programme, 166, 248
Community participation, 170, 172
  result of, 172
Community welfare organisation, 188
Conceptual analysis of Rural Development, 144
Constitutional Amendment Act, 122-124
Construction Programme, 218
Country liquor shops, 113
Cow protection movement, 243-244
Creative Programmes for Peace, 272
Criminalisation, 73
Culmination, 1, 18
Cultural programmes, 31, 195

Democratic society, 76
Department of Gandhian Thought and Peace Science, 89
Development bureaucracy, 177
Developmental functions, 124
Dharma, 8, 45, 58, 66
Directive Principles, 119, 122
Disabilities, 128-129, 131, 144, 199, 270
  management, 127-131
  prevention, 199, 270
Disabled
  child, 128-129
  youth, 131
Disciplined person, 262
Dissemination, 193
District Peace Academy, 275
Dogmas, 1
Domestic violence, 63
Dysentery, 229-230

Ecological problems, 140
Economic development, 53, 133-134, 167
Economic domination, 91
Economic freedom, 211, 271
Economic order, 17, 35, 43, 191
Economic power, 20, 136
Education in Health and Hygiene, 107, 227, 269
Education system in India, 85
Effective participation, 157
Egalitarian society, 19-20
Election Commission, 74, 78
Elementary education, 42, 196
Environmental protection, 58-59, 139
Environmental threat, 53, 55, 63
Exploitation of villagers, 149

Fasting, 109, 243, 247, 281
Films on Sarvodaya and Gandhi, 45
Financial power, 124
Forest protection, 250
Forgiveness, 50, 102
Formal education, 137
Four-fold development, 87
Free India, 205
Freedom
  moral, 12
  spiritual, 7, 12, 190
Futuristic Trends, 267

Gandhi *Bhawans*, 89
Gandhi Diary, 204, 208, 210-211, 213-214, 217, 227, 230, 232-238
Gandhi education, 87
Gandhi Mandram, 31
Gandhi Peace Prize, 128
Gandhi *Samadhi*, 45
Gandhi *Smarak Nidhi*, 27-28
Gandhi Summer School, 279
Gandhi village development, 150

Gandhi, assassination of, 27, 186
Gandhi free society, 13
Gandhi, Indira, 196
Gandhi, long fasts, 230
Gandhian economics, 59
Gandhian ideology, 198
Gandhian method, 70
Gandhian model, 125, 128
Gandhian movement, 39, 46, 185-186, 259
Gandhian philosophy of *Satyagraha,* 95
Gandhian principle, 89
Gandhian Revolution, 268
Gandhian *Sarvodaya,* 4, 6, 10, 17
Gandhian Thought, Relevance of, 188
Gandhigram, 192-198, 250
Gandhigram Model, 192
Gandhigram Rural Institute, 192
Gita, 2-3, 7-8, 10, 90, 273, 280
Global Framework for Sustainability, 164-165
Global Sustainable Development, 163
Gramdan, 27, 39, 107, 186, 248, 255-256, 259, 261, 270

Handicraft, 14, 214, 216
Harijan Sevak Sangh, 14, 180, 187
Harijan, 40, 141, 180, 194, 202-203, 205-215, 219-222, 227, 233, 235, 237-241, 244-245, 249, 257
Harmony
- communal, 77, 101, 105, 182, 262, 274-275, 279
- international, 22
- religious, 194

Hind Swaraj, 56, 65
Hinduism, 207-210, 217, 225, 243
Holistic concept, 140
Homogeneity, 84
Human chain, 277
Human development index, 162
Hygiene, 107, 191, 197, 227, 244, 269

Independence movement, 230-231
India Science Congress, 145
Indian Home Rule, 4, 38, 139
Indian Journal of Traditional Knowledge, 247
Indianization of social work, 199
Indo-Sri Lanka Peace, 50
Industrialisation, 53-54, 56, 133, 136-137
Integrated education, 216
Integrated Rural Development, 193, 248
International Institute of Rural Reconstruction, 161
International Labour Office, 144
International Peace Day, 275
International Year of Eco-Tourism and Mountains, 168
International Year of *Sarvodaya,* 45
Internationalism and *Ram Rajya,* 15
Inter-religious
- festival, 274
- knowledge, 278
- prayer, 194, 272
- songs, 279
- tours, 278

Inter-University Youth Festival, 37
Islam, 4, 10, 207

Joint Caste Council Meeting, 274

Kasturba Gandhi Memorial Trust, 223
Khaddar, 212
Khadi, 14, 30-32, 106, 139, 146, 190, 195, 203, 211-212, 254, 262, 269-270, 279
- and *Shanti Sena,* 27, 186
- programme, 106
- workers, 251

Kisan movements, 235

Koonankurichi village, 173

Land reforms, 253, 255
Landless labourers, 234-235
Leaders
  inter-religious, 278
  national, 10
  religious, 268
  revolutionary mass, 39
Literary education, 215-216, 218
Loka-sakthi-civil power, 166

Mafia, 71-72
Malnutrition, 64, 67, 134, 144, 271
Mandela, Nelson, 26, 185-186, 267
Man-made laws, 286
Marxism, 10, 21
Marxist violence, 247
Mass education, 85, 107, 146
Mass participation, 41, 43
Medical Camp for Peace, 277
Military power, 63, 166
Ministry of Youth Affairs and Sports, 37
Mobile Peace Centre, 277
Model village *panchayat*, 171
Model village, 171, 173
Modernisation process, 133, 137, 139
Moral degradation, 56, 65, 67, 70, 79, 81, 116
Moral power, 219, 224
Moral principles, 22, 57, 62, 65
Moral spiritual education, 199
Movement
  charkha, 204
  ecological, 138, 140
  mass, 176, 234
  resistance, 92
  separatist, 64
  social, 27

Nai Talim, 42, 192, 216, 231, 269-270
Narayan, Jayaprakash, 2, 16, 18-21, 26, 186, 248, 256
Natchikulam Sugarcane Satyagraha, 251
National Flag, 241
National Institute for Leprosy Control, 198
National Institute of Science Communication, 247
National Service Scheme, 37, 271
National Youth Policy, 131
Naturopaths, 246-247
Naturopathy, 228, 245-247
New Testament, 90, 93
Non-cooperation Movement, 110, 113
Non-exploitative society, 18
Non-formal education, 274
Non-formal Education Centres, 42
Non-governmental organisations, 40
Non-governmental schemes, 193
Non-*Harijans*, 194
Non-student youth communities, 36-37
Non-violence, 6, 8-9, 13, 45-46, 48-51, 95-97, 101-102, 185-187, 189-192, 224-225, 252-253, 261-263, 269, 271-272, 274-276
  active, 48, 97
  advocated, 38
  complete, 40, 286
  preached, 139
  realise, 190
  term, 48
Non-violent non-cooperation, 110-111
Non-violent police, 254
Non-violent revolt, symbolic, 115
Non-violent revolution, 42, 251-253, 256, 270
Non-violent self-rule, 204
Non-violent society, 13

Oceanic circle, 38

Ostegaard, Geoffrey, 255-256

Panchayati Raj Institutions, 119, 124-125, 159, 173
Parallel governments, running, 74
Patriotic students, 242
Peace and Academic Curriculum, 276
Peace Arches, 277
Peace Award, defender of, 275
Peace-Brigade, 26, 39, 186, 257-259, 273-274
Peace Education Centre, 275
Peace exhibition, 279
Peace festival, 279
Peace March, 194, 273
Peace Park, 277
Peace Pilgrim, 275
Peace Prayer Club, 275
Peace Slogans and Quotations, 273
Peace worker, 276-277
Peaceful campaigns, 225
Perfect democracy, 120
Perfect education, 84
Philippine Rural Reconstruction Movement, 161
Plague, 114
Political Crisis and Gandhian Solution, 70
Political development, 143
Political education, 215, 217-218, 233
Political participation, 167
Political power, 15, 123, 204
Poverty
  elimination of, 81, 122
  rural, 142, 144
Proliferation, 20
Public education expenditure, 63

Racial discriminations, 92
Rehabilitation programmes, 195
Religious
  communities, 204
  equality, 101
  fanaticism, 16
  heritage, 4
  sanction, 287
Renaissance, 10, 81
Reservation, 123
Revolution
  creative, 268
  peaceful, 261
  violent peasant, 252
Revolutionary concept, 26, 39, 186, 192
Revolutionary programmes, 269
Rishi, 252
Rural communities, 39, 122, 125, 147, 154
Rural development, 120, 122, 141-149, 151, 155, 163, 167, 170, 192-193, 248
  accelerated, 143
  problems, 143
Rural Health & Sanitation, 193
Rural reconstruction, 129, 146, 161, 192
Rural self-Government, 121
Ruskin, 4-5, 10

Salt *Satyagraha*, 106
Salvation, 50, 53, 289
Sanyasi, 238
Sarva Seva Sangh, 190, 203, 247, 253-254, 257, 259, 262
Sarvodaya
  ashram, 257
  centres, 29
  charter, 33
  community, 14
  conference, 45
  day, 275
  leaders, 44-45
  mandal, 2, 27
  movement, 26-35, 43-45, 58, 80, 199, 204, 244, 268
  organisations, 194
  philosophy of, 1-3, 10

political philosophy of, 203
positive concept, 3
samaj, 2, 191
socialism, 18
thinkers, 190, 203
workers, 27-30, 254
youth, 41
Sarvodayites, 26-31, 33, 199
representation of, 33
Satyagraha, 2, 15, 26, 39, 49, 59, 67, 80, 88, 90-98, 102-104, 106-107, 109, 111-116, 290
Satyagrahis, 91-95, 97-98, 101-104, 106, 108-109, 115, 262, 264, 281
Scavenging, 101, 241
Second World War, 63
Self-contained villages, 147
Self-imposed laws, 120
Self-purification, 92, 97, 109, 190
Self-realisation, 8, 12, 15, 96, 189, 281
Self-reliant power, 166
Self-sacrifice
tradition of, 68
woman, 219
Self-sufficiency, 17
Shanti Sainik, 258, 260, 263, 274
Shanti Sena, 26-27, 31, 33, 39, 107, 186, 194, 254, 258-264, 270, 278
Shanti Sena Mandal, 259
Shanti Sena of Satyagrahis, 263
Shanti Sena Rally, 279
Shanti Sena Training Camp, 275
Shastri, Lal Bahadur, 167
Shramadan, 39, 41
Social Action in Gandhian social work, 191
Social case work, 188
Social development, 150, 180
Social justice, 17-18, 141-143, 187, 191
Social ostracism, 113
Social reformers, 187-189
Social reforms, 179-180, 188
Social solidarity, 84-85
Social welfare activities, 106
Socialism, 18-19, 21, 86
Socialist programmes, 255
Societal functions, 178
Socio-economic problems, 39, 129
South Africa, 2, 7, 14, 38, 48-49, 92, 97, 141, 228
South-African Satyagraha Movement, 111
Spinners Association, 14
Spiritual development, 35, 45
Sponsors of Violence, 276
State bureaucrat, 143
State capitalism, 19
Students *Seva* Centre, 251
Summer Youth Festival, 280
Suppression of woman, 220
Supremacy of moral law, 95, 97
Sustainable development, 54, 59, 140, 154-155, 160-164, 168-169, 173, 249
Swadeshi, 17, 58, 66-67, 81, 102, 148, 150, 179, 212, 249, 271, 291

Tamil Nadu *Sarvodaya Mandal*, 244
Task Force on Integrated Rural Development, 145
Terrorism, 50, 64, 67, 79-80
Third world countries, 167
Tolstoy, 4, 6-7, 10, 90, 93, 219
Tourism, 135, 168-169
Transcendental concept, 21

United Nations, 35, 45, 144, 167-168, 263
Unity Sustainable Development, 168
Universal education, 86
Universal laws, 49
Unnatural food habit, 246
Unnatural habit, 246
Untouchability, 12, 101, 105-106, 109, 148, 183, 188, 190, 194, 204, 208-210, 218, 241, 269

removal of, 14, 106, 146, 190, 194, 208-209, 262, 269
Untouchables, 101, 209-210, 239
Utilitarianism, 3

Value-education, 84
Village articles, 213
Village assembly, 272
Village based industries, 135
Village based local government, 135
Village conflicts, 273
Village development programmes, 41
Village economy, 212
Village festival, 274
Village Industries Association, 187, 203
Village Industries Court, 195
Village industries, 14, 106, 146, 190, 195, 212, 250, 254, 269
Village products, 238, 241
Village sanitation, 14, 106, 190, 196, 269
Vinoba Bhave, Acharya, 2-5, 16, 18, 21, 23, 27, 39, 166, 186, 190, 243, 247-248, 251-254, 256, 259
Violence
communal, 77, 273
physical, 51
sporadic, 255
Violent
resistance, 114
revolts, 235
struggle, 257
Voluntarism, 157, 168, 176-178, 180
Voluntary agencies, 43, 86, 177, 182
Voluntary community service, 43
Voluntary organizations, Role of, 181
Vote Bank Politics, 77

Water conservation, 249-250
Welfarism, 68
Western civilization, 56, 65, 136, 147
Workmanship, 213
World Bank, 41, 144-145, 169
World *Sarvodaya* Conference, 45
World Youth Conference, 272

Young India, 91, 204-209, 212, 215, 219-222, 227, 234, 238-240, 244
Young Peace Scientist, 279
Young Peace Workers Scheme, 279
Youth Brigades, 263
Youth club, 273

Zero alcohol villages, 194
Zero Conflict Village, 274
Zone of Peace, 273